WITHDRAWN

Faces of America

Henry Louis Gates, Jr.

Faces of America

How 12 Extraordinary People Discovered Their Pasts

New York University Press
New York and London

NEW YORK UNIVERSITY PRESS
New York and London
www.nyupress.org

Faces of America, with Henry Louis Gates, Jr., is a Production of Kunhardt McGee Productions, Inkwell films, and THIRTEEN in association with WNET.ORG.

Library of Congress Cataloging-in-Publication Data
Gates, Henry Louis.
Faces of America : how 12 extraordinary people discovered their pasts /
Henry Louis Gates, Jr.
p.   cm.
Based on PBS television series Faces of America hosted by Henry Louis Gates, Jr.
ISBN 978-0-8147-3264-9 (cloth : alk. paper) — ISBN 978-0-8147-3265-6 (e-book)
1. United States—Genealogy—Case studies.   2. Genetic genealogy—United States—
Case studies.   3. United States—Biography.   I. Faces of America (Television program).
II. Title.
CS49.G38 2010
920.073—dc22   2010016968

New York University Press books are printed on acid-free paper, and their binding materials are chosen for strength and durability. We strive to use environmentally responsible suppliers and materials to the greatest extent possible in publishing our books.

Manufactured in the United States of America

10 9 8 7 6 5 4 3 2 1

For Liza Gates,

my champion during the summer of 2009.

And for Larry Bobo, Glenn Hutchins, Marcy Morgan, and Charles Ogletree

irrepressible, noble knights.

Contents

Acknowledgments

This project would not have been possible without the top-notch genealogists and DNA scientists who guided its research and grounded its claims. I will be forever in their debt. Of special note was Johni Cerny, who spent years combing over records, crafting family trees, and directing research across three continents. She was assisted by an incredible international team including Jane Ailes, Candan Badem, Valery Bazarov, Tony Browne, Wang Chung-Guang, Junel Davidsen, Mary Ann DiNapoli, Mick Dowling, Dave Emmons, Family Search International, Fiona Fitzsimmons, Roseann B. Garza, Dianne T. Golding-Frankson, Matthew Hovious, Don Huber, Shundou Koga, Raul Longoria, Robert Maloy, Jeff Marshall, Lilly Martin, Jim Matteucci, Father Donough O'Malley, Helen Moss, Rudy Sassine, Sabine Schleichert, Elyse Semerdjian, Vitaly Semionoff, Luri Silvestri, Keiji Sugimoto, Michael Szonyi, Junko Takahashi, and Elena Tsvetkova.

Two excellent companies—23andMe and Family Tree DNA—served as consultants on the project from its inception and did testing and analysis for all our subjects. In addition, the geneticists at the Broad Institute at MIT and Harvard developed a special autosomal DNA test specifically for this project and applied it to our subjects using the data provided by 23andMe. None of this, of course, would have been the least bit comprehensible to me without the invaluable assistance of a team of scientific advisers, including David Altshuler, David Bentley, George Church, Mark Daly, Bennett Greenspan, Brenna Henn, Eric Lander, Joanna Mountain, Nathaniel Pearson, and Joseph Thakuria. They helped analyze the DNA findings and explained to me what it all meant (no easy task). They have my undying thanks.

I would also like to thank Sabin Streeter, who searched through hundreds of hours of interviews and a mountain of scientific data to help identify the narrative threads of the stories found in this book, and a number of scholars and experts who gave considerable time and input to the project, including John Thornton and Linda Heywood of Boston University, Mark Shriver of Pennsylvania State University, Sarah Gualtieri of the University of Southern California, Catherine Daly of the American Family Immigration History Center, Armando Alonzo of Texas A&M University, Lane Hirabayashi of the University of California at Los Angeles, Gary Okihiro of Columbia University, Martin Keane of the Donaghmore Famine Work House Museum, and Ainsley Henriques of the Jewish Heritage Center in Kingston, Jamaica.

Finally, I would like to thank the production team that helped me to create this project and stood by me at every point in its development, including Jane Ailes, Stephen Altobello, Daniel Amigone, Bennett Ashley, Tina Bennett, Lawrence Bobo, Chris Boskin, Johni Cerny, Richard Cohen, Angela De Leon, Michelle Ferrari, Liza Gates, Maggie Gates, Despina Papazoglou Gimbel, Leslie Asako Gladsjo, Barak Goodman, Amu Gosdanian, Vera Grant, William R. Grant, Pat Harrison, Evelyn Brooks Higginbotham, Glenn H. Hutchins, Stephen Ives, Konstantinos Kambouroglou, Joanne Kendall, Paula Kerger, George Kunhardt, Peter Kunhardt, Teddy Kunhardt, John Maggio, Julia Lockwood Marchesi, Michael Maron, Lindsey Megrue, Marcyliena Morgan, George O'Donnell, Charles Ogletree, Amanda Pollak, Tammy Robinson, Amy Rockefeller, Stephen Segaller, John Sexton, Jennifer Snodgrass, Kim Thorson, Sue Williams, John Wilson, Abby Wolf, Donald Yacovone, Titi Yu, Eric Zinner, and especially Dyllan McGee.

Introduction

Looking at Faces

Our complete ancestry is within us. The individual is a result of a long chain of ancestors who are still present within us and exert power over us. Men must go inside themselves, to be connected to what they originally are.

—Gustav Landauer, Mike Nichols's maternal
grandfather (1870–1919)

ON JANUARY 3, 2001, Dr. Rick Kittles, Assistant Professor of Molecular Genetics at the National Human Genome Center at Howard University, sent me a letter that would answer a question that had haunted me since I was nine years old: Where had my ancestors originated in Africa? To what "tribe" or ethnic group did my original African ancestors, who had come to this country most probably in the seventeenth or eighteenth century in the slave trade, belong? For my part, I had longed to learn the identity of my ancestors in this country since July 2, 1960, the day on which my grandfather Edward St. Lawrence Gates was buried in Cumberland, Maryland. Immediately after my grandfather's funeral, my father showed my brother and me the obituary, dated January 6, 1888, of our oldest known ancestor on the Gates family tree, a nurse and midwife named Jane Gates. My great-great-grandmother, she had been born into slavery in 1819. The very next day, I bought a composition book, interviewed my parents, and began to write down the names, dates, and places of birth of all the family members they could remember. I could trace my mother's side of the family, on her mother's line, back to Lucy E. Clifford, born free in 1863. I remember seeing her on her deathbed in 1956. She was my great-grandmother.

After I joined the rest of America in watching Alex Haley's monumental *Roots* miniseries in 1977, you might say that I developed a serious case of "roots envy": I wanted to know the identity of my African American ancestors on this side of the Atlantic; and, as Alex Haley claimed to know, I also wanted to learn the tribal origins of my ancestors on the other side of the Atlantic, back "home" in the motherland of West Africa. Dr. Kittles had told me he could discover this information by analyzing my mitochondrial DNA (mtDNA), the genetic signature that every person, male or female, inherits from his or her mother. I couldn't believe my good fortune, to be alive at a time when the science of genetics could do for all African Americans that which Alex Haley had done for himself: effectively reverse the Middle Passage to recover every black family's long-lost ancestral origins on the African continent. To say that I was excited by this possibility is an understatement.

Dr. Kittles had come to my home in Cambridge, Massachusetts, in the fall of 2000 to take a blood sample, which at that time was necessary in order to collect enough DNA to identify a person's haplogroup. (Today, with more sophisticated techniques, the sample is collected by a simple cheek swab or from saliva.) A haplogroup is a group of similar haplotypes, and a haplotype, as defined by the National Human Genome Research Institute, is "a set of DNA variations, or polymorphisms, that tend to be inherited together. A haplotype can refer to a combination of alleles [variant forms of the same gene] or to a set of single nucleotide polymorphisms (SNPs) found on the same chromosome." Each haplotype or haplogroup is defined by a particular set of mutations.

Joanna Mountain, Senior Director of Research at 23andMe, one of the major genetics testing companies, explains the process: "We identify a person's haplogroup by examining their set of mutations and comparing them to the definitions of all haplogroups. A simple definition of mutation is a difference between a person's genome and the genome of the common ancestor of all living humans." 23andMe assigns about 500 haplogroups for the Y chromosome and another 750 haplogroups for mtDNA. Think of haplogroups as the 1,250 or so branches of the human genetic family tree, and haplotypes (further genetic refinements or variants of these groups of shared mutations) as the leaves on each of those branches. By analyzing a man's Y-DNA (which males inherit from their fathers) or a person's mtDNA, scientists can identify our deep ancestral origins, tracing back thousands of years to a common ancestor from whom those of us with this particular genetic signature or set of mutations descend. As Dr. Mountain explains, "The powerhouses of our cells, called mitochondria, have rings of DNA that are about 16,500 base pairs long. Because no mitochondrial

DNA from the sperm gets into a fertilized egg, the mitochondrial DNA is inheritied only from mother to child, enabling the tracing of a person's maternal line."

It sounds incredible, but it is true, because both Y-DNA and mtDNA are passed down from parent to child without recombining and usually without mutating. So every human being can be assigned to one of the 750 haplogroups on his or her mother's ancestral line, and every man can be assigned to one of the 500 haplogroups on his father's ancestral line. We are living in an age in which not just African Americans but all the people in the world can trace our roots through a test tube. And while we all descend from our original human ancestors who lived in East Africa, most of these haplogroups evolved from genetic mutations in their descendants, who migrated out of East Africa to populate the rest of the world starting some fifty thousand years ago.

Back in the year 2000, when Dr. Kittles tested my DNA, this procedure was new, indeed revolutionary. I could not even imagine what it could possibly mean to learn this information about my African heritage. None of today's commercial genetic testing companies, such as Family Tree DNA, AfricanAncestry.com (Dr. Kittles's company), 23andMe, or AfricanDNA.com (a company I own along with Family Tree DNA), even existed. And the cost of these tests was much higher than it is today. Dr. Kittles was a pioneer both in the history of genetics and in African American history.

At last, my results arrived. And here is where things became "curiouser and curiouser," as Alice put it. I ripped open the envelope and read: "I compared your pattern of variation with those in my database, which now represents over six thousand samples from populations from west, central, and eastern Africa," it began. "No matches or related sequences were observed with West African populations. . . . I hope the test has been helpful and insightful, please let me know if you have any questions."

Say what? I reread his words: "No matches or related sequences were observed." What could this possibly mean? Where in Africa was I from? Wasn't this what the test had been all about? Was I to be denied what I thought of as my "Kunta Kinte" moment? Since family legend had long held that Jane Gates's children were fathered by a white man of Irish descent, if I was going to be able to trace my roots to Africa, it would have to be through my mother's line. I had to be from someplace in Africa; how else to explain my skin color and my facial features, my grade of hair? And if that place of origin was not in Africa, then where in the world could it possibly be?

This surprising and frustrating result of my first DNA test in the year 2000 launched me on a path that has resulted, a decade later, in three four-hour PBS series and a one-hour special on Oprah Winfrey's family tree. Shortly before I met Dr. Kittles, I had gotten the idea of doing a documentary series in which I would trace the family trees of African Americans. My friend Quincy Jones, the music producer, had told me that for several years he had given his friends their family tree as a Christmas present. He told me about the genealogist he had worked with, Johni Cerny, who excelled at analyzing African American family trees. While I was working on a treatment for what I hoped would become a four-hour series, it occurred to me that I could combine my passion for genealogy, born back in 1960, with this new science of ancestry tracing through DNA. It was one of those middle-of-the-night revelations. The next day, I phoned Quincy and asked him if he would be in the series. His interest in genealogy traced back to Alex Haley: Quincy had scored the music for *Roots*, and the two had become close friends. He agreed on the spot. I wrote to Oprah Winfrey, and she phoned me a week later from Quincy's house to say yes. Six other African Americans agreed to join as well, including Whoopi Goldberg, Chris Tucker, Bishop T. D. Jakes, Sarah Lawrence-Lightfoot, Dr. Ben Carson, and Dr. Mae Jemison. That was the origin of the series that became *African American Lives*.

As the series progressed, I began to learn more about the science of DNA testing by having our guests' DNA and my own analyzed by several scientists, among them Dr. Fatimah Jackson, Dr. Bert Ely, Bennett Greenspan, and Dr. Peter Forster, in addition to Dr. Kittles. One of the biggest surprises in my life came the day that Peter Forster informed me that my haplotype is not traceable to sub-Saharan or West Africa at all. It is named T2 (actually, its proper name is T2b2, a subgroup of T2). The T haplogroup originated about forty-five thousand years ago in the Near East "as modern humans first expanded out of eastern Africa," as the 23andMe website says. T2, as Dr. Kittles had told me in his original report, is common both in northern Africa and in Europe. About thirty-three thousand years old, the T2 haplogroup originated in Europe and the Near East and is common among northern Europeans and the Spanish. Perhaps the most notorious person known to have carried mitochondrial DNA from haplogroup T2 is Jesse James! Jesse James and I share an actual common ancestor on our genetic family tree.

How could this be? Well, it turns out that I am one of the small group of African Americans whose mitochondrial DNA and Y-DNA descend from a European woman and a European man, respectively. The man who fathered Jane Gates's five children, just as family tradition claimed, was an Irishman. We now know this as a fact, since my father and brother and I have the R-M222 haplotype on my father's side of the family, which is called the Ui Neill Haplotype and traces straight back to one man, a king, in fifth-century Ireland. (Eight percent or so of all men in Ireland share his haplotype.) I came to understand that fully 35 percent of all other African American men can also trace their paternal ancestors, their Y-DNA, to European men who impregnated an African American female, most probably in the context of slavery. On my mother's side of the family, we descend from a European woman, who was most probably—judging from the number of exact matches in the Family Tree DNA database—from England or Ireland and whose child, our direct female ancestor, was fathered by a black man. In the year 2000, I embarked on a quest to find my long-lost African ancestry through my genes, and it turns out that my roots trace to that African kingdom called the United Kingdom! If someone were asked to judge my "race" simply from the analysis of my Y-DNA and my mtDNA, he or she would conclude that I was a white man.

"Race," I was made to realize, was infinitely more complicated than our superficial definitions—and I wanted to share this knowledge with the public. This new interest in the science of individual genetic makeup enabled me to return with a new disciplinary perspective to the subject of my Ph.D. dissertation: how race was conceived and represented, or "written," in Europe and America during the Enlightenment and, more particularly, how race was related by European philosophers and creative writers to what they saw as the absence or presence of "reason" among persons of African descent. Broadly speaking, my work concerned itself with what we call the social construction of racial identities. Now, some thirty years later, I returned to the academic exploration of this subject, using scientific tools in the rapidly developing field of genetics that weren't available (or even imaginable) when I was an English department graduate student. It turns out that the four or five "races" that scholars postulated back then have absolutely no basis in biology. But it also turns out that genetic variations among individuals are real and biologically identifiable—and are infinitely more complex than anyone could have imagined in the eighteenth century.

The resulting popularity of *African American Lives* led to two sequels, a one-hour documentary on Oprah Winfrey's family and another four-hour documentary in which I explored the ancestry of eleven more African Americans. Among the thousands of letters I received after the airing of these shows, one, from a woman of Russian Jewish ancestry, challenged me to do a series about non–African Americans, about people like her. I consulted with Johni Cerny and other genealogists and with the scientists at Family Tree DNA and 23andMe, and the result was *Faces of America,* which aired in February and March 2010. This companion book to that series allows me to share in much greater detail the results of our genealogical and genetic research into the lives of these twelve people. We identified each person's mitochondrial haplogroup, as well as the haplogroup of each male and that of a male directly descended from the guest's paternal grandfather, and we tested each guest's admixture (the percentage of European, African, and Asian or Native American ancestry) through dense genotyping done by 23andMe and Dr. Mark Daly and Dr. David Altshuler at the Broad Institute in Cambridge, Massachusetts. Daly and Altshuler also performed a special analysis of each guest's entire genome, searching for long identical stretches of the autosomal regions of DNA, which would indicate that two individuals share a common ancestor as recently as 250 years ago. Whereas haplogroups trace back thousands of years, and admixture tests measure an individual's complex genetic ancestry back some 500 years (say, to the time of Columbus), this identification of what I think of as "autosomal cousins" can be even more recent, leading to all sorts of surprises on one's family tree.

In America, who we are is often associated with what we do. I make my living studying and teaching the history and culture of people of African descent. And that's why I was shocked to learn that, though I don't look like it, I'm actually quite a lot more white, genetically, than I am black. As a matter of fact, I am 56 percent European and only 37 percent African —with a sprinkle of Asian/Native American ancestry (7 percent), much to my cousins' collective delight. My father's complexion is so light that his African ancestry is barely detectable; it turns out that his admixture is 74 percent European, 21 percent African, and 6 percent Asian/Native American. And the rest of my family is a multiracial, multiethnic, multicultural gumbo: black and white, African and European, Irish and Yoruba, Puerto Rican and Danish, Native American and Asian. We're the melting pot that is America, in miniature.

The truth is, you can never tell who people are, or where their ancestors have come from, simply by looking at them. Our genetic identity is much more complicated than that: it is buried deep inside us, beneath the surface. It's a product of events and relationships we have very few clues about—things our ancestors did hundreds, and thousands, of years ago.

This gap between who we appear to be and who we in fact are genetically has made me curious about ancestry for as long as I can remember. I am, as anyone who knows me well will attest, a genealogy junkie. As I mentioned, I began making family trees when I was young boy, soon after I first learned that my oldest known ancestor had been a slave until the end of the Civil War. I have since learned from genealogists in the *African American Lives* series that I am also descended from seven pairs of Free Negroes. These people were once slaves—as all our black ancestors were, unless you are descended from a recent, voluntary migrant—but were freed as early as the middle of the eighteenth century. John Redman, my mother's third-great-grandfather, actually fought in the Continental army in the American Revolution, an enormous surprise to everybody in our family.

But just as I had realized that we could combine genealogical research with state-of-the-art DNA testing to trace the roots of living African Americans back in time, across the abyss of the dreaded Middle Passage, to provide a glimpse of our lost African heritage, I came to realize that we could also uncover the ancestors of people of Jewish, Arab, West Indian, German, Italian, Spanish, Irish, English, Swiss, Russian, Chinese, Japanese, and Native American descent—anybody. The appeal was obvious: Almost all African Americans wonder where their ancestors came from in Africa. What languages did they speak? What was their music? Their religion? Their culture? These are questions that generations of us have asked, but until recently the answers were long lost in the abyss of slavery. But that has begun to change. I now realize that all Americans—all people, really—share the same fascination with their ancestry that I had once thought peculiar to African Americans.

I have spent four years conducting genealogical research on some of the most compelling African Americans imaginable. It was a magical experience for me—indeed, one of the most intensely enjoyable experiences that I have had as a scholar. At the same time, it made me realize a larger truth about genealogy and American identity. I learned, in story after story, that America is a giant ethnic mishmash—a series of interlocking families, like my own, that are so thoroughly blended that any notion of racial purity is naive at best and a dangerous intellectual error at worst.

I conceived of the series that became *Faces of America,* a broader and even more ambitious series than *African American Lives,* because I wanted to explore the complexity of race, genetics, genealogy, and identity in American society. I wanted to celebrate the true triumph of American democracy—our ethnic, genetic diversity—by tracing the family stories of Americans of very different backgrounds to see how their unique ancestries shaped both them and our nation. I wanted to tell the stories of people who identified themselves as English or German, Irish or Italian, Arab or Asian, Native American or West Indian, Jewish or Muslim, Syrian or Turkish, to see what it is we all share and what sometimes makes us quite different.

I wanted, in essence, to look at American identity through the lens of our immigrant ancestors. If you scratch an American family, sooner or later you'll find a historically recent immigrant. Even Native American ancestors, like those of my guest Louise Erdrich, migrated to this continent some sixteen thousand or so years ago. Between 1820 and 1924, no fewer than thirty-six million people migrated to the United States. The tide hasn't stopped: more immigrants arrive every day. As a matter of fact, between 1990 and 2000, more Africans migrated to the United States than the 450,000 of our African ancestors who came here involuntarily during the entire history of the slave trade. All migrants bring with them their cultures, their religions, their languages, their traditions, and, thank goodness, their food. Yet they have confronted a nation that is not always willing to welcome them warmly.

There is a great contradiction at the heart of the history of migration to America. America's prosperity has long depended on its immigrants' willingness to make sacrifices—to work long hours, in difficult occupations, often far from friends and family. Yet immigrants themselves have routinely faced discrimination, outright hostility, and sometimes severe hardships on the way to earning the right to call themselves Americans. Traces of their early struggles still surface generations later. The legacy of their experience is our dual identity: we are Americans, but hyphenated Americans, American from another country. Our roots connect us to somewhere else, across one ocean or another.

Faces of America was born out of a desire to explore these issues. The project took shape methodically. I asked twelve remarkable people to join me, people who have made a profound cultural impact on our nation and who come from different backgrounds: Mike Nichols, Meryl Streep, Queen Noor, Louise Erdrich, Yo-Yo Ma, Mehmet Oz, Mario Batali, Elizabeth Alexander, Malcolm Gladwell, Stephen Colbert, Kristi Yamaguchi, and Eva Longoria. I told them all that I wanted to help them understand the journey their ancestors made on the road to becoming an American. What drives people to leave their homeland, their family, everything they know? How did they build new lives once they got here? And how are we, the descendants of immigrants, shaped by the actions of our ancestors? I wanted to explore with them how the experiences of our ancestors—their dreams, their aspirations, and their choices—have carried forward through the centuries. How much do these experiences still shape our identities as individuals and as Americans?

Our genealogists, under the direction of Johni Cerny, and I began by looking at the circumstances surrounding each subject's birth in the twentieth century and then carefully worked our way back through the branches of their family trees, to discover how events long ago and far away transformed their families' future: how the grand, impersonal sweep of world historical events interacted with personal stories to shape who we are as individuals, as families, and ultimately as a nation. The answers came from family stories checked against the historical record. We talked to our subjects' relatives and hunted down marriage licenses and birth certificates, land deeds, estate records, ships' passenger lists, immigration files, and gravestones, tracing their family trees from America back to countries all over the globe. And when traditional genealogy hit a wall and the paper trail ran out, as it invariably does, we turned to genetics to excavate the ancestral record that each one of us carries inside, in each and every one of our twenty-five thousand genes—our very own individual genetic signature. This investigation allowed us to explore the distinctive ancestral legacy that makes each of us unique, as well as the extraordinary genetic inheritance that binds us all together.

This book is a record, in words and images, of what I learned while tracing the branches of twelve very different American family trees. Each chapter looks at one of these families in detail, focusing on the stories and insights that I found particularly meaningful. It is a book about journeys, not destinations—because the secret of genealogy is that every family story, no matter how seemingly insignificant, and the name and identity of each of our ancestors, no matter how seemingly unremarkable her or his life, contain an abundance of revelations, both about them and about ourselves. As Mike Nichols's great-great-grandfather put it, "The individual is a result of a long chain of ancestors." The Temple of Apollo at Delphi in ancient Greece used as its motto the phrase "Know Thyself." After our experiences tracing the family trees of the individuals in this book, I would amend it to "Know Thy Past, Know Thyself."

A Note on DNA Testing

EVERY SUBJECT IN this project was invited to submit a sample of DNA for testing to complement the genealogical research we conducted. All but one of the subjects agreed to participate in the testing. (The Native American author Louise Erdrich declined, after conferring with her family and with other members of her tribe.) The results of the tests were, I think, among the most exciting things we learned from this project. They told a great deal about the connections we all share and illuminated the deep family histories of each subject. DNA testing is not, however, an easy thing to understand, and rather than clutter this book with repeated explanations of how it works, I thought I'd try to provide a simple overview here.

The first test we did on each subject is known as an admixture test. It uses vast databases of genetic information compiled over the past two decades to make a very simple but telling comparison of the DNA profile of each of our subjects with profiles gathered from people all over the world. The resulting matches allow scientists to estimate the ethnic percentages of our subjects' ancestors within the past few centuries, something we could only partially explore using traditional genealogical records. These results are expressed as percentages of European, African, and Asian/Native American ancestry, yielding a far more precise ethnic portrait than traditional genealogy ever could. So, for example, admixture testing of Eva Longoria, whose ancestors are a mix of Spanish and Native Americans, revealed that she is 70 percent European, 27 percent Asian/Native American, and 3 percent African. (Asian and Native American ancestry register identically on these tests because of the history of human evolution: the earliest Native Americans were people who crossed into North America via now-vanished land bridges from Asia.)

After the admixture test, we then examined the mitochondrial DNA in each of our subjects. Mitochondrial DNA consists of thirty-seven genes that all of us—men and women alike—inherit exclusively from our mothers. (Men carry their mother's mitochondrial DNA but do not pass it on to their children.) It is thus a kind of genetic fingerprint, passed down from mother to daughter unchanged for thousands of years, connecting us all back to a theoretical original female ancestor—a mitochondrial Eve, so to speak. We do not all have the same mitochondrial DNA because over the long course of human evolution, small mutations have occurred. As a result, when we look at ancestors from the past few thousand years, mitochondrial DNA is a precise record of family groups and their migratory patterns. Your mother's mother's mother's mother's mother's mitochondrial DNA is exactly the same as yours. And by analyzing it, we can often tell where your mother's mother's mother's mother's mother came from.

Our testing of each subject's mitochondrial DNA yielded two types of information. In most cases, our consultants were able to use their databases to find matches for each of our subjects' mitochondrial DNA with other people living across the globe today. These matches indicate shared recent ancestry. (Malcolm Gladwell's mitochondrial DNA, for example, yielded near-matches with people alive today in Ethiopia, Cameroon, and Gabon; these are Malcolm's distant cousins, related to him by connections that may be as recent as only a few hundred years.) Our mitochondrial DNA testing also revealed which maternal haplogroup each of our subjects belongs to. This information is extremely significant because it is evidence of maternal ancestors who lived in the very distant past, when human beings were first migrating out of Africa.

It's a complicated idea, but, in essence, haplogroups distinguish groups of people who diverged genetically thousands and sometimes tens of thousands of years ago. They relate to the idea of the mitochondrial Eve, the mother of all mothers. Scientists believe that the ancestry of every person alive today can be traced back to East Africa. There, nearly two hundred thousand years ago, human beings evolved out of a single family group. These early humans remained within the confines of Africa until, about fifty thousand years ago, a few of them decided it was time to move, beginning what became humanity's most remarkable migration. Over the millennia that followed, their descendants gradually spread to the east and the north. Some ventured deep into Central and East Asia, eventually getting all the way to the Americas, some sixteen thousand years ago. Others wandered into the heart of Europe. Their DNA evolved as they moved, and each of these sets of mutations was passed on from mother to child. But males do not pass along their mtDNA; only females do.

Geneticists have identified and labeled significant mutations—such as those shared by all the people who migrated across land bridges from Asia into North America—and the people who carry them today are said to belong to the same haplogroup. Each of these major branches on the human family tree sprouted other, smaller branches, over time giving rise to collections of extended families, each of which shares a common genetic signature. Every person alive today descends from these families. And the story of human migration can be best glimpsed through the haplogroups that each of us carries in our DNA. Indeed, it is the only scientific way to look deep into the human past.

The names of these haplogroups start with a capital letter (occasionally, two) designating a major branch on the human genetic tree, signifying common ancestry. That capital letter is often followed by a series of numbers and lowercase letters, each corresponding to a subsequent branch on the tree. So, for example, Dr. Mehmet Oz, whose mother is Turkish, belongs to the maternal haplogroup known as H2a1. It arose in the Near East about fourteen thousand years ago, when the Ice Age was drawing to a close. As the great ice sheets began to recede and the climate stabilized, members of this haplogroup migrated northward through the Caucasus Mountains into the heart of Eurasia. Populations carrying H2a1 then expanded throughout the Ural Mountains, the Central Asian plateaus, and the land bordering the Baltic Sea, probably by about ten thousand years ago. Today H2a1 is most frequent in eastern Slavic-speaking populations such as those in Russia and the Ukraine—and there are some interesting stories in Mehmet's genealogy that suggest how Russian ancestry may have entered his Turkish family.

In addition to mitochondrial DNA testing, we also looked at the Y-DNA of the men who participated in this project and, whenever possible, at the Y-DNA of male relatives of the women who participated. While we all inherit mitochondrial DNA from our mothers, men also inherit Y-chromosomal DNA from their fathers—the Y chromosome, as we all learned in middle school, is what makes a man a man. It is the same kind of genetic fingerprint as mitochondrial DNA, meaning that your father's father's father's father's Y-DNA is exactly the same as yours, if you are male. Our testing of it revealed the same kinds of information that we were able to glean from mitochondrial DNA—information regarding each subject's recent shared ancestry as well as membership in a paternal haplogroup that allows us to glimpse deep into the past. In some cases, this information proved very surprising. The Y-DNA of Elizabeth Alexander's father, for example, revealed that the head of Yale's African American Studies Department is much more European than she might have imagined.

The final DNA test we conducted was crafted specifically for this project by scientists at the Broad Institute at MIT and Harvard. It is a very complex test that looks at what is called autosomal DNA, which is the DNA in the twenty-two chromosomes each of us carries that do not determine gender. In effect, the Broad Institute's test allowed us to look across the full spectrum of each subject's DNA and compare each section of their chromosomes to see if any of the people who participated in this project were related to each other via a common ancestor as recently as the past 250 years. Is Stephen Colbert a cousin of Yo-Yo Ma? Is Eva Longoria related to Meryl Streep? You are going to have to read the rest of this book to find out.

1

Mike Nichols

1931

FOR NEARLY HALF a century, Mike Nichols has been one of America's most creative and influential artists. He is among the tiny group of people to have won all four of our most competitive awards for film, television, theater, and sound recordings—an Oscar, an Emmy, a Tony, and a Grammy.

Mike first gained notice in the early 1960s as half of the legendary comedy duo Nichols and May, skewering this country's middle-class social mores. He went on to become an ever more complex and nuanced artist, a leading film and theater writer and director who has spent four decades exploring and exploding the most deeply held American values. His first film, *The Graduate,* defined the zeitgeist of the sixties. But my guess is that few of that film's millions of fans could possibly imagine that its director's brilliant take on generational change as a metaphor for larger changes abroad in our society was the insight of a man who grew up in an era of total chaos, barely surviving one of history's worst atrocities, the Jewish Holocaust in Nazi Germany.

I approached Mike as soon as I conceived of this project. I wanted to include him because, over dinners on Martha's Vineyard, I had come to learn a bit about his remarkable childhood. I also wanted us to try to investigate the ancestry of a person who was of both German and Russian Jewish ancestry, the latter of which presents formidable challenges to genealogists. I was pleased at how far back we could trace his family on both of these lines. But just as I enjoyed finding that the imagination, careful preparation, and deep intelligence that have characterized his career are actually part of a family tradition stretching back at least four generations, I was dismayed to learn of terrible atrocities committed against several of his ancestors. Members of Mike Nichols's family have suffered a remarkable amount of political persecution from the Left and from the Right, ranging from the czars in Russia in the nineteenth century through the Bolshevik

Revolution in 1917 and the German Revolution a year later, to Stalin's purges in the 1930s and Hitler's insane persecution of the Jews. We found relatives on both sides of Mike's family who faced terrible injustice, suffering, and even execution—yet somehow passed on to their descendants the talent, optimism, and inner strength needed to persevere.

Mike's direct ancestors also seem to have had an uncanny knack for migrating one step ahead of great historical events. His father's family left Russia in 1917, on the eve of the Bolshevik Revolution, eventually settling in Germany. His parents then found themselves forced to flee the Nazis shortly before it became impossible for Jews to leave the country. He has many ancestors who were not so lucky—and who died in these historical cataclysms.

Much of Mike's work, and many of his most memorable characters, have the feeling of the outsider observing people and events from afar, from almost a peripheral vantage point. As we sat down to begin our interview, I asked him if he thought his style was unique among his contemporaries in that way. His answer—modest but clearly thought out—was telling: "I don't think I'm so unique," he replied. "But I'm a Russian German Jew—and I think I do have a refugee sensibility. I think the reason I say 'refugee' rather than just 'traveler' is that if you are a refugee, there's urgency. You need to be hearing and noting how people are doing things —the local customs. And doing that means studying nuances of behavior. I'm very aware that all the time I was growing up, I had that awareness of behavior, of how they do it here. And I was always honing my sense of observation, searching for invisible signs of good things, bad things, anger, pleasure, affection, dislike, the thing you always got an ear cocked for—will it be okay? Those things get sharpened, you know, because it went pretty uniformly badly as I was storing them up." In other words, the subtle manner by which he evokes characters' personalities through the nuances of their behavior and attention to minute detail can possibly be traced to the survival skills he developed as a refugee, even—or especially —as a child.

Mike was born Michael Igor Peschkowsky on November 6, 1931, in Berlin, the oldest child of Brigitte Landauer and Dr. Paul Peschkowsky, a physician. He spent his first seven years as a very sensitive and clever child in an upper-middle-class Jewish family, largely unaware of the dangers his family faced after the Nazis came to power in 1933. By 1938, however, their perilousness was becoming clear. Across the country, Jews were being arrested and sent to concentration camps, synagogues were being burned,

Mike Nichols as a baby in Berlin, with his parents, Brigitte Landauer and Paul
Peschkowsky. (Used by permission of the Nichols family)

and Jewish businesses were being seized. Mike remembers his parents
spending what he describes as an endless amount of time waiting at con-
sulates, trying to get papers to leave the country. Most of the people who
were on those lines with them ended up perishing in the Holocaust.

The Peschkowskys succeeded, as luck would have it, because of Nazi
Germany's infamous nonaggression pact with the Soviet Union, the cyni-
cal, short-lived agreement between two of the twentieth century's most
brutal regimes. "The only reason we were able to leave was the Stalin-Hitler
pact," Mike said with an ironic smile. "During that time, Jews with Russian papers could leave Germany. Nobody else could. And a patient of my

father's—at least this is the legend in the family—a patient of my father came to his office and said, 'They're taking doctors alphabetically, and your initial comes up next month. Get out.' So he did."

We could find no evidence documenting this family legend, though many stories of its kind are true. But we did find shipping records that showed that Michael's father arrived in New York on August 14, 1938. He quickly passed his medical boards, set up a practice, and sent for his family. Mike's mother, however, was ill and could not travel. Fearing the worst, she sent her two boys off alone on April 28, 1939—and then, just as miraculously as her husband's escape, managed to join them the following year.

I showed Mike the manifest of the SS *Bremen*, the ship that left Germany for America carrying seven-year-old Michael Igor Peschkowsky and his three-year-old brother, Robert. "It's very startling," Mike said, looking at this document for the first time and recalling vivid memories of that trip he made more than sixty years ago. "I remember everything about getting on the boat," he said. "We were at the gangplank and about to go down when a Hitler speech began. And, of course, you didn't listen to it on the radio; you listened on loudspeakers on every block, and while Hitler spoke, nothing moved. So they held us back from the gangplank. And I remember mother wanted to give us supplies, and they were all saying, 'Sorry, madam, there's nothing we can do. Nothing happens till the speech is over.' I remember that."

"And then when we were on the boat, we had little purses on cords under our shirts, and they had fifteen [German] marks in them for emergencies. And I knew two sentences in English: 'I don't speak English' and 'Please don't kiss me.' Because we were alone. And I think if you're a kid without adults, people tend to kiss you, because what do you do with a kid, right? So I remember that. And I remember my brother and I got very excited because we'd never had food before that made noise. But Rice Krispies! We were thrilled with Rice Krispies and excited about Coke which—shhhhh—you could hear, and it tasted great. We went nuts for that stuff."

This story fascinates me because it is charmingly revealing about the different ways in which people see—in this case, a child's perspective on even the most traumatic historical events. Mike and his brother were children traveling alone during one of the most dangerous moments in history, fleeing people who wanted to kill them. And what do they most vividly remember? Rice Krispies and Coca-Cola.

"We were basically unaware of what was really happening," he continued. "I do have a specific memory, though, of coming down the gangplank and seeing my father waiting. We're hugging and talking, and across from the dock there's a delicatessen, and it had a neon sign with Hebrew letters. And I said, 'Is that allowed?' And he said, 'It is, here.' So that was the first thing that happened to me in New York, so I must have known something."

We found a surprising number of documents illuminating Mike's family's journey to America. They tell a story that was common in its time but that most Americans today can't quite imagine. Dr. Paul Peschkowsky arrived in the port of New York on August 14, 1938, and signed a declaration of intent to become an American citizen, something he'd have to wait five years to achieve. His declaration says that he was a physician, that he had sailed from France, and that his race was "Hebrew" and his nationality Russian. Shortly after arriving, he changed his last name to Nichols, signing his petition for naturalization "Paul Nichols, formerly Paul Peschkowsky."

When Mike and his brother arrived in New York, they took their father's new name. In yet another telling sign of just how young and innocent he was, or perhaps how deeply traumatic this was, Mike has absolutely no memory of his family's changing his surname, a hallmark, after all, of one's identity: "I don't remember Peschkowsky," he told me with a shrug. "I only start remembering Mike Nichols. Nichols was everything. We were Nichols." But that name change was not without its consequences.

Mike soon learned that Nichols was not a common name among American Jews, instead being prevalent among Protestants. "I became aware that it was not a name that told people easily that you were Jewish, like Goldschmidt or any thousands of names," he told me. "And this was not something I wanted." Where did the name Nichols come from? Mike told me that he believes his father chose it because in the Russian style of naming it was a variant of his patronymic, which he had inherited from his own father (whose birth name was Pavel Nikolaevich Peschkowsky). "My father thought Nichols was perfectly reasonable," Mike said, laughing. "He didn't know that it was a goy name. He just took his father's patronymic, unfortunately making me Michael Nichols—which was not my favorite."

Setting aside his own feelings on the matter, Mike told me that his father was genuinely thrilled to become an American. "He adored America," Mike said, smiling warmly. "And he always did very well. He was an

Naturalization petition signed by Mike's father, Paul Nichols. This document indicates that Paul changed the family surname from Peschkowsky to Nichols soon after arriving in America. (Public domain)

extremely good doctor, and he had very fancy patients. He had [Vladimir] Horowitz. He had Sol Yurick. He was *the* doctor to Russian stars. And he was very good at the dinner table. He told great stories. He was full of life. I still remember his happiness at buying a Packard Clipper. I remember that car with emotion, because he loved it so much and it was so beautiful —black, with a leather interior."

But Paul Nichols did not get to enjoy his new freedom or his new country for very long. Having successfully fled Nazi Germany, he died of cancer at age forty-four. Mike remains angered by his loss, which he believes could have been prevented. "The first job my father got as a doctor in New York," Mike said, "was working for a union on 42nd Street, running the x-ray machine for the union members. And unbelievably, nobody knew about shielding from x-rays. And he got leukemia. It was an occupational death, no doubt. It's hard to imagine that they didn't know, what with Madame Curie dying of radiation and so forth. He was a baby. And I —selfishly—still needed him."

When his father died, Mike's life was turned upside down. The loss of a parent proved far more profoundly disruptive than moving to a new continent or adopting a new culture had. And even though his father loved America, Mike was not so sure how he felt, even as he adapted to his new surroundings. "I lost my accent in two weeks," he said. "I remember being on the school bus and saying, 'What means *emergency*?' And two weeks later there was no problem anymore. That's what kids can do. But I was not happy."

Despite the fact that he spent the first seven years of his life growing up Jewish in Nazi Germany, Mike told me that he never experienced overt anti-Semitism until he came to America. "In Berlin," he said, "I went to a special school for Jews, but I didn't know that was unusual. And once some guys with a swastika on their armbands took my bike in the street. But that was about it. And I don't even remember it as a big deal. I just thought, 'Well, easy come, easy go.'" His parents, he said, sheltered him from what was going on around him. But as he grew up in New York in the forties, the prevalence of casual anti-Semitism shattered his innocence about other people's attitudes toward his religious and cultural heritage.

"I remember I went to PS 87 for a year or less," he said, "and for the first time somebody said something about me being a Jewish kid. It was one of the teachers, and it wasn't in a particularly friendly tone. So I came home a little concerned about it, and my mother was great. She put an arm around me as we were sitting on the sofa, and she told me about Jews and what it meant to be a Jew and what the problems were. And none of this had ever been spoken of before, or she wouldn't have had to have this little talk."

It says quite a lot about the sheltering effects of nurturing families, and the particularity of prejudices, that Mike's experiences as a child in Nazi Germany so little prepared him for anti-Semitism in America. "I didn't think of it as terrible," he says. "I just wondered what she meant. I just had no frame of reference. Because Jews in Germany, before all this, were Germans. They didn't speak Yiddish. They didn't celebrate Jewish holidays. My grandfather, who was in the end a Zionist, spoke not a word of Yiddish, much less Hebrew. All this came to the surface later. I think it was always underneath, as it has been for Jews always everywhere. But I learned little by little."

With his father's death, Mike's problems grew. "I was not happy with myself," he said, "and I was not happy at home. My father was gone, my mother was deeply miserable—as anybody would be whose husband died. She didn't know the language; she had never been alone in her life. And yet from that point, she got it done. She took good care of us. But I never felt pleasure in being with people and being in any situation, really, until I went to the University of Chicago. In line to register, I started to talk to the girl in front of me, a beautiful girl—Susan Sontag. That was the first person I met, and from that point on, because I was at the University of Chicago, I have this shocking experience over and over: 'Oh my god, they're like me. I'm like them. Oh, they're weirdos.' For the first time in my life."

Double consciousness is the capacity to perform a function and watch yourself performing that function at the same time. I believe that all brilliant artists have the capacity to watch themselves watching others. This talent describes Mike Nichols's outsider perspective in a nutshell. Can we trace this capacity with certainty to any one set of experiences? Of course not. Mike Nichols's genius would have manifested itself in one form or another no matter where he may have been raised. But those poignant experiences of exile, alienation, studied adjustment, and redefinition, I'm convinced, have been leitmotifs throughout his remarkable body of work—if not its driving force.

I wondered if this gift for what we might think of as social introspection could be found elsewhere on his family tree. We unearthed a number of stories suggesting that Mike comes from a long line of outsiders and mavericks. But finding these stories was not easy, especially along Mike's paternal ancestry, which stretches back to Russia. Locating records of Russian Jews is among the most difficult challenges in genealogical research. A genealogist once told me that finding the ancestors of Russian Jews is at least as difficult as tracing the slave ancestors of African Americans. For centuries, the forebears of men and women like Paul Peschkowsky were barred from citizenship and its rights. They were confined to Jewish settlements that were subsequently destroyed either by Stalin or by the Nazis in World War II. They did not even have surnames, other than patronymics ("son of" names). In other words, they lived lives without a paper trail, lives almost totally unrecorded. Jews appear in Russian documents only beginning in the nineteenth century, when the czar, seeking to tax them and conscript them, required that they adopt last names.

We began our search by consulting Mike's father's death certificate, which is filled with information given by his wife, Brigitte. From it, we learned that Paul Peschkowsky was born to Russian émigrés in Vienna, Austria, on January 13, 1900, and that his mother's name was Anna Distler. His father is listed as "Nicholas Nichols"—but, as we have seen, this was not his real name. Mike's father was originally named Peschkowsky; in Vienna, we were able to locate his birth record, bearing the name "Nosson Peschkowsky." This record says that Nosson (the Yiddish form of Nathan) came to Vienna from Tomsk, Siberia, where he was born in 1870. We found other records in which Nosson went by the name of Nikolai, probably because it was the closest Russian equivalent. So the fluidity of naming started early in Mike's family, and it involved at least two languages. We also found a wealth of records suggesting that Mike's grandparents traveled frequently between the luxurious European capital of Vienna and the rough hinterlands of Siberia throughout the first decades of the twentieth century.

By this point, Mike and I were both fairly confused. We wanted to know how—and why—his grandparents were traveling so much. Given the state of Russian records, the prospect of unraveling this mystery looked bleak at first. But then we got very lucky: We found the city directory of Irkutsk, one of the largest cities in Siberia. It lists Mike's grandfather, "Dr. D. N. Peschkowsky," as a specialist in venereal disease. We also learned that he was a member of the East Siberia Physicians Society and that his wife, Anna Distler, Mike's grandmother, was a member of the board of the Irkutsk Charitable Society for the Assistance of Poor Jews. They seem to have been very prominent people in Irkutsk. And the source of their status appears to have been the family of Mike's grandmother, the Distlers.

Mike had heard many stories about this line of his family and was eager to learn more. "I'll tell you right now all I know about my grandmother Anna," he said. "And I know it only from the wife of my now deceased Russian cousin. The story is that when my grandmother left Russia in the 1917, she took with her forty pieces of luggage. And in the forty pieces of luggage were fifty gold bars from the family goldmine. But I have no idea if that's true."

The Distler family in Russia. Grigory Distler, Mike's great-grandfather, is in the middle. Mike's father, Paul Peschkowsky, is the young boy on the far right. (Used by permission of the Nichols family)

He then showed me a remarkable photograph of the handsome Distler clan taken sometime in the late nineteenth century, looking almost like an imitation of a period photograph. "My cousin gave me this," he said. "It's like that picture you take of the cast of any Chekhov play. I love it." Its sepia tones cannot contain the extraordinary personalities of some of its subjects. "I said to my cousin, 'Who is this woman in the foreground?' Because she's really interesting looking. And he said, 'That's Aunt whatever, who lived forever. She only died recently, and she was the star of the old-age home; she fucked everybody—she lived for sex. All her life she lived for sex.'" He laughed. "I don't know. I can't verify that, and my cousin's dead. But look at those eyes—of course she lived for sex! Right here in the photograph she's got something going with the soldier next to her."

According to family lore, the Distlers owned a goldmine on Sakhalin Island. After a great deal of research, we were able to verify the essentials of this story. The Distler goldmine was not on Sakhalin Island—it was right in the middle of Siberia. But it existed, nonetheless, just as family legend says it did. And it was the creation of Mike's great-grandfather Grigory Distler.

Records show that Grigory was born in Poland and was exiled to Siberia in 1865 for participation in an anti-Russian rebellion (yet another dissident refugee in the Nichols family). He went to Tomsk, Siberia, an area that was legendary for its lucrative goldmines. At the time, Jews were prohibited from engaging in mining, so Grigory set up a butcher shop instead, and he prospered. His life changed dramatically, in the late 1880s, when the prohibition against Jewish ownership of goldmines was dropped —largely because the mines were generally thought to be exhausted.

Distler decided to try his luck. He started a mine with his five sons. It was an unusual business. Unlike most of the goldminers of their day, the Distlers themselves researched, developed, and traded their final product. They were involved in the entire process from start to finish. And they were wildly successful. Their mine was soon producing three tons of gold a year. Grigory reinvested the profits, acquiring several more mines in the same area. The Distlers were, for a brief time, like the Rothschilds of Russia. And Mike's grandparents Nosson and Anna were most likely traveling the world on her father Grigory's profits from this very mining venture.

The Bolshevik Revolution ended it all. When industry and farming were nationalized post-1917, it wasn't a good time to be a capitalist. The family suspended its mining activities and dispersed. Some of Mike's ancestors remained in Russia, including two great-uncles, Alexander and Vasily Distler, who moved to Moscow.

Mike's grandparents took a different route. After the dissolution of the family business, Nosson and Anna and their son, Paul, traveled east to Vladivostok and then to Harbin, China. This was a common route for Russians attempting to escape the Revolution, and many continued to the West Coast of the United States. But for reasons that remain unclear, Anna and Paul turned west and fled from Harbin to Berlin. They arrived there around 1920 and appear to have lived the remainder of their lives in Germany. We don't know if they arrived with forty suitcases full of gold. We do know that they arrived in Berlin with money that had been earned in the Distler goldmines. Mike's father, Paul, was able to earn his medical degree, marry, have two children—and ultimately pay for the journey to America for himself and his family.

"This is so amazing to me," Mike exclaimed when I told him all of this, "because I always have this picture of my father working his way up once he got to Berlin and somehow getting to medical school—but they really were rich! This really fascinates me. I wish to God I had gotten to know my father better because I had it all wrong."

Mike's great-grandfather Grigory Distler with two of his sons
in Tomsk, Siberia. (Used by permission of the Nichols family)

Although the Distler wealth was able to save some members of the
family, it could not preserve those who stayed behind in Russia. Many of
them simply disappear from the records. Others, like Mike's great-uncles
in Moscow, suffered gruesome fates. They were arrested and put to death
by Stalin for "counter-revolutionary activities." Records show that one of
them, Vasily Distler, was tried and executed on the same day, April 25,
1938, just months before seven-year-old Mike arrived in New York.

"I've never heard about these people," Mike said, looking solemnly
at the execution lists published in a Russian newspaper, complete with

ДИАСАМИДЗЕ Владимир Александрович
Родился в 1916 г. в г.Тбилиси, грузин, б/п, студент Московского геолого-разведочного института. Жил в Москве: Псковский пер., д.3, кв.20.

Арестован 3 марта 1938 г. Приговорен к расстрелу 21 апреля 1938 г. ВКВС СССР по обвинению в участии в антисоветской террористической организации. Расстрелян 21 апреля 1938 г.
Реабилитирован 12 мая 1956 г. ВКВС СССР.

ДИЖУР Макс Захарович
Родился в 1891 г. в г.Киев, еврей, б/п, образование высшее, гл. инженер Гл. управления промышленности растительных жиров и масел Наркомата пищевой промышленности СССР. Жил в Москве: ул.Горького, д.38, кв.286.

Арестован 15 февраля 1938 г. Приговорен к расстрелу 15 сентября 1938 г. ВКВС СССР по обвинению в участии в антисоветской террористической организации. Расстрелян 15 сентября 1938 г.
Реабилитирован 26 декабря 1956 г. ВКВС СССР.

ДИК Иван Осипович
Родился в 1893 г. в г.Бухарест, румын, член ВКП(б), образование высшее, зам. начальника отдела Центрального управления народно-хозяйственного учета Госплана СССР. Жил в Москве: Божедомский пер., д.1, кв.6.

Арестован 5 апреля 1937 г. Приговорен к расстрелу 4 января 1938 г. ВКВС СССР по обвинению в шпионаже. Расстрелян 4 января 1938 г.
Реабилитирован 23 июня 1956 г. ВКВС СССР.

ДИКГОФ Константин Борисович
Родился в 1878 г. в г.Москва, русский, б/п, образование среднее, бухгалтер магазина № 3 московской конторы Гл. управления автотракторной промышленности Наркомата машиностроения СССР. Жил в Москве: Староконюшенный пер., д.28, кв.6.
Арестован 28 декабря 1937 г. Приговорен к расстрелу 3 апреля 1938 г. ВКВС СССР по обвинению в шпионаже. Расстрелян 3 апреля 1938 г.
Реабилитирован 30 января 1958 г. ВКВС.СССР.

ДИМАНШТЕЙН Семен Маркович
Родился в 1886 г. в г.Старая Русса, еврей, член ВКП(б), доктор исторических наук, председатель ЦК Общества земельного устройства трудящихся евреев в СССР (ОЗЕТ), редактор журнала «Революция и национальности». Жил в Москве: ул.Коминтерна, д.10, кв.2.
Арестован 21 февраля 1938 г. Приговорен к расстрелу 25 августа 1938 г. ВКВС СССР по обвинению в участии в к.-р. террористической организации. Расстрелян 25 августа 1938 г.
Реабилитирован 13 августа 1955 г. ВКВС СССР.

ДИМЕНТ Евсей Лазаревич
Родился в 1897 г. в д.Верхиевка Черниговской обл., еврей, из рабочих, член ВКП(б), образование высшее, секретарь парткома завода № 171. Жил в Москве: Трехгорный Вал, д.4, кв.25.
Арестован 29 января 1938 г. Приговорен к расстрелу 9 мая 1938 г. ВКВС СССР по обвинению в участии в к.-р. организации. Расстрелян 9 мая 1938 г.
Реабилитирован 26 ноября 1955 г. ВКВС СССР.

ДИМИТРАШКО Федор Тимофеевич
Родился в 1896 г. в с.Коркмазы Аккерманского уезда Бессарабской губ., молдаванин, член ВКП(б), образование низшее, начальник Всесоюзной конторы по борьбе с амбарными вредителями Комитета заготовок сельскохозяйственных продуктов при СНК СССР. Жил в Москве: 4-й Сыромятнический пер., д.1, кв.8.
Арестован 31 августа 1937 г. Приговорен к расстрелу 15 марта 1938 г. ВКВС СССР по обвинению в участии в антисоветской террористической организации. Расстрелян 15 марта 1938 г.
Реабилитирован 3 ноября 1956 г. ВКВС СССР.

ДИНАМОВ Сергей Сергеевич
Родился в 1901 г. в г.Москва, русский, из служащих, член ВКП(б), образование незаконченное высшее, директор Института красной профессуры литературы, редактор журнала «Интернациональная литература». Жил в Москве: Страстной бул., д.8, кв.27.

Арестован 26 сентября 1938 г. Приговорен к расстрелу 15 апреля 1939 г. ВКВС СССР по обвинению в участии в к.-р. террористической организации. Расстрелян 16 апреля 1939 г.
Реабилитирован 19 мая 1956 г. ВКВС СССР.

ДИСТЛЕР Александр Григорьевич
Родился в 1881 г. в г.Томск, еврей, б/п, образование высшее, горный инженер. Жил в Москве: Никитский бул., д.25, кв.14.

Арестован 18 сентября 1937 г. Приговорен к расстрелу 15 марта 1938 г. ВКВС СССР по обвинению в участии в к.-р. террористической организации. Расстрелян 15 марта 1938 г.
Реабилитирован 30 мая 1957 г. ВКВС СССР.

ДИСТЛЕР Василий Григорьевич
Родился в 1884 г. в г.Томск, еврей, б/п, образование высшее, старший юрисконсульт Главсырья Наркомата пищевой промышленности СССР. Жил в Москве: Гоголевский бул., д.8,

Арестован 28 января 1938 г. Приговорен к расстрелу 25 апреля 1938 г. ВКВС СССР по обвинению в участии в антисоветской террористической организации. Расстрелян 25 апреля 1938 г.
Реабилитирован 6 мая 1958 г. ВКВС СССР.

Russian newspaper article describing the execution of two of Mike's great-uncles, Alexander and Vasily Distler (*bottom right*). (Public domain)

photographs of the executed. "It all died with my father. But I'm so used to knowing that I'm beyond lucky—it's like a joke, this luck. And what a putz to ever have complained of anything for even a moment."

After a long pause, Mike told me something else—something I have very rarely heard discussed in relation to the Holocaust and the immigration of Jewish people from Germany to America. "Very few people know that this has utterly haunted me," he said. "But in order to get a visa to this country—and I don't know whether it's still true, but it was certainly true then—you needed to be guaranteed financially. And my mother had a rich cousin living in this country who did it for us. Without it, you didn't get in. There were some charities who would do it for some Jews who applied. But they were very few, and it didn't happen very much. So money made the difference." He added, "And it's only recently, very recently, that I discovered this. I didn't know it. My mother never told me. But I was so shocked by all this because it's all privilege that we're talking about. It's the same everywhere, always." As we shall see, Malcolm Gladwell, like Mike Nichols, was also shocked at a revelation about the inherited effects of privilege that we discovered on the Jamaican side of his family tree.

We have all read about the collective guilt felt by Jewish people who escaped the Holocaust—the guilt of those who lived while six million died—and I wanted to know if Mike had ever been troubled by this.

"Of course," he replied, "of course there's guilt. I once was at a dinner where I sat next to a woman who had come from Germany roughly the same time I did. And she said that she'd gone to a shrink in New York and said that she didn't know that she could live with the guilt, and he said, 'Well, we found you at last.' She said, 'What do you mean?' He said, 'We've all been looking for the person responsible for the Holocaust.' And this was supposed to be a funny story, but I burst into tears at this dinner table because I never thought about it. I pushed it so far away, and once I discovered this, I had a very hard time for a long time."

He continued, "I never know what's going to trigger it because it's gone most of the time, and then suddenly something brings it up. Guilt, they say, is stronger than love. And that's a horrible but true thing. Of course the only way to deal with guilt other than bury it is to try to do a little something. And so you do what you can find, and you do what you do, and you get by. But of course, the idea that all of this is borrowed time, that I should have been six million and one, is all-pervasive. There's nothing I can do about it except cherish my luck and be grateful for it. I guess I think of myself as that bacterium that survived and somehow bred on. Bacteria is the wrong metaphor, probably. But look what happened: one little organism by chance survived all this and had a whole other opposite life."

At this point, we could go no further down Mike's father's line, but given the challenge of tracing the ancestry of Russian Jews, I was pleased that we had been able to go back this far. So we turned to his mother's side of his family tree and began to focus on the stories of a number of his ancestors whose lives, though also sometimes tragic, suggested some of the exceptional artistic creativity that Mike has himself displayed.

Mike's maternal grandparents, his mother's parents, were Gustav Landauer and Hedwig Lachmann. The couple were fascinating figures in their time. Gustav was one of the leading anarchists in Germany at the turn of the twentieth century. A public intellectual in the truest sense, he wrote about art, literature, and philosophy, as well as politics, and he labored tirelessly to create a more socially just Europe without economic inequities. His wife, Hedwig, was equally impressive: she was a poet, the librettist of the Strauss opera *Salome,* and she translated the works of Edgar Allan Poe and Oscar Wilde into German.

Thinking about the shape of Mike Nichols's career, I found the stories of both these people quite compelling. Gustav was born on April 7, 1870, in Karlsruhe, Germany, the son of a shoemaker. He was well educated, and despite his father's objections, in 1893 he became a journalist and public speaker, championing what he called "anarchist socialism" and traveling across Europe advocating for workers' rights and economic justice for the underclasses. In 1899, he met the thirty-year-old Hedwig, the daughter of a Jewish cantor from Stolp, Pomerania, then a part of Prussia.

Mike knew very little about his grandparents. "I've read a few of her poems in German and a few of his essays," he said, "but although I understand German, I have the vocabulary of a seven-year-old. And *Salome* is interesting to me as an opera—that means a great deal to me. I think it's a great opera, and it's one I love to see. And I'm always startled that it was her work. Of course it's Oscar Wilde, but he wrote it in French, she translated it into German, and she made it what Strauss made it. And my grandfather, I'm told, was a very interesting man, but she was an almost greater star. I mean, my mother got royalties from *Salome.*"

After Gustav was briefly imprisoned in Germany for his political activities, he and Hedwig lived together in England for three years, having their first child, Gudula, while Gustav was still legally married to his first wife, Margarethe. After divorcing Margarethe in 1903, Gustav married Hedwig, and the two had their second child, Brigitte, Mike's mother, in 1906. Soon after, Gustav began publishing a magazine entitled *The Socialist,* which was one of the leading voices of radical politics in its era.

During World War I, the family moved to Krumbach, in southwestern Germany, where tragedy struck. Hedwig died of pneumonia on February 21, 1918, leaving her husband with two young daughters to care for. Later that year, Gustav became involved in the November Revolution, a ten-month civil conflict that swept Germany in the wake of its defeat in the war. The revolution was an extremely fragmented and poorly executed effort to create a liberal socialist state in the power vacuum of postwar Germany. It was briefly successful, especially in the south. Gustav became "Commissioner of Enlightenment and Public Instruction" of a regional government headquartered in Munich called the "Soviet Republic of Bavaria." (His first and only decree was to ban all history lessons in Bavarian schools.) But when the government was taken over by Communists seeking to remodel their state on Soviet Russia, Gustav, who did not believe in Communism, dropped all political affiliation. He nonetheless ended up paying the ultimate price for his actions. In April 1919, Munich was reconquered by the German army. Gustav was arrested on May 1, 1919, and murdered by soldiers one day later in Munich's Stadelheim prison.

We found an account of his death. It reads, "An escort of Bavarian infantry brought him outside. An officer struck him in the face. The men shouted, 'Dirty Bolshie, let's finish him off!' And the rain of blows from the rifle butts drove him out into the yard. He said to the soldiers around him, 'I've not betrayed you. You don't know yourselves how terribly you've been betrayed.' 'Stand back there and we'll finish him off properly,' one of them called and shot him in the back."

Mike's mother, Brigitte, was twelve years old when her father died. According to Mike, she heard the news on a streetcar. Brigitte and her sister, Gudula, were orphans.

"My mother talked about that often," Mike reflected. "They then were taken care of by a cousin who disliked them and had children of her own and treated my mother and Gudula very badly. For a long time she suffered from being, well, a stepchild. After that she became a nursemaid, somebody who took care of little kids, and then she met my father and I think married him having worked just a very short time."

I asked Mike if he connected his creativity and success to his grandmother Hedwig. "Well," he said, "I've thought of it. I've thought sometimes that writing, the ability to write well, is genetic. Because it startles me in my kids. I have three kids. One of them never thought of writing. My son read, as far as I can see, mostly comic books. And yet when he was in high school he was assigned to write a short story, and he sat down and he wrote this really startling story. I mean, you might get it into the *New Yorker*. It was brilliant. I thought, 'Where did this come from?' And my other daughter is a writer. So that's something. I mean, it could be coincidence, but I think something is passed down."

I was curious to discover if this creativity could be found in earlier members of this particular line of Mike's family, but we were able to go back only to Hedwig's grandparents, Mike's great-grandparents: Bär Wohlgemuth, born around 1810 in Westpreussen, Prussia, and Julia Blau, born around 1812 in the same town. We were unable to learn anything more about them. We had more luck, however, with the family of Hedwig's husband, Gustav Landauer.

Gustav Landauer's parents were Herman Landauer and Rosa Neuberger. Rosa was born on October 29, 1845, in the city of Buchau, Württemberg, which had one of the largest Jewish populations in the region. Most were merchants or manufacturers who enjoyed freedoms and civil liberties that were rare at that time for Jews in Germany, including the right to acquire goods. They also had a large cemetery and synagogue, which proved a boon to our researchers. We were able to trace the Neuberger family in this town for many generations, back to the mid-1600s. And along the way, we found that Mike shares a recent paternal ancestor with a very famous German scientist.

It turns out that Albert Einstein's second-great-grandfather and Mike's fourth-great-grandfather are the same person, a man named Nepthali ben David, who was born in 1725! This makes them third cousins twice removed. Nepthali was the son of David; he wasn't called Einstein because, as our genealogist, Johni Cerny, had warned me, it wasn't until the early nineteenth century that European Jews were required to adopt a formal last name so that they could be taxed and conscripted into the army.

"Oh my God!" exclaimed Mike. "This is really amazing! You know how you sort of enhance everything a little bit for your pals? My mother used to say that she or somebody in the family was a cousin of Albert Einstein's. But I thought she made it up. And I have one friend, Alice Arlen, who is always saying something like, 'Well, that's what you would expect from Einstein's cousin.' I always felt guilty and ashamed that I had passed on my mother's little lie." He smiled. "But this is true? Son of a bitch! That's really astounding—to find out that the thing you've been bragging on and thinking you were a liar is true. I'll have to call Alice Arlen immediately. I mean, I have to admit, it is third cousins twice removed, so nobody was bosom buddies here. But blood is blood. Family is family." Mike was ecstatic to learn of the connection, and I was just as happy to have been able to affirm this family legend—many of these legends, of course, in this sort of research, are either impossible to prove or are easily disproved.

Despite the odds, Mike's family had a considerable paper trail: On his paternal line, we had taken his family back to his great-grandfather

Grigory Distler, born in the early nineteenth century in Poland. On his mother's side, we were able to go all the way back to a man known only as Avam, son of Abraham, born sometime around 1665 in Württemberg, Germany.

I then explained to Mike that DNA analysis could tell us even more about his ancestry. We began with the admixture test. I told Mike that his test revealed that he's 100 percent European over the past five hundred years. "Big shock," he replied, laughing. But it wasn't that simple. His DNA also tells us a great deal about what it means to be European and Jewish. I explained to Mike that his mitochondrial DNA falls into the haplogroup K2a2a, which is specific to Jewish populations and especially to Ashkenazi Jews. Haplogroup K2a2a is a subset of a larger haplogroup called K2, which is very common across the globe, especially in Europe. But the uniqueness of the second portion of Mike's mitochondrial genetic signature—the "a2a" part that marks his subset—represents a series of specific mutations that is found almost exclusively in Jews of eastern and central European descent. According to the geneticists we consulted, this means that Mike and 10 percent of Ashkenazi Jews alive today share a common female ancestor within the past two thousand years.

On his father's side, his Y-DNA falls into the haplogroup J2a1b. Today, haplogroup J2 is most common in southern Europe, Turkey, and the Caucasus, and the haplogroup is found in both Ashkenazi and Sephardic Jewish populations. It is, in fact, one of the most common male Jewish genetic signatures. Because this DNA signature is found in Germany and Switzerland, on the west, and in Latvia and Lithuania and the Ukraine, on the east, people of this lineage were most likely deported by the Roman army in about 70 AD from ancient Judea to Italy, where Jews were sold as slaves. Within a few generations, this Jewish slave community in Italy earned its freedom and began slowly to migrate north toward central Europe. Some stayed in Germany, while others moved eastward into Poland at the invitation of King Kazimierz of Poland in the year 1203. A possible limb of this tree might be Mike's great-grandfather Grigory Distler, who we know was born in Poland in the early nineteenth century.

"That's funny," Mike said, "because I spent a lot of time visiting Poland. I've been to Poland about fifteen times. I felt a kinship with Polish people. We had a great time." He held up his hands and waved his heavy-looking fingers. "See those thick fingers? That's real kinship," he said, laughing. We were both fascinated to see how closely our genealogical research dovetailed with the results of his genetic testing. The records that had allowed us to trace his family back to Jewish communities in eastern Europe were mirrored in his DNA.

If the analysis of haplogroups can tell us about our more distant human ancestry, was there any way that genetics could tell us if Mike Nichols is related to any of the other subjects in this book? David Altshuler and Mark Daly, two scientists at the Broad Institute, told me that they could answer it through an examination of autosomal DNA. The results showed that Mike shares a common recent ancestor with one of our other guests: Meryl Streep! The two of them share long segments of DNA on chromosome 13. This result is a moving reminder of just how small the human family actually is. "I'm totally speechless," Mike declared, enormously pleased. "And we look alike. She once said that—it was some ratfuck for me—she said that we share the same nose, and she meant literally there's only one nose for the two of us. But we do."

Mike was also rather startled to learn that he shares smaller stretches of DNA with another one of our subjects, Stephen Colbert, which means that Mike and Stephen's common ancestor is not as recent as the one he shares with Meryl Streep. We then began to discuss the fact that despite this strong connection to Meryl Streep, her admixture does not suggest Jewish ancestry—whereas Mike's DNA clearly reveals a strong and direct connection to genetic populations that define themselves as Jewish. We were both quite fascinated by the way genetic science makes nonsense of any simple classifications based on "race" or notions of some sort of genetic purity. Mike Nichols and Meryl Streep share an identical stretch of DNA because they share an actual ancestor, an ancestor whose mutations or alleles were not what we think of as one of the haplotypes shared by Ashkenazi Jews. In other words, the human community is a complex genetic mishmash. In fact, all humans share 99.9 percent of the same genetic information. And yet cultural and ethnic differences have been such a huge part of human history. People have historically, insanely, justified killing each other in the name of that 0.1 percent genetic difference, and they continue to do so today.

As we thought about the ironies of one's genetic heritage, and its relation to the paper trail that is used to populate a person's family tree, I showed Mike some of the writings we had found by his grandfather, the anarchist Gustav Landauer. In one particularly moving passage, Gustav, who had broken off with his father to lead a life of political activism, wrote, "Our complete ancestry is within us. The individual is a result of a long chain of ancestors who are still present within us and exert power over us."

Mike told me he completely agreed: "I think about that a lot," he said. "I see things of my mother in my son. I hear him say phrases he never heard her say. I'm constantly aware of those who came before us appearing in us. I feel connected to my ancestors. It took me a long time to get interested in the details and the specifics, partly because in our household there was so much chaos, but I feel very connected to them now."

I then asked Mike how much he thought we constructed our own identity and how much he thought our identities were dictated by our ancestors' shared experiences and, as well, the genetic heritage they passed on to us. "I think both," he replied. "I think that, as we know, if you work very, very hard and really concentrate and get lucky, you can change a lot over a lifetime. I'd think we can maybe change as much as two percent of ourselves. And that's doing a lot. I think the die is cast, but together we can do more."

He added, "It's like a good marriage. You are more than you were as individuals. And we just have to multiply that number, and multiply it. I think my grandfather was right that our complete ancestry is within us. 'The individual is a result of a long chain of ancestors who are still present within us and exert power over us.' Do these people exert power over me? Absolutely." But how? This question is what has propelled so many of us to attempt to trace our family tree. I wondered if the other guests in the series would agree.

2

Meryl Streep

1949

IF HOLLYWOOD WERE a kingdom, Meryl Streep would be its queen. There is no more gifted actor today on film or the stage. She has been nominated for twenty-five Golden Globes and sixteen Academy Awards (including wins for both Best Actress and Best Supporting Actress), and she has very deservedly received the American Film Institute's Life Achievement Award. I have admired her since we overlapped as students at Yale in the seventies. Even then, I found her stage presence transfixing, as I would watch from the cheap seats reserved for students. I could see the commitment she makes to re-creating or evoking, through tiny, quirky details, the wide variety of characters she plays or inhabits, from a middle-aged hippie in *Mamma Mia!* to my over-the-fence neighbor in Cambridge, Julia Child. Meryl Streep has the uncanny ability to conjure up a remarkable array of character types, seemingly effortlessly and at will, mimicking their voices, manners, and deepest feelings. I know that all actors are supposed to be able to do this, but it is difficult to imagine one who does so more effectively, with greater range or depth, than Meryl Streep.

When I asked her if I could investigate her family tree, I halfway expected her to have detailed character studies of all her ancestors at her fingertips. I was therefore surprised to learn that she—like all the guests in *Faces of America*—knew very little about her heritage in Europe and relatively little about her family's deep roots in this country. Researching these individuals thus became a remarkably rewarding journey for both of us; and I found it fascinating to watch Meryl, who is famously reserved and chooses her words with great care and thought, being drawn into the excitement of her ancestors' stories, imagining them right before my eyes.

Meryl was born Mary Louise Streep on June 29, 1949, in Summit, New Jersey, the daughter of Harry William Streep, Jr., and Mary Wolf Wilkinson. She's been known as "Meryl" since birth. It's a nickname her mother

The wedding of Meryl's parents, Harry William Streep, Jr., and Mary Wolf Wilkinson. (Used by permission of the Streep family)

picked for her. When I asked her what she thought she would learn about her family's past, she laughed and told me that she firmly believed that she came from well-earned obscurity. But that was not to be the case.

"There were stories on my mother's side," she said, "that somebody was hung in Philadelphia for horse thievery and that one of my grandmothers busted up bars with Carrie Nation in the temperance movement. But that was it. Just rascals, really. And on my father's side, I remember I was once given this genealogy book called *The History of the Streep Family in England* or something like that. And it traced the story of that family. They were all Jews in England who had come over from Holland and took the name Streep, which means 'stripe' in Dutch. But I really didn't know much else." She added, "Growing up, I just always had this vague idea that there was some Brahmin version of an American on our family tree, which had to do with coming on the *Mayflower* or something. And that was a class into which we just never fit in—the debutante world." But it turns out that Meryl's instincts were right.

When I initially conceived of *Faces of America,* I adopted what I thought of as the "Noah approach": selecting two representatives of different ethnic or religious groups, male and female—for example, two Roman Catholics, two Muslims, two Jewish people, and so on.

Like Meryl, I presumed that she was of Dutch and Jewish descent. Meryl seemed genuinely shocked, as I was, when we learned that we had found no evidence for this version of her ancestry. Instead, we were able trace her family tree in considerable detail all the way back to the seventeenth century and to introduce her to relatives from England, Germany, and Switzerland who were among America's earliest settlers. Indeed, on two sides of her family, Meryl Streep descends from founding fathers in Rhode Island and Pennsylvania.

We began our search with Meryl's father, Harry William Streep, Jr., who was born on October 3, 1910, in Newark, New Jersey. Photos show him to have been very handsome and well dressed, a quality I particularly admire. "He loved a nice suit of clothes," Meryl mused. She remembers her father with some sadness—as a man who encouraged her in her acting and loved music and singing but who experienced a rather difficult childhood. Although he died in 2003, Meryl made it seem as if he were in the room with us.

"He wrote songs," she said. "He was a great dancer. We used to dance in the living room, he and I and my brother. And he was a really good pianist when he was a young boy, and he got a scholarship to Brown. But they didn't have any money, and when the Depression hit, he had to leave school. He went for a year. But after that he never graduated from college. It was hard. Everybody had to go out and work. And he had so much potential as a person, but at every turn things kind of ran into a wall. He had a tough time with his parents. His mother was very ill, very depressed. And he had a strong streak of melancholy."

Harry ended up working for almost thirty years in the personnel department of the Merck Corporation, essentially hiring and firing people. Meryl believes it was a difficult job that wore his spirits down. But to begin to understand more deeply the sources of his melancholy, she told me we needed to go back one generation.

Harry was named after his own father, Harry William Streep, Meryl's grandfather, who was born on February 5, 1884, in Irvington, New Jersey, and spent most of his life as a traveling salesman. "He was in the army," she said. "When he got out, I think he sold tires, something to do with the automobile. He was gone a lot. And I know that because my dad was a very stoic person, but when he went to see my son in the play *Death of a Salesman,* when he was in high school, my father just couldn't stop weeping. He said, 'That was my dad. That was my dad.' So I think that life was rough: rough on him for traveling and rough for the two left at home. My dad was an only child, so he was just with his mom."

Harry's mother, Meryl's paternal grandmother, was Helena Huber, born on October 16, 1886, in Newark, New Jersey. She led a troubled life and appears to have been clinically depressed. She was confined to a mental institution for a time because of her depression. Meryl has vivid memories of visiting her home as a child. "It wasn't a happy place," she reflected. "It was tough. When we were kids, my dad dutifully took us there because he was the only son. So we would go every week and visit, but it wasn't fun."

She went on to add the sort of poignant details she might use in preparing a theatrical role: "It was an apartment where the shades were always drawn. My grandmother was afraid of everything, and so there was always just a sliver of light this big. That's the thing I remember best. It was really a sad household. My grandmother would save every single piece of tinfoil and wrap it in a ball that got bigger and bigger and bigger. It would go under the sink when it got really big, to reuse the tinfoil. They reused everything."

We were unable to find out much about Helena or to learn if there was any history of mental illness in her family. We were, however, able to trace her ancestry back several generations on either side. These ancestors were, by all indications, a stable group, arriving in New Jersey in the mid-nineteenth century from Switzerland and Germany and settling into a middle-class existence within one generation.

Helena's father was Balthazar William Huber. He was born in 1852 in Giswil, Switzerland, where records show that his family had lived in the town for hundreds of years. We could trace them back to Meryl's seventh-great-grandfather, Joseph Huber. He was born in the year 1650, and he married Marie Reinhardt. The Hubers must have fallen on hard times at some point in the nineteenth century, because records show that they arrived in America in the steerage class of a ship called *The City of Paris* in 1869. The ship's records list as passengers Meryl's great-grandfather Balthazar, along with his brothers Joseph and Arnold and his father, Felix. At that time, Felix was forty-seven years old, Balthazar was sixteen, Joseph was fourteen, and Arnold was eleven. Barring war or ethnic or religious persecution, prosperous people tend not to emigrate when they are forty-seven years old.

I asked Meryl what it was like to see the records of the actual ship that her ancestors arrived on. "This is like seeing a picture of something I've imagined," she replied. "And it's very touching. I just think those people were very brave. What were they leaving, I wonder? I mean, was what they were leaving so tough that they needed to come for a new chance? That's very meaningful."

I couldn't fully answer her question, but we were able to find some clues. Balthazar came to America with his father, Felix, yet there's no evidence that his mother, Franziska, traveled with them. Franziska and Felix had ten children together, but when Felix left for a new life in America, Franziska stayed behind with six of them—all girls—while Balthazar took the boys. "I wonder if he sent her any money?" Meryl asked, voicing the question that I was thinking.

We can't know for sure why Felix left Franziska and their other children behind, but it seems likely that economic opportunity was at the top of the list, and boys could potentially earn far more than girls could. The lure of well-paying jobs, economic mobility, and the eventual ownership of property was so strong at that time that millions of other Europeans in the "century of immigration" beginning in 1824 did exactly as Felix did, leaving behind families they hoped a newfound prosperity would allow them to retrieve. Often these families were reunited, but sometimes they were not.

It is hard to imagine Meryl's ancestors saying goodbye to spouses, parents, and children, fearing that they might not ever see each other again. And, in fact, the Hubers never were reunited. Franziska died in 1880 in Switzerland.

Going back down Meryl's paternal line, she and I then began to explore a similar story of another branch of her family: that of Harry Streep's grandfather, Meryl's paternal great-great-grandfather, a man named Gottfried Streep, who was the person who brought the Streep name to America. But he did not bring it over from Holland, and he was not Jewish, as

Meryl's great-grandfather Balthazar William Huber and his mother, Franziska Z. Huber. Franziska remained behind in Switzerland when her son and husband emigrated to America in 1869. (Used by permission of the Streep family)

she had been told. We tracked down the record of Gottfried's birth in a village called Loffenau in Württemberg, Germany, in 1815. His birth name was Streeb, but in German, *b* is pronounced like *p*. So the family name became Streep as soon as he arrived in America—from Germany, not from Holland.

We don't know exactly when Gottfried came to the United States, but we know that he married Christina Zelfman in New York City in 1851. She was also from Loffenau, born in 1831, and they might well have known each other there before they came to America. They settled in Elizabeth, New Jersey, and had ten children together.

The 1880 census reports that Gottfried was a laborer who worked at the Rankin Roofing Company and lived in company housing with his wife and children. Theirs seems to have been a very typical immigrant, urban, working-class existence, forging a new life in America, with the father working day by long-working day and the mother remaining at home, making do for all those children. "Poor Christina, is all I can say," Meryl remarked as she looked at her family tree, thinking about this working man's wife taking care of those ten children. At the time of the 1880 census, Gottfried was sixty-seven years old, Christina was forty-nine, and they were living in a home with children aged three, six, seven, ten, twelve, fourteen, seventeen, and twenty. One of them, the twelve-year-old, was a boy named Frederick Streep. He was Meryl's great-grandfather.

The family had left behind a long line of distinguished ancestors in Germany. Gottfried's grandfather, Meryl's sixth-great-grandfather, was named Johann Georg Streeb. We found the records of his marriage to Anna Barbara Stremmor. They were wed on November 18, 1704, and the marriage certificate indicates that Johann was "a citizen and most senior judge" in Loffenau. Records also suggest that at some point he was mayor of the town and that his father, Simon, was likewise a "citizen and most senior judge."

"Wow," says Meryl. "That's why I'm so bossy. Look at that. Judges! Oh, my dad would be so happy!"

We were able to go back even further on this line—as far back as her eighth-great-grandfather Johann Jacob Streeb, who was born early in the seventeenth century, in the year 1607 in Loffenau. Much of what we learned came from church records of baptisms, marriages, and deaths. These were Lutheran church records; everybody in this line of Meryl's family was Lutheran. Had she been Jewish on her father's side, as Meryl had thought, she would likely have had a much shorter paper trail, as we saw with the family of Mike Nichols, for similar reasons.

Meryl's family, on the other hand, has a continuous paper trail from her birth in 1949 to her eighth-great-grandfather's birth in 1607. I assured her that this was unusual. Most American families cannot trace their ancestors this far into the past—and most certainly very few, if any, Jewish families can, and absolutely no African American families, at least on their African side.

As I told Meryl, I think it's fascinating to try to imagine what happened to the Streeb family fortunes in Germany over the century after Johann Jacob was born. They had real importance in their town in Europe, at a time when the Puritans and the Pilgrims were braving the high seas and wandering through the wilderness, trying to build their city upon a hill. What's more, her family continued to thrive in that region for more than two hundred years. But then something drastic occurred that led them to move. Were they fleeing one of Europe's many wars? Was it financial disaster or the widespread rumors of America's unparalleled financial opportunities? We can't tell. But they decided they needed to leave. And they ended up in Elizabeth, New Jersey.

"My dad didn't know any of this," said Meryl. "I mean, that's sad.

He just didn't know anything about his family. He would have been so amazed."

As we turned to her mother's side of her family tree, Meryl quickly joked, "Now we're going to look at the horse thieves." But again, our research recovered stories quite different from what either she or I had expected. Meryl's mother, Mary Wolf Wilkinson, was born on July 30, 1915, in Brooklyn, New York. Her father, Meryl's grandfather, was a man named Harry Rockafellow Wilkinson, born in 1882 in Bucks County, Pennsylvania. His roots in the area ran very deep—as a matter of fact, the lovely Wilkinson Road in Bucks County is named for the family. We both wondered what the Wilkinsons had done to merit this honor.

We interviewed Meryl's cousin Stephanie Wilkinson in an effort to learn more about this line of her family. Most families include at least one person who has taken a strong interest in the family's history, and we always start our research by interviewing this person. Stephanie did not disappoint us. She told us that Harry's nickname was "Harry Pop" and that he was a very smooth talker who enjoyed himself—a "good-time Charlie," as she said. Meryl agreed. "They were all Quakers on his side," she told me. "They all said 'thee' and 'thou' in my grandfather's home. But he was kind of a black sheep."

Meryl herself remembers many colorful stories about her maternal grandfather. "He made big gestures," she said. "They lived in Madison, New Jersey, and he would work in the city and come out on the commuter train. My mother would go down to meet him, and one day he went to the back of the train where there was a cargo car, and he opened the door and out came a little pony. He lost all of his money, eventually. But, oh, she loved him. She was wild about him." Meryl also remembers that one of her favorite aunts told her a story about how, when she was going to marry Harry Pop's son, the old patriarch took her out drinking. "He took her to a bar," Meryl recounted, "and he sat her down and regaled her with jokes—just to see if she could fit in with the general family way of doing things."

Our research, of course, is generally unable to verify stories such as these, but they all had the ring of truth. There were certainly enough of them. And there was certainly plenty of evidence suggesting that Harry Rockafellow Wilkinson was a renegade in a long line of mostly otherwise reputable Quakers. But it turns out that Harry Pop wasn't the only renegade in this line of Meryl Streep's family.

Moving back in time, we focused on Meryl's fifth-great-grandfather John Wilkinson. John was born in Wrightstown, Pennsylvania, in 1711.

John's life was a familiar one in colonial America. It consisted of following the seasonal rhythms of farming his land, attending service at the Quaker meeting-house, and raising his family. He was a prominent farmer and a cooper—which meant he made barrels, an important part of the colonial economy at that time. In 1740, he married a woman named Mary Lacey, and they had five children. He seemed to be thriving. But the 1770s, with the outbreak of war with England, changed everything.

Though a Quaker, John became a Patriot and was deeply involved in the Revolutionary War. He never took up arms because of the Quaker prohibition against it. But he did take an active part in supporting the American cause. Records show that beginning in 1774, as relations with England were rapidly deteriorating, John joined a series of local committees that took ever stronger positions against the Crown. Then, in July 1774, he was elected to represent Bucks County, Pennsylvania, at the provincial meeting of deputies in Philadelphia. It is unclear what John's precise role was, but he must have made an impact, because just days after the Declaration of Independence was signed in 1776, he was made a delegate to the Pennsylvania Constitutional Convention. This convention immediately drafted a document ending Pennsylvania's status as a colony of England. John signed it, along with Benjamin Franklin, who was the convention's president. This is one of the most important documents in early American history. I don't think I've ever actually met anyone whose ancestor signed something this historic. I was thrilled for Meryl. I explained to her that this meant that her fifth-great-grandfather was one of the founding fathers of the Commonwealth of Pennsylvania. "This makes me so mad," Meryl mused, wistfully, echoing what she had said about her father, "because I can't tell my mother that there's some good news in the back history."

One would think that John would have been widely revered and respected for his leadership role in the Revolution. But in the minutes of the Wrightstown Quaker meetings we saw that it was not necessarily true. Because Quakers are pacifists—it's against their faith to do violence of any kind or to support it even indirectly through politics—the Revolutionary War was anathema to them, as was joining a political party. As a result, John had a long and painful confrontation with his fellow Quakers over his political beliefs. The minutes of the Wrightstown monthly meetings show that John was seriously criticized for his involvement with the patriots and was repeatedly warned to cease his political activities.

The struggle ended in a manner that must have been intensely painful to Meryl's ancestor. In the spring of 1777, less than a year after the signing

The Pennsylvania Constitution, signed by John Wilkinson, Meryl's fifth-great-grandfather, as well as by Benjamin Franklin. (Used by permission of the Historic Society of Pennsylvania)

of the Declaration of Independence, John's fellow Quakers decided to initiate an expulsion process against him, which began with gathering formal testimony. Then the Quaker elders went to his house, demanding that he immediately renounce involvement in the Patriot cause. But John was caught up in a personal crisis: his son, also named John, was at home dying. The elders were undeterred and entered his house to confront John

Minutes of the Wrightstown Quaker meetings describing the expulsion of John Wilkinson, Meryl's fifth-great-grandfather. (Public domain; thanks to the Friends Historical Library of Swarthmore College)

with their demands. Outraged by their insensitivity, John told the elders that he would rather follow his conscience and defend his country than remain true to his faith. Accordingly, in November 1777, the Quakers formally expelled him as "unworthy of Christian fellowship." John Wilkinson lost his son, and he lost his church, in the midst of war.

John was not the only Quaker to be expelled in this manner. It happened to a great number of people who participated in some aspect of the Revolution, on both the British and the American sides. Many Quakers were reinstated after the war; sadly, John died on May 31, 1782, at the age of seventy-one, before the war was over and before he was able to rejoin the church. "That's cold," said Meryl. "My grandmother is buried in the Friends Meeting Grounds. I wonder if they know that the family was kicked out?"

John was very a principled man. The records suggest that he was deeply conflicted and did not want to abandon his faith. In meeting after meeting, he alternated between defiance and apology—repeatedly promising to end his political work but then finding himself unable to do so. In the end, his country was more important to him than his religion, and he did what he felt was the right thing, the moral thing, to do.

He was recognized for his patriotism in his time, if not by the Quakers. He received a prominent obituary in the *Pennsylvania Gazette* celebrating him as a "unanimously chosen member of our convention" who "served in the assembly with zeal and integrity." However, the obituary also notes that John's conflict with his fellow Quakers troubled him for the rest of his life. It closes with the words, "We trust he is now in those mansions where the wicked cease from troubling and the weary are at rest." Although his family was reinstated after his death, John died disowned by the Quakers. And he was not buried in the Quaker cemetery as later generations of Meryl's ancestors would be.

Meryl spent a long time looking at this obituary. "They were such thoughtful people," she finally said. "Everything counted. Everything counted about what you believed in this conflict—between your conscience, what you think is right, and God, what you think is called for by your duty to your congregation. I mean, it's an amazing little record here of his moral dilemma. It's so sad."

Moving back even further on the Wilkinson family tree, we focused on another rugged individual: Meryl's eighth-great-grandfather Lawrence Wilkinson, born in England in 1620, the year the *Mayflower* landed at Plymouth Rock. Lawrence was her oldest immigrant ancestor on this line, but we could not discern the exact year that he arrived in this country. We know only that he was one of the first settlers of Rhode Island, and we can trace him there just twenty-five years after the Pilgrims landed in Massachusetts. The earliest record of his presence in the colony is in a document called "The Second Book of the Town of Providence," which he signed in 1645. It was appended to the original Civil Compact formed by the very first settlers of Rhode Island.

Though in England he seems to have come from "well-earned obscurity," as Meryl had put it, Lawrence prospered quickly in the colonies. Records show that in 1659 he became involved in local politics, first as what was called a "jury man"—a sort of local councilman—and then as a member of the Rhode Island legislature. We also found more than ten documents that record his steady acquisition of land in and around Providence, more than a thousand acres in all. "That's wild," says Meryl. "I'm thinking of my dad going to Brown, having to drop out because he didn't have any money."

Of course this was land that originally belonged to the Native Americans, to a tribe known as the Wampanoag. And as a result, Lawrence was caught up in one of the transforming events of early America: Metacom's War, also called "King Philip's War" after the English name for the Wampanoag leader, Metacom. This was very significant and tragic conflict in its time. Metacom was the son of Massasoit, the chief who negotiated the first treaty between the Pilgrims and Native Americans living around Plymouth, Massachusetts. The peace was short-lived. By the time Metacom became chief in 1662, Wampanoag lands had been drastically reduced by pressure from expanding English settlers in the east and the powerful Iroquois Confederation to the west. In 1675, after being forced to make a series of humiliating concessions, Metacom and his warriors struck back, attacking settlements all over Massachusetts and Rhode Island, terrifying the settlers, and killing some eight hundred of them (although as many as three thousand Indians died in the conflict). It turned into the deadliest war of the century for the English in North America.

The fight came to Lawrence Wilkinson in March 1675, when Metacom's warriors approached Providence. The total population of the city was only about a thousand people, most of whom fled for their lives. But Lawrence, with a few of the town's leaders, remained defiant; and while the Wampanoag burned thirty houses in the town, Wilkinson and his property were miraculously untouched. He died of natural causes in the year 1692. We don't know where he was buried—probably somewhere on his land in Providence. Metacom did not fare so well. He was killed in the swamps near Bristol, Rhode Island. His body was quartered and hung in the trees, and his wife and son were sold into slavery.

"Lawrence, this guy, he was stubborn," Meryl reflected, admiring her ancestor's willingness to stay and protect his property, when so many other settlers fled. At the same time, she expressed concern at how her ancestor had acquired his land: "But you know, it's brutal. It makes me feel sort of like it's my fault at some level. And, really, we're so ignorant of our back history. I've been to Rhode Island, of course, many times. I've been all over this part of the world. I never knew what happened there to my family— or any of this history. We're very busy with our own lives, but this connects us to those days."

She's right, of course. This war is one of many tragic events in early American history. Discovering our ancestors' participation in events such as these offers us an effective way to reconstruct and understand the large and seemingly impersonal events in American history. We are all descendants of people who did their share of terrible things and noble things, mostly unknown to us. So when we learn that one of our ancestors actually was a participant in an important historical event, we can only embrace history's complexity, and the complexity of our ancestry, as openly as Meryl has done.

As we paused to think about Lawrence Wilkinson's role in Metacom's War, I told Meryl that she had one of the most detailed family trees of American colonial ancestors that I've ever seen. But I had one more story to tell her, and it too involved early encounters with Native Americans. On her maternal grandfather's side, we were able to trace her roots all the way back to her eighth-great-grandfather, a man named William Crispin. He lived in England at about the same time as Lawrence Wilkinson, and his life was also closely connected to significant events in colonial America. Born in 1627 in Yorkshire, William joined the British navy when he was only fifteen years old and rose to be a captain serving under Admiral William Penn, the father of William Penn, founder of Pennsylvania. When Crispin was twenty-five, he married Rebecca Penn Bradshaw, becoming first cousin by marriage to William Penn. As a result of this connection, Penn chose Crispin to be the chief justice and one of the four first commissioners of Pennsylvania.

Crispin set off for America in 1681, but his ship was blown off course, and he ended up in Barbados, where he fell ill and died. This isn't the end of the story, however. William Penn then appointed Silas Crispin, Meryl's seventh-great-uncle, to be the first assistant deputy governor of Pennsylvania. Silas, born in 1655 in London, was also a "First Purchaser" of the first five hundred thousand acres of land that Penn offered up for sale in America. He died on May 31, 1711, in Dublin, Pennsylvania, a prominent and influential citizen, one of the original settlers of the colony. As such, Silas played an intriguing role in the colony's initial dealings with the Native Americans. Penn was unusual among our country's founders because he was determined to treat the Native American people fairly— to buy their land at an honorable price and to negotiate equitable treaties with them. This policy held during Penn's lifetime (it later disintegrated under the leadership of Penn's sons), and Meryl's ancestor Silas Crispin embraced it.

We found a deed from the year 1682 recording the first English purchase of land from the Lenape Indians, signed by Silas Crispin. So just seven years after Meryl's eighth-great-grandfather Lawrence Wilkinson fought alongside his fellow Rhode Island colonists in Metacom's War, Meryl's seventh-great-uncle in Pennsylvania was trying to avert such bloodshed by negotiating peacefully with the Native Americans. Though Penn and Crispin's efforts eventually came to naught (in the end, the Lenape were almost entirely driven out of their homeland), they represent a vision that was exceptional among European settlers in America. Whereas Meryl was somewhat distressed to learn of Lawrence Wilkinson's role in Metacom's War, she was visibly relieved that Silas Crispin had evened the score, as it were, in her family's relations with the earliest Americans.

"My God," she exclaimed. "I was so afraid you were going to find, you know, slaveholders and horse thieves. But my family is going to be so very proud and very happy to hear all this. They really are. And they're going to be shocked."

Meryl Streep had rediscovered a wide array of ancestors on several lines of her family tree, deep into her collective family past, including founding fathers as well as the aspiring, working poor. She reflected on her desire to know more about these people: "I thought that all of our family stories had to do with the people who screwed up. It really is very, very touching, you know. They were preeminent in their time, and that kind of makes me proud of them and the little acts of bravery that it took to get to that place. But also I'm honestly more intrigued with their households, with their wives, with the invisible history of the women that came alongside this august journey. I feel connected to them, because I'm a woman, and to their invisible life—how interesting it must have been. To look down the list of names of all the women: Susanna Kohler, Anna Barbara Trimmer, Maria Barbara Zeldman, Margareta Mongler, Christina Velch, Plain Wickendon . . . Her name is Plain! I long to know what the human connection is, what their lives were like."

Turning to Meryl's DNA testing results, I told her that although we could not illuminate the lives of these specific ancestors any further, her genetic makeup does hold a great deal of information about who she is. Her admixture test revealed zero Native American ancestry and zero African ancestry. Like Mike Nichols, Meryl is 100 percent European over the past five hundred or so years. She was somewhat confused by this result at first. She wondered how it was possible—given that the human species began in Africa—that she could have absolutely no African ancestry. This is an excellent question, one that it took me a long time to wrap my head around. The answer is that we are all related if you go back far enough. We all do share descent from a genetic Y-DNA Adam and a mitochondrial Eve, as it were, who lived in Africa nearly two hundred thousand years ago. But each of us inherits half our genome from our mother and half from our father. If we do the math, it is easy to see why our African genetic heritage isn't appreciably measurable through an admixture test in Meryl's case or in Mike Nichols's. Essentially, we get much more genetic information from our recent ancestors than we do from our ancient ancestors, which is why an admixture test on someone like Meryl or Mike can produce a 100 percent European result, since this test measures ancestry over about five hundred years.

To clarify this explanation, I showed Meryl the results of her mitochondrial DNA testing, which indicated that she belongs to haplogroup K. Scientists, I explained, believe haplogroup K emerged thousands of years ago when an ancestor of Meryl's was a member of a small group of hunter-gatherers who left Africa heading into the Near East. This group later branched out into Europe and then were part of the Celtic expansion into the British Isles, after the end of the last Ice Age some five to nine thousand years ago. Today the K haplogroup is common around the European Alps and in Great Britain. Given what we learned about Meryl's maternal ancestors in England, the paper trail and the DNA results, as in Mike Nichols's case, seem to confirm each other.

Meryl understood all this and was pleased to learn that haplogroup K is a very distinctive genetic signature, found in only about 9 percent of all the European people. "We're the ones that can do the accents," she said, laughing.

The Broad Institute's testing of Meryl's autosomal DNA revealed that she shares recent ancestral connections to Mike Nichols (of four million base pairs on chromosome 13) and to Eva Longoria (of five million base pairs on chromosome 2), as well as an extraordinarily close ancestral connection to Stephen Colbert. Indeed, Meryl and Stephen share thirty million base pairs—a huge stretch of identical DNA.

"Isn't that wild!" she exclaimed, delighted. "We're practically the same person. That is a thrill. I'm going to read about it more and tell the kids. It's just wild. And I never—I mean really never—knew any of this stuff. Here I was getting all ready for something really interesting out of eastern Europe, you know, and Russia and Poland—but no. It's a good story, but it didn't happen."

I asked her the same question that I had asked Mike Nichols at the end of our interview: what she thought of her relation to her ancestors now that she had a fuller understanding of who they were. I wanted to know if she felt in any way directly influenced or shaped by them or if she felt that their experiences had helped to form her. Her response was as thoughtful as anything I could have hoped for.

"I think we are nothing *but* them," she replied, casting her hand across her capacious family tree. "I am nothing but these people. As an actor I'm always trying to call up lives, and the reason that I think I know these things that I know as an actor is because I have the DNA of all these crazy people who were brave and cowardly and who were murderous and who were ambitious and avaricious. I'm everything—I'm all of that. We all are. We all carry the choice within us. That's the great thing about being human. You have the choice to decide who you're going to be, what you're going to do."

She went on: "And I think we are the sum of all the people that have lived before us. It's the source and seed of the great human quality of empathy, which we neglect but which art brings out. So for me, for an actor, I access that ability of us to look at people that don't look like us and to imagine how they feel. I'm channeling them in a way." She concluded quite thoughtfully: "Think how many lives we all carry around with us. Everything that they learned, everything that wounded them, everything that made them stronger, everything that made them happy, we contain in our little corporeal selves. So that gives me a rush and a kick. I am my people —good and bad."

3

Queen Noor

1951

LISA HALABY CAPTURED the world's imagination when, in a storybook marriage to King Hussein of Jordan, she became Her Majesty, Queen Noor. After King Hussein's death, she continued to command universal respect for her ongoing role as an outspoken advocate for world peace and justice. She plays an active role in promoting international understanding of Arab and Muslim culture and politics, Arab-Western relations, and conflict prevention and recovery. When she agreed to participate in this project, she told me her primary interest was to learn about the family of her Arab ancestors before they left for America in the 1890s. But, in the end, the stories we uncovered were perhaps most revealing of her ancestors' unique journey within America itself.

Queen Noor was born Lisa Najeeb Halaby on August 23, 1951, in Washington, DC. Her father, Najeeb Elias Halaby, was the only child of a Syrian immigrant father and a mother whose roots stretched back to France. The Queen's mother, Doris Carlquist, was the descendant of recent immigrants from Sweden and Great Britain.

Although she knew that the majority of her ancestry was European, Noor told me that for as long as she could remember, she felt very attached to her Arab roots. "People consider me to look Swedish, like my mother," she said. "But I was always more attached to the idea of being an Arab American than anyone else in my family. And I was the one member of the family who wanted to go discover that world—not to say my sister and brother weren't interested, but I was the one who made that a goal—and it came to pass in ways I never anticipated."

We began by looking at the source of both her Arab roots and her middle name: her father, Najeeb Elias Halaby, Jr., who was born in Dallas, Texas, on November 19, 1915. He was the son of a Syrian immigrant, Najeeb Elias Halaby, Sr., and Laura Wilkins, a Texan. Noor believes that her father was heavily influenced by the death of his own father when he was

Queen Noor and King Hussein with their four children: Prince Hamzah, Princess Raiyah, Prince Hashim, and Princess Iman. (Used by permission of Corbis Images)

very young. She believes that, left without a strong role model, he became especially ambitious and eager to provide security for his family.

"He was constantly striving for perfection," the Queen told me, looking at an old photograph of her father. "He was constantly striving to be of service and to make of himself more and more and more. He was driven. To my father, nothing was ever good enough. That drove him from his origins in Dallas to Stanford University and then to end up at Yale Law School—in a class that was distinguished for having a large number of American statesmen and others who had an extraordinary impact on the United States. That one class was highlighted in *Life* magazine once, and all the heads were circled of people who either were serving in government or had gone on to excel extraordinarily. And my father excelled professionally in a range of different ways."

Najeeb did indeed excel, distinguishing himself in both the military and politics. He served during World War II as a navy test pilot—a dangerous job that required young men to risk their lives in brand-new, unproven aircraft before they saw combat. "I think my father probably would have loved to have seen action," she said, "but he was serving his country and serving it in the best way with the best skills and talents he had. He flew some of the first supersonic jets. He was never happier than when he was in a plane."

After the war, Najeeb embarked on a remarkably successful career as a public servant and aviation specialist. He served under Presidents Truman, Eisenhower, Kennedy, and Johnson in various roles, among them deputy assistant secretary of defense and head of the Federal Aviation Administration. He may have been the first Arab American to hold so many prominent government positions. He was certainly the first member of a minority group to run a federal agency. When he took up the reins of the FAA he was instrumental in moving for the desegregation of all U.S. airports. He was also the CEO and chairman of PanAm from 1969 to 1972.

Despite this illustrious career, Noor does not believe that her father considered himself a pioneer of minority rights. To the contrary, she told me that her father strongly identified himself as an American, not as a Syrian or as an Arab American. Because of Najeeb's success, the Halaby family moved frequently, and the Queen herself grew up with only a limited sense of her roots. "We didn't grow up in an Arab American community," she said. "And I don't know that he would have thought of himself in those terms. No doubt he was aware of it, and as time went on in his career, he felt more and more of a responsibility to serve that community and to be someone who could help others in that community realize their potential. But my father was a passionately patriotic American. He reveled in his public service; he blossomed in that. It was the fulfillment of a dream, and he thought of himself first and foremost as an American. He was always conscious of opportunity—of how America had been a land of opportunity for his family and so many others and a land of freedom and tolerance and of infinite possibility."

We found some evidence that Najeeb's views were perhaps more complicated than he let his family know. In 1983, when he was interviewed by the author Gregory Orfalea for a book called *The Arab Americans,* he

The Queen's father, Najeeb Elias Halaby, Jr., with President John F. Kennedy. Halaby served four different presidents and was the first member of a minority group to run a federal administration. (Used by permission of the Halaby family)

described his identity in a complex way: "I've gone through several phases," Najeeb told Orfalea. "One is like my father, trying to be more American than American. That first generation of the immigrant Arabs really wanted to be 100 percent pure American then—they changed their names, they changed their religions even. They totally assimilated. They wanted to be in the Rotary and the Shriners and the country club. And they wanted to arrive socially, politically, professionally. And so when you're raised in that kind of atmosphere, you wanted to be all American. And yet underneath you sensed a deep, ah, the buzzword is heritage. It's also probably genetic as well."

After I shared this passage with Noor, I asked her if she thought her father ever felt a tension between his Arab heritage and his American identity. She nodded thoughtfully. "He was always trying very hard," she said. "He was constantly struggling to improve his ability to contribute, to improve himself. He was constantly aspiring to perfection. That is actually a spiritual quest as much as anything else. Every faith is exhorting us to aspire to perfect ourselves, to become nearer to God, or however it might be described. Though he would not have put it into religious terms, it was very similar to a spiritual quest." She reflected on the toll this aspiration could take: "It's an impossible struggle. It pushes you to push yourself, sometimes more than anyone should push themselves. He was constantly struggling to prove himself, to himself and to the rest of the world, because he did come from a heritage that was an anomaly in most of the circles in which he found himself, educationally and professionally and otherwise."

I asked Queen Noor if, when she was growing up, her family retained any cultural traditions from its Syrian past. She replied that there was a portrait of her grandfather that hung in the dining room. "He looked tall and dark, handsome, an extraordinary face," she said. But aside from that portrait, she told me there was virtually no evidence of her ancestry in her childhood home. "Arab Americans," she added, "were not a vital, dynamic community back then. They were still trying desperately to assimilate because, even like Jewish Americans, there'd been so much prejudice and so much resistance. When my father first lived in Washington, Jews and Arabs, all fellow Semites, weren't able to join various institutions—clubs and so forth. And that was true for a long time, even longer for the Arabs."

"I remember," she said, growing animated, "when we arrived in Washington—we're talking early 1960s—and *Parade* magazine always had a column of riddles on Sunday. And one Sunday, it was, 'What is a Najeeb Elias Halaby? Animal, vegetable, or mineral?' And that was my father. It's not my nature to take offense easily, so it wasn't that I was offended or hurt, but I was puzzled by it. And then I realized, of course, that my father's name and our name were very different from any of my friends' names. They were all pretty much white Anglo-Saxon Protestants or the Jewish American equivalent. But there was no one really from any other part of the world. So that is the first time when I realized that perhaps we might fall under a category like Arab American."

I was astonished at how crude and insensitive that magazine had been, without being self-conscious about it. It never occurred to the editors to apologize. It would have been incredibly painful for me to read that riddle in that magazine about a member of my family. So I asked Noor how her parents explained it to her. She told me that they did a small amount of damage control but that there was really nothing to talk about. Her father, she believes, must have been hurt, but at that same time, she is convinced he wanted his family to move past the incident as quickly as possible.

We can only wonder at the range of Najeeb's feelings on seeing his name in that riddle. It meant that he was important enough to be a clue in a quiz published in a widely circulated national magazine. But the insult of being compared to a vegetable or an animal in the well-known children's game would have been unmistakable. The most generous interpretation of the item is that the author was implying that Americans are ignorant of other people's cultural heritages; but I don't think so.

Najeeb, like so many hyphenated Americans, would have had a complicated relationship with his ethnic heritage. He was part of a generation —the culmination, in fact, of several generations—that wanted to assimilate into American society. His mother was of European descent, and so was his wife. And yet, at some level, he clung to his roots. Perhaps the best example of this is the subtle role he played in his daughter's courtship by and marriage to King Hussein of Jordan in 1978. At the time, it seemed like a fairy tale to everyone in America. But to the Queen herself, it was something simpler: a logical extension of her childhood desire to come closer to her heritage—to return to her ancestral home. And her father helped make it happen.

"We met quite naturally," she told me, launching into the story of her meeting with King Hussein. "He was trying to build an airline from scratch in Jordan, and he had a Lebanese aeronautical engineer helping him, a gentleman named Ali Handoor, who also knew my father and brought him in as an aviation adviser. So the building of that airline was a creation of three men for whom aviation had been a passion, in the case of my husband and my father, from their teens. And we met at an airport, perchance at a ceremony. I was working in Iran and was passing through Jordan on my way back to the United States for a brief stop, and my father suggested we meet in Jordan. While we were there, my father and I were invited to a reception for the first Boeing 747 to arrive in Jordan. And I met my husband there."

This meeting occurred in 1976. It was not, Noor recalls, in any sense a romantic meeting. She was twenty-five, and Hussein was forty-one, happily married to his third wife. But months later, his wife died tragically in a helicopter crash, and over the course of the following two years, Hussein began to court Noor. "On several occasions," she said, "he came to the United States and said that he wanted to see my father. There were preparations under way for an international peace conference on the Arab-Israeli conflict. And he was working very hard to pull together the different strands of this conference. And it first it did not occur to me that it was a courtship at all. It seemed it was a friendship based on long discussions about Middle Eastern politics, about the search for peace in the region, about the people and the history and the heritage of the region. I just thought that he needed someone to talk to." Their relationship developed slowly: "We would have long conversations. I'd often get a phone call asking if I'd like to come up for dinner. I would go up for dinner. We would stay up talking or watching a movie. He was a night owl, so I'd end up back in my apartment around twelve or one in the morning, and then I'd have to wake up at six the next morning. By the time I married, I'd lost about ten pounds."

Queen Noor told me that perhaps the greatest obstacle to their courtship was her own fear that her being an Arab American would cause problems for King Hussein. "I was worried," she said, "about how the people of Jordan would react to me because of having grown up and been educated in the United States—because American foreign policy in the Middle East was a subject of such controversy, such frustration. But he showed so much faith in the idea of us, and of what we could do together, and he just grew that love in me, I guess. I don't know how to describe it, but I accepted his proposal."

It turned out that the Queen's fears about the Jordanian response to her wedding were completely unfounded. "I was welcomed as a Halaby," she said, "as an Arab returning home. And that is just natural for the Arab world and for Arab culture and society, and it does make sense now that I know it so well. But I was very worried."

She then told me that she vividly remembers, as she was moving halfway across the globe and resettling in a very different culture, that she took comfort in knowing that she was participating in her ancestors' cultural history—except that she was moving in the opposite direction, from west to east. "I understand it is not unusual for the third generation to do that, to go home. And I was consistent with that. I guess I'm just a cliché really. But I realize that is a pattern for the children of immigrants often."

The Queen's grandfather Najeeb Elias Halaby, Sr., just before his death in 1928. (Used by permission of the Halaby family)

It is not difficult to imagine the depth of pride her father must have felt on her wedding day, as his daughter was reuniting their family with their Middle Eastern roots. Moving one generation back on their family tree, we started to explore Noor's deep Syrian roots. We focused first on Najeeb's father, Noor's grandfather. Najeeb Elias Halaby, Sr., died in 1928, when he was just forty-eight years old. The Queen had little knowledge of his life. She'd heard family stories that her grandfather and his brothers had emigrated from Syria through Beirut and then arrived at Ellis Island. As a result, she told me that she had always assumed that he was born in Syria, but she was eager to know more.

After a bit of digging, we found Najeeb's obituary. It indicates that he came with his family to America from his birthplace in Damascus, Syria, when he was eleven years old. There is no reason to doubt this—and it is striking because at the time, Damascus was a province of the Ottoman Empire, which included modern-day Jordan, Noor's country of adoption by marriage. "That's fascinating," Noor commented when I showed her the obituary. "I have often thought that my family origins were in fact in the region that I returned to and married and raised my family in."

The obituary also suggests that her grandfather came to New York with his father, Elias Halaby, and his elder brother, Habib, around 1891. We could not find a record of their arrival, because the point of entry for immigrants arriving in New York between 1855 and 1890 was Castle Garden on the southern tip of Manhattan, not Ellis Island (which didn't open until 1892). And unfortunately, the records for Castle Garden are not nearly as extensive as they are for Ellis Island, so tracing ancestors who arrived there can be difficult, if not impossible. This meant we had to look elsewhere. To my surprise, we found a great deal of documentation. It seems that the Arab immigrant community in New York was given ample coverage by the popular press in the 1890s. Our research turned up illustrations and articles showing that the American audience found these new immigrants quite interesting and exotic. We even managed to find a *Boston Daily Globe* article published on June 30, 1894, specifically about Najeeb's father, Elias, revealing that he left behind an important job as a treasurer or magistrate in several provinces in the Ottoman Empire.

Elias, Noor's great-grandfather, is described by the *Globe* as "well born" but possibly having fallen on hard times. In one intriguing passage, the article states a bit cryptically, "The future promised so little for him in his own land he has been prompted to come to America, with a view to educating his family as he would wish them to be."

Religion may have also been a factor in Elias's decision to emigrate. In the article, he praises the Ottoman Sultan, Abdul Hamid II, as a wise and progressive ruler, but he also says that Christians are "at a growing disadvantage" with Muslims, or "Mahometans," as the author calls them.

"I'm not an expert on Turkish history," Noor demurred, "but I know there was definitely an emigration of Christians out of the Ottoman

CROWDED OUT OF SYRIA.

Elias Halaby Comes from Ancient Damascus.

Mahometans Now Educated Enough to Take Christians' Offices.

Through Interpreter He Tells His Story
—His Reverence for Harvard.

One of the most interesting emigrants that ever came to America is Elias Halaby.

Mr Halaby, who arrived in this country about three years ago, has within a few days come to Boston, and a Globe reporter had the opportunity of hearing him talk about his old and new homes, at his present residence on Chandler st.

Mr Halaby himself played a silent role through much of the interview, for although he knows several languages besides his own, which is the Arabic tongue, thus far he has acquired no speaking knowledge of who come altogether empty handed, and sometimes empty headed and almost empty hearted.

He does not wonder that already those here who are conserving the best interests of the country resent the unlimited coming of hordes who not only can do next to nothing for themselves, but who are hardly conscious of wishing to do anything for their own betterment.

If Mr Halaby could but speak English he would be in great demand as a lecturer, for he knows his country from ancient days down to the present time.

He talks most interestingly of the manners and customs that obtain among all classes, from the nomads on the desert in the interior to the Mohammedan ladies who still go abroad veiled and enveloped in their native cloaks, but who in their homes wear the dress of American women, imitated more or less closely, and are certain before long, says Mr Halaby, to walk abroad with their faces uncovered.

He disposes of a great deal of the nonsense that is written about his people by those who merely scamper through the country and then write a book about it.

In common with nearly all foreigners, he knows a great deal more about this country than the majority of our people know about

MR ELIAS HALABY AND TWO SONS.

Boston Daily Globe article from June 30, 1894, about the immigrant experience of the Queen's great-grandfather Elias Halaby. (Public domain)

Empire—and the majority of Arab Americans are Christian at this time. I think it may be 90 percent of those who immigrated to the United States are Christian."

My guess is that most Americans do not know this; I certainly had no idea until I began research for this project. We all tend to assume that an Arab is a Muslim. But the Queen's ancestors, like most Arab immigrants of their generation, were Christian, even though she herself converted when she married King Hussein and is now a devout Muslim.

Whatever her ancestors' reasons for emigrating, economics was almost certainly among them. The Ottoman Empire, which had been the vital center of Eastern and Western relations for six centuries, was in serious decline in the late nineteenth century. As the Western powers jockeyed to expand their fields of influence in this once-great empire, it was probably clear to the Halabys that they might benefit from a change.

The very first known family of Syrian immigrants arrived in New York sometime around 1878. The Halabys came in 1891. So, in a very real sense, her ancestors were pioneers. Americans seemed to welcome them in surprising ways. We found dozens of articles in American papers portraying the Arab immigrant community in the 1890s. They are remarkable for a number of reasons, most notably for their relative lack of xenophobia or ethnic chauvinism. The illustrations show that the American audience found these new immigrants interesting and exotic, but they are treated with a far greater level of respect than the ancestors of many of the other subjects whose family stories are found in this book. Popular articles about Asian, Irish, and Italian immigrants, for example, often caricatured their subjects in demeaning ways—in the case of the Irish, as quasi-simians in the same way black people were caricatured. But in these articles the recent Arab immigrants are represented as a noble people, worthy of our admiration and, implicitly, of a place in American society.

The Queen and I were both surprised by this. The articles represent America showing its best face to immigrants—Americans at our most welcoming and least xenophobic. "I would have liked to have had this material post-9/11," said the Queen. "It would have been lovely to refer to it during a period when Arabs—whether they were Christian or Muslim or even if they weren't Arab but just looked Arab—were being profiled and attacked."

We then focused on her ancestors' experiences in the United States. The Halabys first settled in lower Manhattan, in what was then a small Syrian quarter, near Battery Park and Wall Street, very close to Castle Garden, where they had first disembarked. It was America's first Arab neighborhood. Many of the mostly Christian Arabs in this new immigrant community earned their living as peddlers. The neighborhood had everything they needed for their work: goods, suppliers, housing, community life, and places of worship. New York's first Syrian Orthodox church services were held on the street where the Halabys lived. They were at the center of their community. Records suggest that the Halabys thrived by importing goods, probably textiles and curios, to supply the Arab peddlers.

In August 1894, just a few months after the Queen's great-grandfather was interviewed by the *Boston Globe*, her great-grandmother Almas Mallouk Halaby—who had been left behind in Syria—arrived in New York with her younger children. But just two and a half years later, the Queen's great-grandfather Elias Halaby died. He was fifty-three years old. His teenage sons, Najeeb and Habib, inherited their father's business. It must have been a great challenge, but they clearly met it. In 1900, the family was living in downtown Manhattan, near the East River. Ten years later, they appear in the census as living in Brooklyn. This was a definite step up for Arab Americans of that era, as they moved from the warehouses and tenements of lower Manhattan to larger apartments and homes just a ferry ride away.

Something else important had changed in those ten years. Shortly after the Queen's grandfather Najeeb turned twenty-one, he became an American citizen. We found his oath, which reads in part, "Najeeb E. Halaby, petitioner, do declare an oath, it is my bona fide intention and has been for two years next proceeding this application to become a citizen of the United States and to renounce forever all allegiance and fidelity to every foreign prince, potentate, state or sovereignty whatever, particularly to the Sultan of Turkey of whom I am now a subject, so help me God."

This oath was signed by Najeeb in 1902. Citizenship was not an automatic consequence of immigration in that era (as indeed it has never been in any era). The Naturalization Act of 1790 allowed only "free white persons" of "good moral character" to become naturalized citizens of the United States. After the Civil War and the end of slavery, the Naturalization Act of 1870 extended that right to "aliens of African nativity and to persons of African descent." This meant that anyone else—including Arabs, Asians, even Native Americans—could be considered an "alien ineligible for citizenship."

The Syrian community in New York was very aware of its tenuous status. Government officials scrutinized all immigrants very closely, asking what race they were—white? black? neither? If they were neither black nor white, they were excluded from the right to citizenship. In the early 1900s, Arabic-language American business directories featured extensive discussion of this issue and, indeed, of almost every aspect of naturalization law. They included translations of the Chinese Exclusion Act and articles about the "Gentlemen's Agreement" between the United States and Japan. Arab Americans knew what they were up against. Because America was not sure how to classify Arab Americans, the immigrants themselves mounted a campaign to prove that they were "white"—and the Queen's ancestors played a role in this effort.

In 1909, Noor's great-uncle Habib Halaby wrote a letter that was printed in the *New York Times*. It reads, in part, "It cannot be said that simply because a people reside on the continent of Asia, or in any particular part of that continent, that they are Mongolians. . . . It seems to me that if the Syrians are refused citizenship upon that ground, it shows a weakness on the part of the Government. . . . The Syrians are very proud of their ancestry, and believe that the Caucasian race had its origin in Syria, and that they opened the commerce of the world, and that Christ, our Savior, was born among them, in which fact the Syrians take high pride."

The same year that Najeeb's brother wrote this letter, the first of several cases went to court to decide whether Syrians met the racial requirements for U.S. citizenship. Although people of other races tried the same tactic, more of these so-called racial prerequisite cases were filed by Syrians than by any other ethnic group. For the most part, the Syrians succeeded—just like Najeeb and his brother. It was a situation that is hard to understand today. As University of Southern California professor Sarah Gualtieri, an expert on Arab American history, told me, "Race wasn't really one of the primary ways that they understood themselves in the Middle East. They tended to understand themselves in religious terms or place-of-origin terms. But when they came to the United States, which of course was a highly racialized society, race became very important to them, and they realized the privileges of whiteness."

The Queen had never heard about this history. She had no idea that her ancestors had once had to argue that they were essentially white in order to gain citizenship in America. "I don't know what to say," she said, taken aback. "Among the Arab populations, the Syrians actually are known for being fair-skinned. It's the mixing of races: European, Mediterranean. But was the color of the skin really a determining factor for immigrants to this country?" I assured her that it was—that color has played a much greater role in determining who has been considered an American than is widely known. The issue of color did not concern only American blacks and whites; it is a much larger part of our shared past, involving members of virtually every ethnic group that has entered this country.

It is also an issue that the Queen's family seems to have moved quickly past, much as her father moved past that vicious magazine riddle about his name. The Halabys were strivers. They embraced assimilation as a means to a better life, and they thrived in this country. Citizenship and a growing business would have been more than enough achievement for most immigrants, but Najeeb was no ordinary man. Soon after his family moved to Brooklyn, he struck out for new horizons—in Dallas, Texas. There, he met and married the Queen's grandmother, Laura Wilkins, a Texas-born woman of northern European descent. It was pretty daring for a young Texan of her generation to marry a Syrian immigrant like Najeeb. But records show that by 1919, the Queen's grandfather was working as an oil broker, which attests to how quickly he must have gained the trust of the Texas business community. He even converted to his wife's religion, Christian Science.

By October 1928, Najeeb owned three homes and was doing so well that he and Laura opened a rug and interior-decorating business called Halaby Galleries on the fourth floor of the Neiman Marcus department store in downtown Dallas. Sadly, the Queen's grandfather died in December 1928, so Halaby Galleries shut down almost immediately. Still, Najeeb's ascent up the American social ladder is astonishing. And his son, the Queen's father, only furthered that ascent. "They were truly blessed," said the Queen, reflecting on her grandparents. "Their courage and adventurous spirit and determination and faith in themselves and in their ability to make a new life in a new country is something I've always admired—and admire even more now that I know more about it."

The racial classification on her grandfather's death certificate is "Caucasian"—something that did not surprise or disturb the Queen. Although she knows her father and his father were tremendously driven to assimilate, she also knows that they took tremendous pride in their Arab heritage. Najeeb married a Texan woman, converted to Christian Science, and lived an all-American lifestyle. Yet he kept his Arab name. As we saw in the story of Mike Nichols's family, and know from those of countless other immigrants, many people arrived on these shores eager to shed their names. The Halabys did not. About this, the Queen said simply, "I always was thankful for that."

It proved to be very difficult to find out more about the Halaby family's origins in Syria. The earliest Ottoman population records do not include vital information about ordinary families and individuals. When Western-style reforms were instituted in the 1840s, local offices began recording persons' names in connection with property rights, but unfortunately most of those records have been destroyed.

We knew that the Queen's great-grandfather Elias was born in Syria around 1844, but we didn't know where. The Halaby name suggests that the family came from Aleppo (which is called "Halab" in Arabic), but there were also indications that the Halabys may have come from Zahle, Damascus, or Beirut. Even if the surname correctly identified them as "from Aleppo," there was no way of knowing when they might have adopted it. It could have been generations earlier. (We encountered very similar problems researching the ancestry of Dr. Mehmet Oz.)

In the end, we had researchers search for her ancestors in Damascus, Aleppo, Zahle, and Beirut. They looked for Halabys in church and civil records, examining archives in the local headquarters of several Christian faiths. They also looked for traces of the Queen's great-grandmother Almas Mallouk, the wife of Elias Halaby. She was the daughter of Constantine Mallouk and Helen Midany, both born in Syria in the 1840s. Yet we could go back no further than their generation. Finally, we sent researchers to look at the Ottoman records stored in Istanbul. We knew it was a long shot, but since we had read in the *Boston Globe* article that Elias was a provincial treasurer or magistrate for the Ottoman government, we hoped that we might get lucky. Our researcher collected records for every Halaby he could find. We found some who were religious figures, others who were clerks, murderers, bandits, even an alleged embezzler. Yet the dates and details never fit. "Thank goodness," Noor responded, smiling.

I then told her that I was forced to conclude that we would never be able to trace the deep origins of her Arab roots. Her great-grandparents took the mystery of those origins to their graves. I was able to tell her that her great-grandfather Elias was buried at Holy Cross Cemetery in New York on January 14, 1897. In 1925, when his wife, Almas Mallouk Halaby, passed away, Elias's remains were moved to Greenwood Cemetery in Brooklyn so they could be buried there together. In addition, the remains of Noor's grandfather Najeeb Elias Halaby were moved to this burial site from Texas. The three graves are still there today. The Queen was not aware of this family burial plot, so after our interview we visited the site, where she prayed in honor of the couple who brought her family here so long ago and in honor of her grandfather.

Moving back down the paternal line on her tree, I asked Noor what she knew about her father's American family and, in particular, her father's mother, Laura Wilkins, who was born in Graham, Texas, on April 23, 1889. The Queen told me that she had known her grandmother well and had what she politely described as an "up and down" relationship with her. "My father was an only child, so he and his mother were very, very close," said the Queen. "She was a very artistic and creative and independent-minded and opinionated individual. But I discovered another facet to her character to my shock. In the early '60s, when we were living in Washington, she had a little place in Centerville, Virginia, and I was visiting her one weekend. It was when they were attempting to desegregate the University of Alabama. And Martin Luther King came on television to comment on the confrontation between the police and the African Americans and the standoff between George Wallace and the White House. As he was finishing, I said, 'Isn't he wonderful?' And my grandmother said, 'Oh yes, isn't he?' It took a few moments before I realized she was talking about George Wallace. She was talking about Wallace, I was talking about King."

Noor's expression conveyed a hint of her long-ago shock. "I had never come face to face with racism before. We had this knock-down, drag-out fight over the civil rights movement and over race—and I was stunned. And when I realized that there was no common ground between us, there was no meeting of minds, I rushed off to my room. I'm not sure we spoke or I visited her again for quite a while after that. I was completely devastated."

This is an astonishing story—all the more so because Laura Wilkins had married a Syrian immigrant half a century earlier. "I know," Noor admitted. "I've thought about that often. It's extraordinarily admirable. Even if she didn't have those feelings about race that she'd been bred with, obviously it had been part of her upbringing."

The story became even more surprising when we researched the life of Laura's father, John T. Wilkins, who was born in 1847 in Henry County, Tennessee. We found records showing that he enlisted in Duckworth's 7th Tennessee Cavalry, part of the Confederate army, in Lawrence County, Alabama, on October 9, 1863. He was only sixteen years old. The company he joined had originally been formed in Henry County, Tennessee. So the Queen's great-grandfather traveled some two hundred miles to join this unit of the Confederate army—probably because he had friends and neighbors among its troops.

John Wilkins saw action almost immediately. His regiment staged a daring raid against Union forces along the Memphis and Charleston Railroad, attacking the federal garrison at Collierville on October 11, 1863, and ambushing a train carrying General Sherman and his entire staff. Then, over the next year and a half, John fought with Duckworth's 7th Tennessee Cavalry in battle after battle through Mississippi, Alabama, and Tennessee. Finally, on May 4, 1865, he and the other surviving members of the 7th Tennessee surrendered to Union forces in Citronelle, Alabama. This was the last sizable Confederate force to surrender in the Civil War. Even to-day reenactors still relive the moment. After everything the Queen's great-grandfather had been through, at the end of the war he was still months shy of his eighteenth birthday.

The Queen had absolutely no idea that she had an ancestor who fought so passionately for the Confederacy. And she was not exactly thrilled with the news. "I don't feel any connection with him," she said. "Clearly his blood does not run heavy through my body." I asked her if she thought he was wrong to have fought for the Confederacy. Her reply was thoughtful and measured: "I have a feeling," she said, "that there is no way of knowing what his circumstances were as a sixteen-year-old. Every war is a tragedy. And I feel to this day when I look at war and conflict, whether it's in the Middle East or anywhere else, that every single soldier is a victim of politicians. I feel compassion for them no matter what side they're on, because I know that they think that they're doing their duty according to what they've been told, and that is usually highly politicized propaganda. And they're children—innocent young men and women sent to fight battles that they don't really know the reason for."

I told Noor that I feel very strongly that there is no shame in our ancestral past. We may carry some of their DNA, but we are not responsible for our ancestors' actions. All we can do is look at the facts of our family's past and reflect on them, emulating and embracing some, doing our best to avoid others. How are we to judge the dead? "I learned to live with my grandmother," said the Queen, nodding in agreement, "and to appreciate her other finer qualities."

Fortunately for us in our search for her roots, Noor's father wrote a memoir late in his life. In it, he describes the reaction of his Texas grandparents, John and Mamie Wilkins, when their only daughter, Laura, announced that she was marrying an Arab American named Najeeb Halaby. According to him, Mamie was suspicious of Najeeb, since she saw him "as an adventuresome stranger in a somewhat mysterious and not very solid business, with a suspicious nationality." Surprisingly, though, he goes on to say that John Wilkins, the former Confederate soldier, was not opposed to the match. In fact, John saw his new son-in-law as a kindred spirit and "a fellow seeker of freedom and advantage."

"Interesting," Noor mused. And, of course, I share her curiosity about this intriguing reaction. It is fascinating to think that an old Confederate soldier could welcome an Arab son-in-law so readily. From our vantage point today, this seems a credit to John Wilkins's open-mindedness.

We were able to trace John T. Wilkins's family back more than nine generations. It contained some very illustrious figures, including Queen Noor's third-great-grandfather, a man named James Roper Randle, who was born in the year 1793 in North Carolina. James moved to Tennessee when it was still a wild, unsettled frontier. In the early 1820s, he became the first mayor of Paris, Tennessee, which is the oldest incorporated municipality in the western part of the state.

The farthest back we could go on the Wilkins's line was to Noor's ninth-great-grandfather, a man named George Symes who was born in Winterbourne, England, in the year 1643. Around 1672, only a few years before Meryl Streep's ancestor William Crispin left England for the New World, George Symes and his brother also left England, when their father received a land grant in Antigua. At that time the English had been on the Caribbean island of Antigua for only about a decade.

George flourished in Antigua, eventually becoming a merchant and a member of the legislative assembly. He met and married a fourteen-year-old orphan named Dorothy Everard. Dorothy's family had come to Antigua from Meath, in Ireland, when Oliver Cromwell appropriated their estates in the 1650s. Although she was too young to marry legally, she and George eloped. Their first son, George Symes, Jr., was Noor's eighth-great-grandfather. And although the Symes family was doing quite well in Antigua, George Jr. must have shared his father's willingness to take risks, which seems to be a leitmotif in all of Queen Noor's bloodlines. In 1687, he left Antigua for the colony of Virginia—the new land of opportunity, just as Antigua had been for his ancestors. He started out by working in exchange for the cost of his passage, but soon he established himself comfortably in the colony, paying his own "head tax," as it was called, from 1694 on.

Like Meryl Streep, Noor had never known that she had ancestors in colonial America almost a century before the Revolutionary War. The most astonishing aspect of Noor's ancestry, however, was still to come. Her seventh-great-grandfather Adam Symes, the son of George Symes, Jr., married a woman named Mary Isham. Her family line traces back to some of the most famous names in the history of Europe. As a result of this connection, we were able to show that the Queen's twenty-first-great-grandfather was Edward I, king of England. Her twenty-fourth-great-grandmother was Eleanor of Aquitaine, queen of England. Her twenty-seventh-great-grandfather was William the Conqueror, Duke of Normandy and king of England. Her thirty-seventh-great-grandfather was Charlemagne, emperor of the Holy Roman Empire (an ancestor she shares with another of the subjects in this book, the African American poet Elizabeth Alexander). When King Hussein married Lisa Halaby, unbeknown to both, he was marrying a princess.

Finally, I told Noor that we had established a continuous paper trail between her and her forty-eighth-great-grandfather, Childeric I, king of France in the fifth century. Since the European royal families intermarried for centuries, her full pedigree includes kings and queens of Spain, Sweden, Finland, Flanders, and many other countries.

I well remember marveling at the news of a Princeton graduate's marriage to King Hussein, and this new information seemed like a fairy tale to me. The American descended from hardworking immigrants marries a king descended from an ancient and illustrious family line. Well, guess what? Hussein was marrying royalty, and perhaps he intuited this all along.

"I must say that this list is extraordinary," said the Queen, almost speechless, "and quite a surprise. I know that it seems everybody is descended from royalty these days. At least you're constantly hearing of people related to the queen of England or this or that. But this is fascinating, and it means I have to become much more familiar with the history of Europe, just to try to place some of these characters in here who are not familiar to me. You've given me a lot to do, a lot to think about, especially given my life today and the issues that are important to me. This is fun — this is a gas."

I then asked her how she felt knowing that we could trace her Wilkins roots back to the beginning of Western civilization, but on the Halaby line, we're stuck in 1844. "I'm frustrated by that," she admitted. "I would love to know about the Halabys, because Syria and where I live today, Jordan, have been a crossroads throughout time. And it would have been wonderful to be able to see the component parts of different groups passing through and whether they intermarried, because everybody was intermarrying probably. But I can understand why that's so difficult to chart."

Queen Noor's family tree shows the astonishing cultural diversity of America, a nation of immigrants. To recapitulate: On her paternal grandfather's side, we found the names of her Syrian great-great-grandparents

Constantine Mallouk and Helen Midany. We couldn't learn any more about them, but we found a wealth of documentation regarding their son, Elias Halaby, who was born in Syria in 1844. And then on her paternal grandmother's side, we traced her ancestors all the way back to a fifth-century king of France. On her maternal grandmother's side, we found her second-great-grandparents John Ackroyd and Jane Brooks, both born around 1822 in England, as well as her third-great-grandparents William Peddie and Janet Brand, born in Scotland around 1776 and 1781, respectively. On her maternal grandfather's side, the Swedish side, we could trace back from her great-grandfather Carl Johan Carlquist, who was born in 1841, all the way back to her sixth-great-grandparents Mans Mansson and Ingred Samuelsdotter, born in Sweden in 1661 and 1664, respectively. Queen Noor's ancestry is just about as diverse as one can imagine.

Turning to our DNA testing, I told the Queen that her admixture test revealed that she has no recent African or Asian ancestry. She, like Mike Nichols and Meryl Streep, is 100 percent European.

"That's a little boring," she said, laughing, just as Mike and Meryl had spontaneously remarked. I found this reaction quite intriguing, given the striving to be "white" that has characterized so much of American history, including immigrants from Ireland, Italy, and the Middle East.

Her mitochondrial DNA further confirmed this part of her ancestry. She belongs to the I2 haplogroup, which is widespread throughout Europe. The Family Tree database found that she shares a common ancestor with one individual living today in Poland, one in Russia, and two individuals in England.

Because Noor is female, we do not have any of her father's Y-DNA. But we found a male cousin of hers to trace her paternal grandfather's line. Test results from this cousin showed that her family's Y-DNA haplogroup is G, which is common among Palestinians, Moroccans, Georgians, and Ossetians. Indeed, the databases show that she has one twelve-marker exact match today in the Palestinian territory—meaning that there is a person living in the Palestinian territory who exactly matches her father's Y-DNA at this number of markers, indicating that they have a common ancestor a few thousand years ago.

The autosomal DNA testing done by the Broad Institute revealed that Noor shares an ancestor as recently as the past 250 years with two people in this book: Mario Batali and Stephen Colbert (who at this point seemed to be related to just about everyone, having already showed matches with Mike Nichols and an extremely close match with Meryl Streep).

I explained to Noor that she and Mario Batali share DNA on their second chromosome, from base pair 213 to base pair 221, which translates into eight million base pairs, which is a close match. She also shares DNA on chromosome 5 with Steven Colbert, matching base pairs 37 to 42, which translates into five million base pairs with everyone's favorite Irish cousin and late-night comedian. "I wish I had his humor," she responded. "I wish I'd inherited that."

As we said goodbye, I asked Noor the same question that I had asked Mike Nichols and Meryl Streep: if this experience meeting ancestors she never imagined she had, people with whom she shares a direct and recent genetic heritage, had changed the way she thought about herself. "I have a greater degree of admiration for my ancestors," she said, beaming, "because I've learned more about what they dealt with. Now they're people in my mind; they're not just numbers on a genealogy chart. And what I love is the entrepreneurial spirit on so many different sides of my family. I admire the courage. I know many of my ancestors were forced by economic and other circumstances to leave their homelands. But so many of them showed such grit and imagination. That fills me with admiration for them."

"But has it changed me?" she asked. "I don't know. It's too soon. I define myself as someone whose heart lies in several worlds. I am American in my heart, and I am Jordanian in my heart—in part because wherever I have lived and worked in the world, I have been able to feel at home. Maybe because I never had one community I was a part of, I don't need a large community to feel a part of a place. From a young age, I felt that I was —though the expression probably hadn't been coined yet—a global citizen. That's how I feel, and I think the healthiest future for all of us would be if everyone could see themselves as part of a global citizenry and feel a responsibility to contribute to that as well as enjoy all the riches and the privileges that come from that possibility." I can only hope that uncovering the cultural and ethnic multiplicity of contemporary Americans' ancestry contributes even in a small way to this worthy goal.

The truth, I told her, is we all have multiple identities. And the manner in which Lisa Halaby embraced hers is deeply inspiring, a model for a genuine multiculturalism—one lived each day and not just theorized about.

4

Louise Erdrich

1954

LOUISE ERDRICH IS the author of thirteen novels as well as volumes of poetry, short stories, children's books, and a memoir of early motherhood. Her novel *Love Medicine* won the National Book Critics Circle Award in 1984, and *The Plague of Doves* was a finalist for the Pulitzer Prize in 2009 and won the Anisfield Book Award for Fiction. She is, I think, one of the great novelists writing in this country today.

She is also the product of a fascinating, truly American family. Her novels are steeped in the traditions of both her Ojibwe and her German ancestors, and many of her works draw directly from her own family's past to chronicle the tragic interaction between Native Americans and the European settlers who took over their land. She agreed to participate in this project, she told me, because she wanted to learn more about these ancestors. I knew this would be a steep challenge for our researchers. But in the end, I was thrilled with the results and hoped that she would be as well.

Unlike most of the other subjects of this project, Louise already knew a great deal about her genealogy when we met. She grew up hearing stories about her illustrious ancestors, particularly the Ojibwe men on her mother's side who played vitally important roles in the history of their tribe. But we were able to track down other relatives—some very illustrious ones at that—about whom Louise knew nothing at all. And moreover, I think we were able to shed some light on the profound dichotomy between the European and Native American ancestors on her family tree.

At first glance, this dichotomy appeared straightforward. On one side of Louise's family tree were the Erdrichs, a German family whose experience seemed to reflect the classic American immigrant narrative: coming to this country in search of a better life, more freedom, and a future for their children. On the Ojibwe side of her family, by contrast, seemed to loom the terrible costs of that familiar narrative: the displacement and persecution that Native Americans suffered at the hands of the European

Louise at an Ojibwe tribal dance. (Used by permission of the Erdrich family)

immigrants, invaders of their land. But that dichotomy, as it played out in Louise's family, was not quite so simple.

Karen Louise Erdrich was born on June 7, 1954, in Little Falls, Minnesota. Her mother, Rita Joanne Gourneau, is a member of the Turtle Mountain Band of the Ojibwe tribe. Her father, Ralph Louis Erdrich, is the son of German immigrants. I began by asking her how her parents' marriage was viewed by the older generations of her family. Intermarriage between Native American and immigrant families is not unusual, but it can be a source of significant tension. "What I always observed," she said, "is that both families were very happy with each other, and all the people were happy with one another. I think it may have been a unique situation, but I don't know. All I saw was that the German side of the family was fascinated with the Native side of the family. The Chippewa or Ojibwe side of the family was interesting, maybe exotic—and so they were anxious to meet everyone."

Louise told me that she did not know if it was hard for her mother to marry outside the Ojibwe people. "She made it look easy," said Louise, "but it had to be hard. She had this loving family around her. She left her parents to live in a town that was largely non-Native, and she suddenly had

Louise's parents, Rita Joanne Gourneau and Ralph Louis Erdrich.
(Used by permission of the Erdrich family)

children and wanted them to live as full human beings and to be proud of
who they are and who their ancestors were. And she was immersed immediately in this life; she was nineteen when I was born, and she had my
siblings shortly thereafter. I would think it was overwhelming to her, but
she carried it off beautifully. And my parents are still married. They are *so*
married. They made it all work."

"History is a messy place," she added, with a knowing look. "Isn't it?
To make sense out of it, you need a love story. And that's my parents."

We then leapt into this messy history, looking first at her paternal line. Louise's father, Ralph Erdrich, was born in Ellendale, Minnesota, on August 6, 1925. His father, Louise's grandfather, was Ludwig Friedrich Erdrich, born in Pforzheim, part of the Baden region of Germany, on June 8, 1895.

Louise was only five years old when her grandfather Ludwig died, but she remembers him vividly. "He was a great, solid strong man," she told me. "I was about up to his knee, and he seemed to tower over everyone. And I remember he ran this incredible meat operation—this butchering, sausage-making operation. I can remember his laughter. He had a great sense of humor. Instead of handing out treats on Halloween, he had a big kettle of fresh wieners, and he'd give out sausages."

It is not surprising to me that Louise can still conjure up memories of her grandfather fifty years after his death. She's written a novel about Ludwig, *The Master Butcher's Singing Club*—one of her best works, in my opinion. But he was more than an inspiration for this novel; his remarkable life had a shaping influence on her entire family.

The Erdrich family in Germany. Louise's grandfather Ludwig is standing, in uniform. (Used by permission of the Erdrich family)

Ludwig was the son of Franz Ludwig Erdrich and Katharina Barbara Bäyer, born in Pforzheim, Germany, in 1872 and 1873, respectively. Franz was a butcher in the town, and Ludwig grew up planning to follow in his father's footsteps. World War I interrupted his plans. Conscripted into the German army, Ludwig fought in several of the bloodiest battles along the Russian front. In one, he witnessed the death of his best friend, a man named Emil. The exact circumstances of Emil's life and death are unclear, but the ensuing events are not. When the war ended, Ludwig returned home and almost immediately married Emil's widow, Elisabetha Ruf, known as Liesel, and adopted Emil's son. Liesel was Louise's grandmother, and this story, understandably, has long fascinated Louise. It was the basis for her novel about her grandfather, and it has a fairy-tale quality when she tells it.

Ludwig and Liesel, however, did not live a fairy-tale life for long. The harsh reality of postwar Germany overwhelmed the young couple. In 1919, following the failed November Revolution (in which, as we saw, Mike Nichols's grandfather Gustav Landauer participated and which eventually claimed his life), a constitutional assembly established what is now remembered as the Weimar Republic. Designed as a liberal democracy, it was largely unable to deal with the myriad problems facing Germany as the country almost immediately fell into a severe economic depression. By early 1922, with the economy crippled, currency almost worthless, and the government in shambles, Ludwig and Liesel felt forced to make a choice: to remain in their homeland and barely subsist or to leave their families behind and take the risk of emigrating to America.

They chose quickly and decisively. Records show that Ludwig sailed without his wife (just as did Mike Nichols's father, Meryl Streep's great-great-grandfather, and Queen Noor's great-grandfather) from Hamburg on the SS *Caronia*, arriving in New York on July 23, 1922. He was followed a few months later by his wife and adopted son. They settled in Ellendale, Minnesota, and had three more sons together—one of whom was Louise's father, Ralph.

"I can't imagine what it was like for them," Louise remarked as she looked at the records of her grandparents' journey. "It must have been so strange. I was told that my grandfather kept looking at people when he embarked, and he thought they must have some sort of nervous habit because they were chewing all the time. Well, gum chewing hadn't caught on yet in Germany, although people were chewing gum in New York. It's just impossible to imagine. They were from such an intricate little world where

Louise's paternal grandmother, Liesel Ruf, in Germany. (Used by permission of the Erdrich family)

everyone knew everyone, and they left. But they had no choice. My father has said it: his father desperately wanted a decent life, and he wanted the entire family to survive. And it was all on his shoulders."

In Minnesota, Ludwig opened a butcher shop, the trade he had learned from his father, and settled down to raise his family. Though his business flourished, his wife, Liesel, Louise's grandmother, died in 1935. She was only forty-two years old. Ludwig, suddenly the sole caregiver for four boys, faced another fateful juncture in his life. His parents still lived in Germany, and he had many relatives there. The Nazis had taken power,

Ludwig Erdrich, Louise's grandfather, outside his home in Minnesota. (Used by permission of the Erdrich family)

and the country's economy was stable. At the same time when Mike Nichols's father and mother were being implored to flee Germany for New York, Ludwig received a series of letters from his family back home encouraging him to return or—at the very least—to send his sons back to be raised by their extended family. Louise's father, Ralph, was at this time eleven years old.

"If my father had gone back," said Louise, "he would have been the right age to fight on the Nazi side eventually. And I think I know what would have happened. I think of it many times, and about that narrow opportunity for redemption that they had."

Ludwig politely refused his family's offers. He remarried and kept his family in America. And during World War II, his four sons all served in the U.S. military, fighting against their ancestral homeland and their relatives who had been conscripted by the Nazis (just as Kristi Yamaguchi's father and uncle ended up fighting against relatives in the Japanese navy). In two short decades, the family's cultural identity and national allegiance had been transformed.

"It's extraordinary," Louise remarked, thinking about the way that the world wars split families right down the middle, as the Civil War did to

American cousins born in the North and in the South. "I always find it so moving—what it says about this period in history and about the experience of this family coming over."

I told her that I had never thought about this issue before I researched her family and Kristi Yamaguchi's. The great century of immigration into the United States also involved a profound transfer of national loyalties. To think that Ludwig fought for Germany in World War I and then encouraged his sons to fight against it in World War II—it's difficult to comprehend the cultural dissonance this must have provoked.

When I asked Louise how her family confronted this duality, she replied, "What I understand from my father is that my grandfather loved both his American life and the people here. And I am sure that there must have been a great division in him, but he had the choice and he made it. He must have had to compartmentalize himself. But they were all, including my father, extremely dutiful people: they're people of their word and people of duty. And so I think that's how they moved forward."

Ludwig's four sons all survived the war, returned to America, and started families of their own. Sadly, his parents did not: Franz and Katharina Erdrich, Louise's great-grandparents, were both killed in the firebombing of Pforzheim by the Allied air forces early in 1945. "As I understand it," said Louise, looking at a photograph of the rubble that was once her great-grandparents' home and butcher shop, "she went into the flaming building after him—he was trapped there. And they both died there."

Louise's grandfather Ludwig died on October 4, 1959, in Morrison County, Minnesota, the patriarch of a large and prosperous family. His immigration experience, as painful as it must have been at times, is ultimately a story of salvation and prosperity. In exchange for his allegiance, America afforded him and his offspring an opportunity to survive and thrive. It's a stirring story. And when we looked back at Ludwig's ancestry, we got an even better understanding of how profoundly difficult his transfer of allegiance must have been. The Erdrich family had very deep roots in the Baden region of Germany, stretching back at least nine generations, to Georg Erdrich, who was born in 1631 in the town of Güdisbach. Her grandmother Liesel's family went back to just over a century later—to a man named Karl Mundorf, who was born sometime around 1765 in the town of Jagstfeld, where his family was very prominent for several generations. (Louise's fourth-great-grandfather Heinrich Joseph Mundorf was mayor of the town in the early nineteenth century, just as Meryl Streep's sixth-great-grandfather Johan Georg Streeb had been the mayor

The Erdrich butcher shop in Pforzheim, Germany. Louise's great-grandparents Franz and Katharina Erdrich lived above this shop and were both killed here during firebombing by the Allied air forces in 1945. (Used by permission of the Erdrich family)

of Loffenau.) It is somewhat surprising that Ludwig turned his back on such deep roots to seek his fortune in America—but that is the promise of America, and, for some people, it has proven extremely rewarding.

Moving from Louise's paternal German roots to her maternal Native American roots, we began to look at the darker side of this promise. While Louise's grandfather Ludwig was running a butcher shop in Minnesota in the 1950s, her mother's father, Patrick Gourneau, was tribal chairman for the Ojibwe tribe on the Turtle Mountain reservation in North Dakota, fighting for his tribe's very existence.

Louise remembers Patrick very well. "He was a vigorous man," she said, "even in his later years. I think he taught more than anything else a kind of resiliency, and that can be seen in his children. You'd see a pow-wow, and there'd be dozens and dozens of dancers. There was a time when all religious expressions of Native belief were outlawed, when dancing was frowned on, when it seemed that Native culture in many places had been eclipsed and that there might be no coming back. But he insisted on being who he was and on expressing it. He had enormous pride in his culture. He was defiant, but he was a wonderful politician as well. He made friends with everyone who set foot on the reservation. He made friends with the governor, he made friends with lawyers in the neighboring towns, he even made friends with General Omar Bradley. He was very, very good at what he did."

Patrice "Patrick" Gourneau was born on February 11, 1904, on Ojibwe lands in Belcourt, North Dakota. By the time he became chairman of his tribe in the early 1950s, Native Americans had been regulated by the federal government for more than a century through the Bureau of Indian Affairs. For most of that period, living conditions on the reservations were extremely poor. Late in the 1940s, an investigation found that the bureau's mismanagement, not the Native Americans' actions, was to blame. The solution was a policy called "termination," which sought to dissolve the federal government's relationship with Native American tribes. Termination seems like it might have been a positive policy for Native Americans, because it promised to reduce their dependence on an inept and corrupt government agency. But Patrick was very opposed to it.

"We had been reduced from huge hunting territories to tiny reservations like Turtle Mountain," said Louise. "And having been told they had to have a new way of life, having had their children removed to boarding schools, Native people were not doing so well. When you change a people's entire way of life, and when there is a historical trauma of this sort, where people have been reduced by disease after disease, it takes generations to come back from that. And they were not coming back. Unemployment was as high as 90 percent in some places."

Louise doubts the new policy arose from concern about Native conditions: "I think the U.S. government got tired. I think there was a weariness with the Indian problem. The solution was 'Let's just make them into mainstream Americans.' But there's always a subtext. The subtext here was 'You will be able to sell your land.' But, of course, holding onto land is crucial to Native nations. When all the land was in federal trust, they could sell only among Native people, which meant the reservations would remain intact. But with termination, the one possession of these people who were very, very poor would be their land, and it could now go to the highest bidder. My grandfather recognized that this would be the end of the Turtle Mountain Chippewa as a people."

Patrick was an extremely prescient leader. About a hundred tribes were terminated, and in almost every case, the impoverished Native Americans quickly sold their land for pennies on the dollar. But Louise's grandfather saw this coming and fought against it as hard as he could. He was eventually called to Washington to testify before Congress against the policy —and he was successful in convincing the government to spare the Turtle Mountain reservation. Today the reservation is still a place Louise's family calls home. Louise and her siblings are currently working to restore the family's ancestral home, one of the oldest on the reservation.

"I feel a great admiration for my grandfather," Louise said warmly. "I have his letters. I look at his beautiful script, and I think, How did this man with an eighth-grade education write so beautifully? How did he know when to act? How did he understand so much about the political climate? I don't know. He saw the downside, and he acted. He did not foresee what would actually happen: in fact, out of termination came an incredible resurgence of Native sovereignty. But he just fought so hard."

Louise's grandfather was also responsible for her decision to enroll in her tribe—a decision that many of her generation declined to make. "He wrote a really beautiful letter to my parents," Louise recalled, "wondering whether I should be enrolled or not. He knew how deep his Native identity went. He lamented sometimes in his letters that he was one of the few dancers at the time who would come out and dance, and he belonged to the traditional Ojibwe religion, the Grand Medicine Society. He knew that enrollment was not maybe desirable at that time, but he ended up saying since I had black hair and his kind of nose— 'If she looks so dang much like her grandpa, then list her with the Chippewas.' And so we did."

Patrick Gourneau was by no means the first in his family to struggle with the U.S. government. Indeed, his ancestors had been engaged in similar conflicts for centuries. Patrick's grandfather, Louise's great-great-grandfather, was Joseph Gourneau, Sr., known as Soozay. Soozay was born in 1825, in the Minnesota Territory. Over the course of his upbringing, that area saw a tremendous influx of white settlers, and Soozay was among the first in his community to seek some accommodation with these newcomers. He appears in the 1850 federal census, listed as "Joseph Gornon, age 25, occupation hunter." By this time, he had become a commercial buffalo hunter, working with and for white people. He was trying, it appears, to make the best of a bad situation. He raised his children as Roman Catholics. His son Joseph Jr. was even an altar boy for a traveling missionary. But he was unable to stay on his ancestral lands.

Seeking to learn more about this man, we found a document called "The Old Crossing Treaty." It was signed in 1863, the same year that Abraham Lincoln issued the Emancipation Proclamation. In it, the Red Lake and Pembina Bands of Ojibwe Indians in Minnesota sold all rights to their land to the federal government. The treaty bears the mark, among others, of Joseph Gornon, as well as his designation as "Warrior of Pembina." Louise later told me that she was stunned when she saw this.

We found a map of all the land that was conveyed by that treaty— seven million very valuable acres, a popular area for traders, accessible by steamboat and slated for railroad development. I wondered why Soozay would have agreed to sell it. "These people were probably desperate," replied Louise. And research suggests that she's right. The 1860s were a terrible time for Native Americans in the Minnesota Territory and, indeed, across all the northern and western United States. After years of aggression on the part of the American government, and countless treaties that had led to the loss of valuable land and widespread starvation, the Sioux nation had finally struck back, waging a bloody but unsuccessful war in 1862, in the second year of the Civil War. In its aftermath, the country was particularly unsympathetic to Native Americans, regardless of their tribal affiliation. During the months leading up to the Old Crossing Treaty, the governor of Minnesota was offering official bounties for Indian scalps. This was meant to exact revenge on the Sioux, but the offer made no distinction between scalps of the Sioux and scalps of the Ojibwe. Militias across the territory began hunting down the Ojibwe people. So it was under considerable duress that they entered—or were forced to enter—treaty negotiations.

Historians generally agree that the negotiations also involved outright deceit. I showed Louise the published transcript of a speech made by a man named Alexander Ramsey, who was the former governor of Minnesota and a U.S. senator, at the beginning of the treaty negotiations. It reads, in part, "He [President Abraham Lincoln] does not want their lands at all if they do not want to part with them. He has more land now than he knows what to do with. He simply wishes that his people should enjoy the

"The Old Crossing Treaty," signed in 1863 by Louise's great-great-grandfather Joseph Gornon and other members of the Red Lake and Pembina bands of Ojibwe Indians in Minnesota. (Public domain; thanks to the National Archives and Records Administration)

privilege of traveling through their country on steamboats and on wagons unmolested."

Soozay and all the other Native Americans who signed the treaty had been told by Senator Ramsey that they were merely giving the federal government a right of way. But in the fine print, the document actually ceded the entire seven million acres to the United States. The Native Americans had been deceived out of this vast territory, a territory that they had roamed for generations.

Senator Ramsey knew very well what he was doing. He wrote to Washington about the land stolen by this treaty: "The whole of this area may be regarded as ultimately available for agriculture and settlement, the soil being generally of extraordinary fertility. It embraces all the present paths of commercial travel, and the designated routes of projected railroads and telegraphs." He also kept a journal that contains translations of some of the speeches made by the Native American chiefs at the signing. Soozay was not recorded, but we can imagine his position from the words of his peers. One statement reads, "Ever since I can remember, and perhaps since the world was made, the river has given me sustenance. Since steamboats were put in it they have driven away the game and made me poor. You say that the land is not of much value to us. It is of great value to us. By your use of it you have made a great deal of money. That river furnished me a living. I drank its water. The beasts that engendered on its shore gave me clothing that I wore. You say it was of no value to us. It is there we used to get everything we had."

"I just tremble inside," Louise commented, looking stricken. "Because I identify with my ancestors. I always have. And knowing that it's not just Joseph Gourneau, it's their children, their wives—and imagining the life that they were now going to lead. It's extremely painful. I think it's a myth that they somehow had no understanding of the owning of land. They had a different relationship with land. They used their land. They hunted their land. They knew everything about the land. They and the land were inextricably intertwined. In a way, it's difficult for other people to understand."

It's heartbreaking to read about the devastating impact that our government, especially under Abraham Lincoln's leadership, had on Louise's ancestors' way of life and the great deception of this extraordinary transfer of land—seven million fertile acres, which could have transformed the economic future of the Ojibwe people had they been able to exploit it in the way that white settlers were able to.

I asked Louise if perhaps the recollection of this event inspired her grandfather Patrick, two generations later, to fight against termination. "I think he well knew that his was the final stand," she replied. "He only had two townships left on this tiny, tiny morsel of land, but the people of the Turtle Mountains would not leave. They wanted their homeland."

Louise's mother, Rita, told us about the patriarch of her family, a man named Old Wild Rice. He was, according to Rita, Louise's fourth-great-grandfather, born around 1750. He is known to have had some of the earliest contact with white settlers among anyone in his tribe. In the late 1700s, he worked as a guide for the North West Fur Company. He was also a prominent chief and has even been called the George Washington of the Turtle Mountain Band. He seems to have been quite a character. He is mentioned in trappers' journals, in tribal histories, and in Louise's family's oral histories. Unfortunately, we could not find any documentation that could take us back to his parents. We were, however, lucky enough to find the baptismal record of his son, Louise's third-great-grandfather. He was called Little Thunder within the tribal histories and "Joseph Georges" at his baptism as an adult in 1799. It is unclear whether Little Thunder was actually the son of Old Wild Rice. His baptismal record lists his father's name as "Joseph Grenon," and oral history tells us that the family adapted the surname "Grenon" into "Gourneau," connecting Little Thunder to Old Wild Rice. (Louise gave me a bag of wild rice, which has great cultural significance for the Ojibwe, following our interview in her wonderful bookstore in Minneapolis.)

Little Thunder, therefore, was as far as we could trace the Gourneau line with certainty. But by moving back across Louise's maternal family tree to Soozay, we were able to go much deeper, by exploring the family of his wife, Judith Delorme. Judith is Louise's great-great-grandmother. She was born sometime around 1830 in the Minnesota Territory and was part Ojibwe and part French Canadian. Her Canadian roots stretched back to Louise's sixth-great-grandfather François Fafard dit Delorme, a Frenchman born about 1660 in Quebec. At this point, I couldn't help thinking about Meryl Streep's ancestors arriving in the New World soon after the *Mayflower* landed and, as we shall see, Eva Longoria's family (like Louise's, a mixture of Native American and European) settling here well before 1620. I was astonished, actually, at how many of my guests could trace their ancestry virtually to the beginnings of European settlements in the New World and how very little they had known about their forebears before our genealogists rediscovered their histories.

We learned that François was a translator and Indian interpreter for the French king, Louis XIV—and that he participated in some of the first encounters between French and Native Americans in the New World. "I'm really astonished," Louise turned to me and said, repeating a refrain that became quite familiar in these twelve interviews. "I knew nothing about this."

We found a contract dated May 28, 1701, securing François's services to interpret the Ottawa language for the explorer Antoine Cadillac at "the pleasure of the King." At this time, Louis XIV wanted to keep the English out of the fur trade in the upper Great Lakes, so he sent Cadillac to establish a stronghold in this territory. Cadillac was instructed to build a fort, bond with the natives, work out land agreements, and exploit any resources he could find. He needed a translator—and Louise's fourth-great-grandfather filled that role. In early June 1701, just days after signing the contract, François set off from Montreal with Cadillac and about a hundred other men in twenty-five canoes, heading for land that they would name Detroit, where Cadillac established a fort called Pontchartrain. This means that Louise's sixth-great-grandfather was one of the founders of the city of Detroit, Michigan. "My mother's going to flip!" Louise exclaimed when she heard this. "The love of cars runs through that side of the family. That's incredible."

But there was more to the story. We found a map showing the land grants given to these early settlers. Lot number 28, located near the present-day intersection of Jefferson Avenue and Shelby Street in downtown Detroit, was given to François. He also received a land grant for a farm outside the city in what is now the famously wealthy suburb of Grosse Pointe. Today, there's even a plaque in Hart Plaza, just a few blocks from the site of lot number 28, that lists all the men who first settled the area. Among the names is François Fafard dit Delorme.

Further research revealed that this very same François Fafard dit Delorme was the grandson of Jean Fafard, a man who was born in Normandy, France, sometime around 1598 and who died there in 1696, having lived almost a century. He never came to the New World, but Jean Fafard, it turns out—in one of those six-degrees-of-separation situations—is a distant relative of one of the other people in this book as well: Mario Batali. Louise Erdrich and Mario Batali are ninth cousins once removed. "This explains my daughter," Louise joked. "She loves, loves, loves Italian food. And she *cooks*. I can't believe it. This is wonderful. We love him! I'm so hungry."

Moving down Louise's maternal line, we then began to explore the family of her grandmother Cecelia Mary Lefavor. She was Patrick Gourneau's wife, born on May 4, 1913, in East Grand Forks, Minnesota. Her ancestry can be traced back to Louise's tenth-great-grandfather, a man named William Sargent, who was born in Bath, England. William is reported to have traveled with John Smith to Virginia in 1614, not long after the English settlement of Jamestown was founded in 1607. We could not find any documentation of his journey, but that is not uncommon, as many documents from this era have been lost. However, we did find evidence that once William arrived in the New World, he made his way to the Massachusetts Bay Colony, where he prospered. He helped found the towns of Ipswich and Amesbury, Massachusetts. With William Sargent, we had connected another guest to a colonial founding father, just as we had with Meryl Streep.

We don't know why William came here, but in the early 1600s it was becoming common for members of the rising middle class in England to flee the regimented English class system in search of greater economic mobility in the New World. It seems highly likely that this could have been the reason for William's journey.

Going back even further in William's family tree, we found that Louise is directly descended on her mother's line from Alfred the Great, king of England. He is her thirty-fourth-great-grandfather, born in the year 848 in Berkshire, England. His wife was Ellswith, queen of England, born in 852 in Kent. And their lineage ties Louise Erdrich to roughly twenty English and Scottish kings and queens, just as with Queen Noor.

As I explained to Louise, Alfred the Great is quite a distinguished ancestor. He ruled from 871 to 899 and is the only British king to have been granted the honorific "the great." He famously fought off invading Vikings and founded England's first navy. But he's best known for his love of scholarship and literature. He encouraged his subjects to learn to read in English, and he made available English versions of all the great scholarly works, some of which he translated from Latin himself. He also commissioned something called the "Anglo-Saxon Chronicle," which is the first history of the Anglo-Saxons written in English. It survives today and is the most important source for this period in English history. He was a man of power, a man of authority, and a man of learning. Alfred was also a pious man, venerated as a saint by the Roman Catholic Church.

"My mother is fainting," said Louise, smiling broadly, "and I feel like I could fall over. I'm very touched when I hear that he was a translator, that all along we've been translating. It's as though this has been in our familial connection going all the way back—and that he loved learning and that he made certain that people's histories were known to them at that time."

Many people research their genealogy hoping to find a distinguished or even mythological progenitor. They want to trace themselves back to some important historical figure—George Washington, Abraham Lincoln, Thomas Jefferson, the early settlers, the *Mayflower* Pilgrims, a Cherokee princess, Chaka Zulu, the Nubian Pharaoh, Taharqa, or a king of England. Most people are disappointed in this quest. Most, myself included, find that our roots past a few generations are either unknowable because of the absence of a documentary record or because our ancestors were "justifiably obscure," as Meryl Streep put it. But Louise, like Queen Noor and Elizabeth Alexander, actually has a family tree filled with such figures. She's related to kings, to a saint, to early settlers in America, founding fathers of three cities—and, of course, she is directly descended from Native American chiefs. She has the American fantasy family tree. And the people on her family tree have been affected by both the best and worst this country has had to offer.

"I've always valued this," she said, looking over the branches of her enormous tree. "I've always valued the different people in my ancestry. It really helps me as a writer. The thing about being a writer is you can't leave anybody out of your sympathies—the criminal, the rich or the poor or the downtrodden or the destitute. So that has to be all inside of you."

Louise is the only subject I interviewed who declined to take our DNA tests. She had already documented the Ojibwe part of her ancestry to prove her affiliation with her tribe. And as she explained it to me, it's her tribe and her family who really make her who she is, and they have, she said, an "internal pie chart," a reference to the graphic of the admixture test I shared with each of the other subjects in *Faces of America*.

She explained her choice in more detail. "I really feel that identity is a very complicated mixture of what you grow up with and what you find out about yourself. I didn't want to add any confusion to it. It wouldn't do me any harm, but when I asked my extended family about this, and I did go to everyone, I was told, 'It's not yours to give, Louise.' Still, I wanted to be part of this, because I really wanted to find out more about myself, and I've found out a great deal."

Hearing this, I asked Louise whether what she'd learned had changed her sense of her own identity. I had shown her an extensive number of limbs and branches on her family tree, stretching back into Germany, England, and France. The Native American branch was a deep one, of course, but it was only one among several. She told me it was too early for her to tell what impact her new knowledge might have on her sense of herself.

"I don't know," she said, like all my guests thus far. "I haven't absorbed this yet. You hear things about who you are, and you form your identity. But it takes time. When I walk into a room, people just see a white woman. That's all they ever saw. But when I started writing, I wrote about what I

knew and what my background was. I didn't really think about being cat-
egorized. I thought of it as a natural part of my existence, and it surprised
me when I started being put into the category of Native American author.
I didn't know that I really fit there or that I really fit anywhere, because I
saw myself and still see myself as a writer—as a world writer. I try to write
the human destiny of each small person that comes into my consciousness.
And so I think the thing about identity is that it transcends so much—and
that it'll just take a while to absorb this. But I am very glad I did it."

In closing, I asked her the question I was finding myself asking all my
subjects: Is learning about one's ancestors important, and if so, then why?
What is the value of learning about one's deep roots? Most of us know our
parents, of course, and it certainly helps to know our grandparents, but who
cares about our seventh-great-grandfather or tenth-great-grandmother and
what they did? Why bother looking into it at all? And why are so many
people, myself included, obsessed with it?

"I think because we want connection," she responded, wisely. "We all
want connection. And I think it's partly because of what we call our American melting pot. I don't think we really want to melt into an amorphous
mass. We want to be ourselves. We're all really imagining that there is some
key to the self in this. And maybe there is, I don't know. But we really want
the connection. I've been so fortunate because the connection we want is
to feel a certain amount of belonging or peace in this country. And I have
that. I have a homeland, and I have a home. And I know who I am. I think
that's what we all need."

5

Yo-Yo Ma

1955

YO-YO MA IS among the most recognizable and beloved musicians on earth. The greatest cellist of our time, he has performed on every continent and at hundreds of significant events, including President Barack Obama's inauguration; he has won innumerable awards and sold more records than most rock stars. He is a hero in Asia and America and an inspiration to countless young musicians around the globe. Yet I was surprised when I first met him, several years ago, to learn that he knew almost nothing about his family's past beyond having visited the graves of his grandfather and great-grandfather. He was even curious about the source of his generational first name.

"There's a Chinese tradition," he said with a shrug, "that all the siblings from one generation share one character in their names in common, or one syllable. In my generation, it was 'Yo.' So my sister's name is Yo-Chang Ma, and either my parents had a sick sense of humor or they did not know that 'yo-yo' was the name of a toy or they had no more ideas—but they just said, 'Okay, Yo-Yo!' So that ended up being my name. And I know that *Yo* means 'friendly,' but I don't know where the name comes from."

When I started this project, Yo-Yo was the first person I asked to join me, both because I wanted to visit his ancestral cemetery and because I wanted to help him find out where that "Yo" came from. But more than that, I wanted to see what kind of family could produce such a modest, playful international icon of musical genius. I have been fascinated with the astonishing sweep of Chinese history since I was in graduate school and read Joseph Needham's multivolume *Science and Civilisation in China,* so I was cautiously optimistic that we'd find something interesting in the Ma family tree. We were rewarded to see a rich musical tradition unfold against a background of remarkably hard work—along with some very good luck.

Yo-Yo Ma was born not in America or China but in Paris, in a tiny one-room apartment on October 7, 1955. His mother, Lo Ya-Wen, and his father, Ma Xiao-Jun, were expatriate Chinese musicians living in France, eking out a living as teachers. They were poor and struggling—their virtuoso career dreams had not come to pass—but they were determined that their new son would share their passion. "Music was so basic in the house," Yo-Yo recalled. "It wasn't just the lesson and then the rest of the time no music. Music was always, always around. Both my parents wanted their children to have music in their lives. And I think they were both pushy parents in different ways." He smiled. "My father, being a violinist and composer, was a brilliant teacher. And my mother, the singer, was more the emotive type, who really responded emotionally to music. My sister, of course, played everything—and being older she was also smarter and wiser, so that was another aspect of what I experienced."

Despite this environment, Yo-Yo said that he almost ended up having no musical career at all: "My older sister played violin, and my father played violin, so I started the violin. I hated it—I couldn't play. It sounded awful, and I gave it up. I was three. So my parents thought, 'Kid's not talented. Done. Lost cause,'" he said, laughing. "But then when I was four, we went to the Paris Conservatory to visit somebody, and there was an oversized double bass. Just like kids all want to play with fire engines, I saw this double bass—which went up literally as high as the ceiling—and I thought, 'This is a really cool instrument.' So, 'Please, please, can I play double bass?' The compromise was the next-to-largest instrument, the cello."

Within weeks, Yo-Yo was taking daily cello lessons from his father—and it is hard to overstate the influence that Xiao-Jun had on his son's development. "He was a workaholic," Yo-Yo said, "both for himself and for me. He was in many ways a traditional Chinese parent, and I was scared to death of him, because he had his point of view, and in the traditional way, obedience is the way to go."

Yo-Yo's father was born on July 11, 1911, in Xianxiang, a tiny village in southeast China, about 35 miles from the city of Ningbo and roughly 150 miles from Shanghai. As a young boy, he discovered Western classical music and dreamed of becoming a great concert violinist. He showed talent, and his family was wealthy enough that they could afford to send him to study music, first in the nearby city of Nanjing and then, beginning in 1936, in Paris, France. At that time, China was experiencing intense political chaos; a civil war was being fought between Nationalist and Communist forces, and the Japanese, who had invaded once in 1931, were preparing to invade again. Paris must have seemed like a respite from war to Xiao-Jun. But it didn't remain one for long.

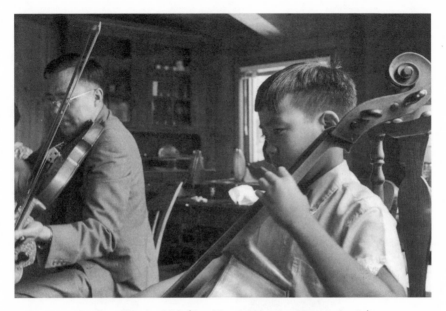

Yo-Yo practicing the cello as a child. (Used by permission of the Ma family)

"My understanding," said Yo-Yo, "is that he went to France to study in 1936, and he was in Paris when the Nazis came in. And so I think he couldn't leave. He was in Paris all the way through, from 1936 until 1945. One of the things he told me about that time remains very much as an image for me. During the war, there were blackouts. You were not allowed to turn on the lights, so basically you had to do what you had to do in the dark. A lot of his friends went to the countryside, but he stayed in Paris in some garret attic apartment. He would memorize Bach during the day and play music on his violin at night in the dark, because that was one way of giving comfort. And so to this day I think one of the purposes of music is to give comfort, to give meaning, to heal."

That's a lovely anecdote. It shows that Yo-Yo's father was much more than a disciplinarian. He was an artist, and a humanitarian, and Yo-Yo justifiably admires his great passion for art and learning. "He was all about studying and doing things," Yo-Yo remarked, emphatically. "Whether it was piano or cello or handwriting or calligraphy or French, it was constant learning. So hardworking. I remember when I was taking German in college, he was actually studying German too. Just an incredible person that way."

The wedding of Yo-Yo's parents, Lo Ya-Wen and Ma Xiao-Jun.
(Used by permission of the Ma family)

Xiao-Jun returned home to China briefly after the end of World War II, but the civil war was still raging. He realized the country was not safe and decided to return to Paris in 1947 to further his career. There, a chance encounter led to his engagement to Yo-Yo's mother, Lo Ya-Wen. The story, as Yo-Yo tells it, is that Ya-Wen got a scholarship to study voice in Paris. She took a boat from Hong Kong and on the journey met Xiao-Jun's younger sister. "So they met," said Yo-Yo, "and the rest is history."

Lo Ya-Wen and Ma Xiao-Jun married in July 1949 and began to raise a family in France. I asked Yo-Yo if his parents ever thought of returning to China. "That's an interesting question," he replied. "I think both of them were very patriotic. Growing up during this time of turmoil, my father was idealistic; he wanted to apply this newfound knowledge in ways that would serve his country. I think he was actually set on going back to China to teach around 1951. They had saved enough money to buy two tickets to go back. But then my sister was born, and they couldn't afford the extra fare. So they stayed."

This turned out to be a fateful decision, one that most likely saved the lives of Ya-Wen and Xiao-Jun—and that almost certainly allowed their as-yet-unborn son Yo-Yo to become the brilliant artist he is today. By staying in Paris, the family avoided the mounting terror of Mao Zedong's Communist Revolution. After more than two decades of civil war, Mao had taken control of China on October 1, 1949. His rule, which lasted until 1976, is believed by historians to have caused the deaths of at least fifty million Chinese citizens. It was almost three decades of mass murder, planned famine, and political terror—perhaps the most deadly regime in a century of genocide, from the slaughter of the Armenians and the Jews to the slaughter

Yo-Yo and his mother, Lo Ya-Wen, in Paris. (Used by permission of the Ma family)

of the Tutsis in Rwanda. Mao's various campaigns targeted anyone with ties to Western culture, including classical music. If Yo-Yo's parents had returned to China, it's unlikely they would have escaped persecution.

Mao's reign nonetheless had an enduring if unintended impact on the course of Yo-Yo's life. In 1962, his uncle Xiao-Jong, an electrical engineer who was living in Rochester, New York, announced that he intended to return to China to be with his wife and children. Yo-Yo's father was terrified. At this point, the extent of Mao's brutality was just becoming known, and Xiao-Jun feared that his brother would never survive under Communist rule. He decided to take his family to New York and dissuade his brother in person. For Yo-Yo, who was almost seven years old, it was a momentous trip. He remembers it vividly even today—indeed, it is a central, treasured part of his life story.

"My uncle came to the States to study electrical engineering, leaving his wife and young child in Shanghai, which was quite the norm at that time. So, many years later, after he got his engineering degree and a job, he said, 'Now, I want to go home.' My father, who was the older brother and had a knack for seeing things and calculating risks, thought this was the absolutely wrong decision. And he thought the only way to convince my uncle not to go back was to show up in person and tell him he couldn't go. And so with funds that came from under some mattress, he took the family to the States. We arrived in New York and went to Rochester, where my father persuaded his brother not to return to China."

Here is where fate took a hand in Yo-Yo's life: "And then we went on this train trip, through Chicago, and the last stop was New York City. On the last day, I think, my sister and I played a concert somewhere on the Upper West Side of Manhattan. The founder of an elementary school, a Franco-American lady, who was looking for a music teacher, came to the concert. She saw my father teaching and setting up the concert and was so impressed that after the concert she offered him a job to teach at her school, on the spot. And that's why we moved to the States. If that meeting had not occurred, I would have grown up in France."

This is Yo-Yo's immigrant story. Like Mike Nichols's escape from Nazi Germany and many other stories I encountered researching the family histories of the people in this book, it shows the fascinating ways our lives can be shaped by pure luck as much as by diligent work and hard-headed determination. It's enough to make you believe in fate. That chance meeting with the head of an elementary school in New York changed the destiny of the entire Ma family. Once Yo-Yo's father was in this country, despite

Yo-Yo and his family at the home of his uncle, Ma Xiao-Jong, in Rochester, New York. This photo was taken during the Ma family's fateful trip to the United States in 1962. (Used by permission of the Ma family)

being a recent immigrant, he made connections with a number of remarkable musicians who recognized his son's talents, including Pablo Casals and Isaac Stern. Within a year, Yo-Yo was invited to Washington, DC, to give a televised recital at a benefit with Presidents Dwight Eisenhower and John F. Kennedy in the audience. What a remarkable transformation for a seven-year-old boy who had just left a Paris garret and could barely speak a word of English!

"It was a thrill," said Yo-Yo with enthusiasm. "I mean, all of these new sights, new people, a new language—everything was exciting. We went to the White House, and we saw Kennedy. And obviously we were told they were important people, but then everybody was important. It was just thrilling." Yo-Yo had not remembered that President Eisenhower was also in attendance at his concert until I showed him a film clip of the event.

By early 1963, Yo-Yo was studying with Leonard Rose and Janos Scholz at the renowned Juilliard School and was well on his way to success.

His family never returned to Paris. He told me that he now believes the move was difficult for them, especially for his father, who had spent more than two decades in France and was suddenly forced to relocate and support his family in a new country at the age of fifty-one. Yo-Yo also believes it was hard on his sister, who, being four years older, had developed more of a life in Paris. But for Yo-Yo himself, the move was a pure blessing: "I had great advantages because I didn't have much of a history. I'd never gone to school, so I started second grade in the States. It was all new and fresh, and so I was lucky."

Hearing Yo-Yo tell his story, I'm impressed by his effortless charm and the easy way in which he constantly downplays his accomplishments— making his great success seem like a matter of luck and chance. I wanted to find out more about the generations that laid the foundations for this success, because I felt there had to be more to it than that. But whenever I asked Yo-Yo, he just responded that the two keys to his success were constant practice and "never doing anything for any particular reason."

To explore his ancestry, I traveled to China, to the tiny village of Xianxiang, where Yo-Yo's father was born in 1911. I went there to see the Ma ancestral home and the home where his father was raised in Xianxiang, to try to piece together the fractured family history that Yo-Yo himself has never really understood. I was fortunate enough to be introduced to a man named Wang Chung-Guang, an adjunct professor of local history at the University of Ningbo, who has researched the history of the Ma family. He had discovered the tombs of Ma's grandfather and great-grandfather while wandering through a bamboo grove looking for the remains of an American pilot shot down during World War II. He took Yo-Yo to these tombs for the first time during his official visit to Shanghai, which Professor Wang had conceived shortly after learning that Yo-Yo's father had been born nearby. Yo-Yo's sharing his feelings about this pilgrimage, at a dinner party in Cambridge, had given me the idea for the PBS series and this book. So finding Yo-Yo's ancestors had a special importance for me.

Professor Wang explained that my task was going to be very difficult. Genealogy, it turns out, is much harder to do in China than it is in the United States. Here we can trace families back two or three hundred years, if we are lucky, using census records and official documents of births, deaths, marriages, tax records, land deeds, and so on. (The process is similar for most European nations.) But records like these don't exist in China. Instead, the Chinese tradition is for middle- and upper-class families themselves to keep private genealogies. And although fifty years ago, virtually every family of note had an official family genealogist, most of those records were destroyed during the 1960s when Mao's policies made possessing them a crime.

Professor Wang told me that he doubted the Ma family genealogy could be found, but he said he was willing to help us try. What happened next was nothing short of a miracle. Wang sent researchers throughout Xianxiang and the surrounding towns, looking for members of the Ma clan and asking if any of them knew what had happened to the family genealogy. In a small village called Hou Ma, one of Wang's researchers found a distant cousin of Yo-Yo's named Ma Yo-De. He knew the location of the only copy of the four-volume genealogy—because he and his father had hidden it in the wall of their kitchen several decades earlier.

It was an astonishing discovery, perhaps the most exciting genealogical story I have ever heard. The Ma genealogy was consolidated and written down sometime around 1755, during the Qing Dynasty, by Yo-Yo's fourth-great-uncle, a man named Ma Ji-Cang. For reasons that are unclear, Ji-Cang decided to dedicate himself to compiling the family stories of his ancestors, recording the recollections of his elders, and noting the strengths and weaknesses, the triumphs and the foibles, of his male siblings and his male children. (Only men are named in the genealogy; women are referred to simply as "female.") He even decided to send messages to the future, dictating the generational names for thirty generations of Mas yet to come.

According to Ji-Cang's instructions, the clan genealogy that he initiated was to be updated by the male head of the Ma family every thirty years. His descendants proved quite willing to carry out his orders; it seems his genealogy was, in fact, updated more or less every thirty years for the better part of two centuries—and that each generation followed his naming dictates faithfully. Then came Chairman Mao. By the mid-1960s, during Mao's Cultural Revolution, the family genealogy was in the hands of Ma Yo-De, and he faced a serious dilemma. The Red Guards, acting on Mao's decree that certain factions in the Communist Party were counter-revolutionaries seeking to revert to capitalist or feudalist ways, were engaged in a campaign to destroy the "Four Olds": old culture, old traditions, old habits, and old thoughts. Possession of a traditional clan genealogy happened to fall under all four of these "olds." Ma Yo-De knew that he would risk being hauled in front of his townsmen and publicly humiliated, imprisoned, or even beaten to death, if he failed to destroy the family genealogy; but to do so would be to obliterate centuries of information about his ancestors.

After hushed discussions with his father, the two decided to hide the four-volume genealogy in a wall in their home. They fooled the Red Guard —but then they fooled themselves. They forgot about the genealogy, which ended up spending roughly three decades in the wall, absorbing dirt and moisture like a sponge. Finally, in the early 1990s, Ma Yo-De, like many peasants as China's economy was modernizing, decided to renovate his home. Tearing down a wall, he was astonished to discover the four volumes that he and his father had tucked away there for safekeeping.

At first, it didn't seem much of a discovery. The volumes had so much water damage and were so filthy that Yo-De assumed they were ruined. (He later told me he thought they actually were going to fall apart in his hands as he pulled them out of the wall.) Yo-De started to throw them away, but something stopped him—respect for his father's memory, respect for his ancestors, a sense that the books were valuable in spite of their condition. So he put the whole mess in a box and ritually placed it in the Ma Family Hall located in the middle of the tiny village of Hou Ma.

This is where Professor Wang's researchers found it. Then Wang himself journeyed to the town and opened the box in a special candlelit ceremony. And although the books did seem damaged beyond repair, it turns out that because they were written on bamboo, they were salvageable. The water in the walls of Ma Yo-De's house would have completely destroyed volumes made of wood-based paper, but damaged bamboo can, through a complex process, be brought back to life.

The volumes were quickly sent to restoration experts at the Tianyige Library in Ningbo. This library, built by Fan Qin in the Ming Dynasty between 1561 and 1566 and maintained by the Fan family for thirteen generations, is the oldest private library in China, the oldest in all of Asia, and one of the three oldest in the world. The restoration department at Tianyige made a duplicate copy of all the pages that were immediately salvageable, amounting to two of the four volumes, and is working to restore the rest.

In the end, more than half the material in the Ma genealogy was made available to our researchers, and even given that limitation, the genealogy is an incredible resource—a remarkable historical and social record. It includes essays, moral guidelines, poems, and biographies. It traces all the people with the surname Ma, through the paternal line. The Ma name is said to have originated with one common ancestor who lived in the third century BCE, a legendary warrior prince named Zhao-She who, after winning a crucial battle, was rewarded with the title Lord of Ma Fu.

This connection between Yo-Yo's family and Zhao-She is not documented in the genealogy and is probably fanciful. But the genealogy did allow us to travel back in an unbroken well-documented line to Yo-Yo's thirteenth-great-grandfather Ma Lin-Guan, who was born in the Ming Dynasty in 1435, fifty-seven years before Columbus discovered the New World. The genealogy contains a detailed description of Lin-Guan which reads, in part, "Our ancestor disdained the city with its noisy bustle and liked the solitude of the countryside. Living an upright life and without holding an official post, he accumulated virtue and cultivated goodness. And thus he laid the foundations for the family for ten thousand generations to come, whether the descendants might labor in the fields, study, fish, or chop wood."

Yo-Yo had never heard of Ji-Cang or Lin-Guan or indeed of almost any of the ancestors whose lives are chronicled within the genealogy. Yet the genealogy contained the answer to the question Yo-Yo had asked me when we first began our journey. His name—and those of his children—originated within it. Writing in the middle of the eighteenth century, Ji-Cang mandated the generational names for all his descendants, including "Yo" for the generation born in the first half of the twentieth century, "Bing" for their children, and the generational names for thirty generations more. Yo-Yo's son and daughter, as he was instructed by his father upon their birth, do in fact bear the name Bing. The instruction was passed along orally from father to son, even as the family was divided by war, revolution, and migration—even as the genealogy itself was entombed for more than thirty years.

Looking over the copy of the volumes, Yo-Yo was moved. "I have always wondered about this," he said. "And to have all of this gathered in one spot and for this man to have buried it, forgotten it, and then rediscovered it is actually very touching. I feel like I'm in the middle of a Dickens novel. I can't believe you found all this. I'm forever grateful."

Yo-Yo's father had a wonderful saying: "It takes the wealth of three generations to make a musician—the first to work the fields, the second to go to school, and the third to master an instrument." I've seen this quoted several times, and I've always wondered to what degree it was reflective of the Ma family's experience. The genealogy showed me that it was, essentially, an exact translation of their experience, adding just few extra generations.

According to the genealogy, Yo-Yo's great-great-grandfather Ma De-Zhang was born in 1805 and grew up in dire poverty. He and his older

Yo-Yo and his father, Ma Xiao-Jun. (Used by permission of the Ma family)

brother, De-Zai, worked for years as knife sharpeners and were so poor that when their parents died, De-Zai sold himself as a laborer to pay for their funeral. Over their lifetimes, however, De-Zhang and De-Zai began to build up their family's wealth, becoming blacksmiths and running a tool-making business for local farmers. They were, in effect, the first generation in Yo-Yo's father's saying. They devoted their lives to labor. De-Zhang is even quoted in the genealogy as saying that "success comes from hard work, failure comes from laziness and carelessness."

De-Zhang's son, Yo-Yo's great-grandfather, was Ma Yong-Jin, born in 1844. His father died when he was just twelve years old, but his uncle De-Zai took care of him. And when Yong-Jin grew to manhood, he did not have to go into the family tool-making business. His uncle had enough money to allow him the luxury and prestige of becoming a scholar. Yong-Jin's son was Ming-Yang, Yo-Yo's paternal grandfather. By the time he was born, in 1889, the Ma family was quite prosperous; in 1897 they built the home in Xianxiang where Yo-Yo's father, Xiao-Jun, was born in 1911. Xiao-Jun, of course, became a musician—mastering the violin and leaving behind forever the tiny town in which his family had lived for at least six centuries. "That's pretty amazing" was all a stunned Yo-Yo Ma could remark.

I told Yo-Yo that there was another surprise coming. I had assumed that Ji-Cang's genealogy would take us as far back as we could go on his family tree. But using it as a starting point, our researchers were able to locate another genealogy at a private library in the city of Ningbo that allowed us to trace the Ma family all the way back to a man named Ma Yuan-Yan, who was born in the year 1217, during the Song Dynasty. He was a scholar and a high-ranking government official. He is Yo-Yo's twentieth-great-grandfather.

We found a letter appointing Yuan-Yan head of what was known as the Imperial Examination Office. This appointment was so significant that it was signed by the emperor Du-Zhong himself. It reads, in part, "Owing to his prodigious learning, while in service let him be our close assistant; on retirement let him find repose, and may his virtue be abundant. He has our confidence in his new appointment, and he receives our benevolence. We look forward to his being able to rest on retirement; let him forever enjoy longevity and good health."

In Yuan-Yan's time, the civil examination system was the only merito-cratic part of the Chinese government. (It continued to be so for centuries, right up until 1905.) Students were tested on their knowledge of Confucian classics, military strategy, civil law, taxation, agriculture, and geography. Any male who took the exam and did well enough could receive a coveted government appointment and a guarantee of official employment for the rest of his life. The only other ways to get such an appointment were to inherit it or to be given it as a favor or bribe. The talent of the government bureaucracy therefore came from the people who did well on this exam. And Yo-Yo's ancestor was, for a time, essentially the gatekeeper—the person who ultimately determined the fate of everyone who took it. To have obtained this position, Yuan-Yan himself must have passed the highest level of the examination, which means he must have been a person of extremely high intelligence, power, and prestige." I can imagine the robes," said Yo-Yo, laughing. "He'd be walking around with one of these hats. Actually, no, I can't imagine. I can't believe you found all this."

Yuan-Yan lived in Hangzhou, the capital city of China in that era. Marco Polo, who visited China twice—once in 1266 and again in 1277—described Hangzhou as "preeminent to all others in the world in terms of grandeur and beauty, as well as in its abundant delights, which might lead an inhabitant to imagine himself in paradise."

We had now documented Yo-Yo's paternal line directly back to the thirteenth century. Considering that I had been led to believe we'd be lucky to find any paper trail at all, this was one of the most rewarding research experiences in all the genealogical work I have done. Unfortunately, as I mentioned earlier, in Chinese genealogy, only the male lines are followed. Each woman is identified only as a "female" with the last name of her father's family. This practice is, of course, a strong indicator of the role of women in traditional Chinese society. It also made it essentially impossible to trace Yo-Yo's maternal line.

Turning to our DNA testing, I told Yo-Yo that his admixture results showed that he was 100 percent Asian, which was perhaps no surprise, and this was also reflected in our Y-DNA analysis, which showed that he has exact matches with people living today in China, as well as in Indonesia, the Philippines, and Taiwan. In addition, I told him that his paternal haplogroup, O1a1, which is a subgroup of O, is the dominant haplogroup in East Asia. The O group originated about thirty-five thousand years ago in southeastern Asia and then spread into India and Central Asia. In the past four thousand years, it has traveled from Taiwan through the Philippines and Melanesia to the Pacific Islands. This information confirmed what the genealogical record had already told us.

Yo-Yo's mitochondrial DNA results, however, were more unusual. They showed five exact identical matches with people living in contemporary Asia (the majority in China), along with additional matches to people in the United States, Canada, and Mexico.

"That's unexpected," said Yo-Yo, smiling. "But, you know, people do do things that are unexpected in terms of migration and procreation. In that sense it's not surprising, but it's actually in some ways gratifying."

I told Yo-Yo that I was surprised by the Mexican match. There are plenty of Chinese immigrants and their descendants in American and Canada but relatively few in Mexico. When I talked to the scientists who analyzed the results, they said the match was probably the result of shared Native American ancestry. They pointed to Yo-Yo's maternal haplogroup —haplogroup C—which arose in Asia more than fifty thousand years ago. Today C is most common in Siberia, Central Asia, and China, but it is not uncommon in the Western Hemisphere. Ancestors who crossed the Bering land bridge, linking Siberia and Alaska during the last Ice Age, began moving south from the Arctic into the heart of the North American continent. Within a few thousand years, the new arrivals had carried haplogroup C down to the tip of South America. Approximately fifteen thousand years ago, the group diversified into the subgroups C1b, C1c, and C1d. Today these three branches are widely dispersed throughout North and South America as a result of the haplogroup's association with the initial peopling of the two continents. And this is why Yo-Yo has so many matches with Native Americans.

Interestingly, when we submitted Yo-Yo's autosomal data to the geneticists Mark Daly and David Altshuler at the Broad Institute, they indicated that as recently perhaps as within ten generations, Yo-Yo shares a common ancestor with Eva Longoria, who is almost 30 percent Native American. The two match on chromosome 3 from base pair 47 to base pair 59, which translates into eight million identical base pairs that they share.

"You have to give me her phone number," said Yo-Yo, joking. "I'm having a family party, come on over!" Then, growing more serious, he lowered his voice and turned his attention once more to the enormous genealogy spread out before him. "It makes me proud," he said. "But I'm hoping that it won't change my life one bit. You know what I mean?"

I told him that I was somewhat confused. Was he just being modest? Did all these ancestors intimidate him or overwhelm in some way? Or did he prefer to think that he owed his success largely to the efforts of his parents? Or to chance? "It's funny," he replied, "because we all had ancestors who were alive in the thirteenth century. Whether we can identify a name or profession, we all had them. And one of the things my wife and I talk about is that, as much as we can possibly determine, we want to be the same people with the same values and character regardless of whatever position we find ourselves in socioeconomically, politically, or whatever. We hope that in adversity or in good fortune, we are the same people to our friends, to our families, to people that we know."

Now I knew exactly what he meant. And I told him I understood. Given all that he and his family had been through—crossing continents and cultures, changing languages, continually reinventing themselves—it made complete sense that he felt most grounded within his own small nuclear family.

"I'm going to walk out of this room the exact same person that walked in," he said, "just knowing that much more. We're always searching for unknowns. But having an important person in your family generations ago, we still have to prove ourselves right now every day in our era. Does it give sustenance? I don't know. You know, my family gives me sustenance. And you've given me just unfathomably important information about my family."

The one constant in Yo-Yo's life has been music. Before we said good-bye, he picked up his cello and offered me a brief, private concert, playing for the next twenty minutes to express his feelings at this reunion with his ancestors. It was some of the most moving music I've ever heard.

6

Dr. Mehmet Oz

1960

DR. MEHMET OZ is so famous as a media personality that it is easy to forget he is also one of the nation's preeminent surgeons and professors of medicine. Vice Chair and Professor of Surgery at Columbia University, he performs over two hundred heart operations annually and also directs the Cardiovascular Institute and Complementary Medicine Program at New York Presbyterian Hospital. He has cared for a number of people I know, and I can say with certainty that the accolades he's received are entirely justified. He's a passionate doctor, consumed by learning about virtually every aspect of health—and concerned, genuinely, with the lives of his individual patients as well as the millions who watch his television show, read his columns, or listen to him on the radio. I can think of few doctors I'd trust more.

As anyone who's even vaguely familiar with his work knows, Mehmet's medical philosophy combines traditional Western techniques for treating disease with alternative ideas about healthy lifestyle choices. He attributes this philosophy in part to his Turkish ancestry, which he says has allowed him to see his work—and indeed his world—from a different perspective than that of most of his American colleagues. I asked him to be in this project to explore that idea in greater detail. I wanted to learn about the cultural differences between Turkey and America; and I wanted to see how, exactly, they had shaped Mehmet. I got a lot more than I'd bargained for.

In making the PBS series and writing this book, I've been fascinated by the ways in which many of my subjects have pursued professions that reflect their ancestral roots. In America, we have a tendency to think that the past is irrelevant and that each generation can, and should, transcend the past, if not completely reinvent itself. This is part of our cherished belief in the possibility of self-invention and the idea of unlimited personal progress. In America, you do better than your parents did—usually by doing something totally different. It's called climbing the ladder. I've done it myself. My father worked two jobs so that my brother could become a dentist and I could become a professor. We love our father, and respect him, but neither of us ever thought for a moment about following in his footsteps working in the Westvaco Paper Mill by day and then as a janitor at the Chesapeake and Potomac Telephone Company in the evenings.

And while I've uncovered a number of stories in this project to support that formula, some of my subjects have creatively subverted it. Yo-Yo Ma, as we've seen, was the son of musicians who believed that their children's musical talents were the fulfillment of generations of work. Mario Batali, as we'll soon see, grew up cooking with his father and essentially making a world-renowned living out of his grandmother's favorite occupation and with some of her recipes. The novelist Louise Erdrich is the self-acknowledged heir to generations of storytellers. And Mehmet Oz belongs in this group, too. His roots are deeply intertwined with the medical profession. He has achieved tremendous accomplishments, but he has done it in close dialogue with his heritage.

"My father is a doctor," said Mehmet, immediately warming to the idea that his career choice might be a product of his ancestry. "A very obvious and perhaps the most compelling of all ancestral links is if your father does something that you love doing. But my mother's side of the family had been involved in pharmaceuticals for generations. And I like the idea of that: if you have a problem, I can talk to you about it, look into your eyes, figure out what I might be able to help you with, and then give you something for it. And I do think our personalities, although driven a lot by environment and how we were raised, may have some genetic links. So the fact that my ancestors like to give people potions might be reflected in my desire to help you."

After only a few minutes of conversation, I was struck by how reverently Mehmet speaks of his parents, with a deep warmth and respect. It's the way most of us feel about our parents, and yet I still find it oddly touching. Mehmet's mother and father are clearly the shaping influence in his life, and he told me that he was aware of this even at a very young age.

"The catalyzing moment for me happened when I was seven years old," he recalled. "I was in an ice cream store with my father. The kid in front of me was a ten-year-old—at that age, three years older than you, they're like a monster. This kid is waiting to get his ice cream, and my father asks him what he wants to be when he grows up. The kid said, 'I don't know, I'm ten,' which is a very reasonable answer to give. And my father very politely lets the kid get his ice cream and move on, but as I'm going to get mine, my father turns to me and says, 'Don't you ever give me the answer that kid gave me. I don't care what you're going to become. I don't care if you change your mind a hundred times, but you always have to know what you want to be, because otherwise you can't aim that direction.' And then he asked me what I wanted to be. And I'd seen my father making rounds in the hospital. I'd scurry along next to him as he went to see patients. I'd see the looks in the patients' eyes when he came, it was a look of hope—that someone had come actually to help—and I thought it would feel so good if I could do that too. So I said, 'I'll be a doctor.' And I never changed my mind."

This, I thought, was a very moving and powerful anecdote. It reminded me of countless conversations I've had with my parents, with my children, and, perhaps most of all, with myself. After we reach a certain age, we all strive to figure out what it means to have values and to try and pass them on to the next generation. It is a conversation that speaks to the core of the human experience. And over the course of our interview, I learned just how powerfully this anecdote illuminated the relationship of Mehmet to his father and to his uniquely crafted identity.

Mehmet Oz was born in Cleveland, Ohio, on June 11, 1960. His parents, Mustafa Oz and Suna Atabay, were recent Turkish immigrants. As we might expect, this fact informed almost every aspect of his childhood. "My father had come to the States in 1955," he told me, "and so he had at least created a little bit of a foundation for himself. But my mother had come from Istanbul less than a year before I was born. So she had left the country that she loved dearly for one that she also knew she would love, but she was not yet comfortable here. She was not only inexperienced at raising children but inexperienced in the land, in the culture, in everything here. As I grew older, I would see my friends do things I'd never heard of or thought of; I would hear words—I remember not knowing what the word *pantry* meant. I'd never heard the word used in my house, because we would use the Turkish word. And so I would slowly but surely, throughout the course of my upbringing, begin to integrate more with my friends who were Americans and with what their lives were like, what their families were like. But it was a process."

Mehmet does not know if his parents experienced any discrimination in this country. He does not recall them speaking about it—but he does not believe they would have told him even if they had experienced it. He himself recalls being made aware that he was different from a very young age and struggling to assimilate, sometimes even getting into fistfights

Mehmet with his parents, Mustafa Oz and Suna Atabay. (Used by permission of the Oz family)

with classmates who teased him—not for the color of his skin but for the strange customs in his home. Even as he struggled, Mehmet recalls that his parents instilled in him a strong attachment to his Turkish roots. "I remember one particular moment," he said. "I was five at the time. I was sitting in the back of the car, and I heard my parents speaking in Turkish, and I remember saying jibber-jabberish back to them and asking, 'How come you always speak in that weird language?' And I think it struck a chord for them. They realized they needed to have me understand my Turkish heritage, or else I would lose it forever."

The following summer—and every summer after that throughout his childhood—Mehmet spent three months in Turkey with his extended family. He believes these summers were among the truly formative experiences of his youth, the times in which he grew the most as a person and most fully came to understand who he was and what he could be. He also told me that the trips were a tremendous education for him about the great class differences between his mother's and father's families.

"When we first started going to Turkey in the summers," he told me, "I would always stay with my mother's side, and I began peppering them with questions: 'When did this house come into the family?' 'Why do we move over here?' 'Tell me more about my grandparents.' Everything was somewhat luxurious—this was my mother's family, and my father would stay behind in America working. But at age ten, my dad said, 'Enough. You're being pampered by your mom, and you're not actually seeing Turkey, not living in Turkey, not being a Turk. So I want you to go spend time with my family. They don't speak a lot of English. They are more typical and traditional in their habits.'"

The young Mehmet was surprised by what he found. "It was culture shock, because they had dirt floors and . . . well, I wasn't at all expecting what I ran into. It was the contrasting stories of the two different cultures. Because they were from different parts of Turkey, and Turkey is really two different countries. My mother's family was from a very old Istanbul family that had been there for several generations, had come from some wealth,

Mehmet's mother's family in Turkey, the Atabays. (Used by permission of the Oz family)

and had done well in life. My father had been born into abject poverty—I'm talking about the kind of poverty where you're not worried about passing clothes down, but you're worried about food. And that's the kind of poverty you don't forget too readily."

Researching Mehmet's family tree, the divide between the two families—and the impact of each family on Mehmet—became clear. His father, Mustafa Oz, was born in Bozkir, Turkey. According to Mehmet, *Bozkir* means "mess up and break." It is a small town in the Konya Province of central Turkey, near the Taurus Mountains, a very rough-and-tumble place. There, as Mehmet said, Mustafa grew up in dire poverty. He does not know his own birthdate, but believes it was sometime in October 1925. We could not verify the date because there are no records of his birth or that of any of his brothers or sisters. Indeed, the Konya Province produced almost no written records in this era.

Mustafa's parents were Mehmet and Fatma Oz. Mehmet, our Dr. Oz's grandfather, was born in Bozkir around 1886. His wife was born in another village in the Konya Province, Akseki, around 1897. Though Mehmet was named after his grandfather, he knows little about him. He died when Mehmet was only two years old. Mehmet was, however, very close to his grandmother Fatma. He vividly recalls her telling him how she met her husband.

"I get goose bumps telling this story," he told me, excitedly. "She was thirteen years of age, and visitors came from another town, a man who wanted to marry and was looking for a woman in that township who might be eligible. She was not allowed to see him—that was tradition—and he wasn't allowed to see her. They weren't allowed to meet until it was already arranged by the parents. So the man comes into the foyer—this is my grandfather. He's not allowed to see her, but she's peeking at him from behind a curtain. She's peering out and seeing that he's sort of a good-looking guy: good stature and might be reasonable." He laughs. "And my grandmother's mother goes out to him and says, 'You know, my daughter's too young. I don't think it's right for her to get married yet.' The man is insistent, so my grandmother's mother comes back and has a discussion with her, a very open discussion, saying, 'This man wants to take you to a different town. I'll probably never see you again if you go with him.'" More than romance was at stake: "My grandmother's father was dead. One of the reasons my grandfather wanted to marry her is that the Turkish army was mobilizing, and he'd already been mobilized several times. There was a rule that if a man was married to a woman without a father, he was allowed

Mehmet's paternal grandmother, Fatma Oz, in Bozkir, Turkey. (Used by permission of the Oz family)

to stay home and take care of her. So it was a very savvy move to marry a woman without a father. And so he put her on a donkey, she rode behind him, while he never looked back, supposedly. They went across the Taurus Mountains, in southern Turkey, from her town of Akseki to his town of Bozkir. And she never returned to her home again. Although the trip took a couple of days back in 1913, I actually drove that route in about an hour and a half."

Dr. Oz was right: this was a fantastic story. I wanted to find out more about Fatma and her family, but I was unfortunately unable to do so, because prior to 1934, the Turkish people—like Jewish people in Russia, as we saw with Mike Nichols's ancestors—were not required to have last names. (Mehmet's grandfather chose the family name "Oz" himself; the name of a nearby town, it means "strength.") And without a surname, it is virtually impossible to trace a genealogy. So we could not go back any further along the lines of either of Mehmet's paternal grandparents. We were, however, able to learn a great deal about the life of their son, Mustafa, Mehmet's father.

Mustafa was one of a dozen children, half of whom died in childhood. His early years were almost unimaginably harsh, and they seem to have forged in him a kind of iron will. "They had to make tremendous sacrifices to survive," said Mehmet. "My father grew up knowing that the only prayer he had to succeed was to outwork everybody else. It has colored every aspect of his life. It's one of the reasons he can't retire even now, at age eighty-five."

Though Mustafa's parents were uneducated farmers, they were determined that their children would lead better lives, and they correctly perceived that education was the means to this end. They encouraged their oldest son, Mustafa's brother Hakki, to migrate to Nazi Germany, where he worked and studied engineering. Hakki was treated terribly by the Nazis but was nevertheless given an opportunity to study and to earn money. He sent all his wages back to his family. They used them to buy food and, as much as possible, to educate young Mustafa.

According to the family, Mustafa claimed that he knew from a very early age that he wanted to study medicine, and he applied himself with an all-consuming zeal. At the primary school in Bozkir, he graduated at the head of his class. Then, in 1938, when he was about thirteen years old, he left his town to attend a government boarding school. After graduation, he won a scholarship to study medicine at the Istanbul University Faculty of Medicine. The scholarship required that he serve at least four years as a government physician, so he took a position in the small town of Gülşehir, in the Nevşehir Province. He was soon appointed to serve in the Turkish capital, Ankara. It was a significant promotion, but his ambitions were by no means fulfilled.

Mustafa wanted to become a surgeon, which required further training. The best way to accomplish this was to find a residency at an American hospital. So he started applying. He did not know English, but even this did not deter him. He had a secretary in the U.S. embassy in Ankara write letters and fill in the forms for him. To the question of whether he knew English, he invariably replied "yes," with the hope of learning it quickly. Meanwhile, according to Mehmet, his father's friends were teasing him constantly, saying that he was wasting his time—that even if he was accepted, he'd never last. He and his friends all knew people who had left for America and come back to Turkey, unable to continue their studies. Mustafa proved them wrong. He was accepted by Western Reserve University Hospital in 1955—and he came here, and he stayed.

"I'm sure he was insecure," said Mehmet. "I'm sure he was troubled.

Mehmet's father, Mustafa Oz, as a medical student in Istanbul in 1950. (Used by permission of the Oz family)

He was from a generation that grew up during the Second World War. The world was not a friendly place. That was Einstein's great quip: 'We have a fundamental decision to make in life: is the universe friendly or not?' And my father growing up didn't think the universe was a friendly place. So the opportunity to get out of Turkey, a country which he loved dearly but did not think he could succeed in, and come to a country where he thought he could get an education that would be unparalleled was what compelled him to do what he did, which was to uproot. It's hard. He did it though."

Mehmet, smiling broadly, then told me the story of his father's journey to America. It was one of the most touching things that I heard over the course of this entire project.

"My father went to the airport to leave for America," said Mehmet. "His mother, my grandmother, wearing a burqa, accompanied my father to the airport and insisted on speaking to the pilot. So they dragged the pilot out of the cockpit—you can just imagine this: the captain doesn't want to be bothered by anybody—and my grandmother says, 'Please take this brown bag. It has my son's lunch. I want to make sure you give it to him. And I want you to take this big plane and fly it very, very slowly, stay low to the ground.' That was a story my father has told many times in his life. It's difficult to imagine, growing up in a place where there are no automated vehicles period, and the next thing you know you wake up in Cleveland, Ohio. But this man was willing to make that move."

Mustafa arrived in Cleveland in June 1955, unable to speak English and without a friend or family member to guide him. He was nonetheless able to persuade school officials that they should let him stay. Part of this was sheer luck. At that time, America was experiencing a shortage of physicians, and doctors from other countries were being recruited and accommodated wherever possible. Nonetheless, luck was not the only factor in Mustafa's success. He clearly had great talent and personal charm. He also encountered people who were willing to help.

"They quickly realized," said Mehmet, "that either my father couldn't read the application or he had falsified it, because he didn't speak the language. Actually I think he didn't understand the questions even. But they figured, 'You know what? We already paid for him to come here, and he seems willing to work.' And so—and he tells this story with tears in his eyes—on his first day, he was paged, and he hears, 'Dr. Oz.' So he picks up the phone, they say something to him, he has no idea what they're saying, and then at the end they say, 'Hang up.' And he's thinking, 'Well, what does that mean—hang up?' So he held the phone up. In the air. And they said, 'Dr. Oz, hang up the phone!' So he got on a chair and held the phone up to the ceiling, wondering what the heck else could he possibly do to get the phone up. He knew the word *up* but nothing else that they were saying to him. And he held it up until a colleague of his came along—and this is I think what has in many ways colored his experience in America: there was so much completely unwarranted kindness. I think it speaks beautifully of our culture. A man who was walking by said, 'Dr. Oz, it's an idiom,' and he showed him how to hang up the phone. And that's how he learned.

Dr. Mustafa Oz, Mehmet's father, as an intern at Western Reserve University Hospital in Cleveland in the 1950s (*seated at right*). (Used by permission of the Oz family)

"You know, he had many experiences like this," said Mehmet, smiling at the thought of the treatment his father received from strangers who had probably never met a Turkish person in their lives. "At my parents' wedding, they had no money, but a patient of his paid for his honeymoon. People just wanted to help other human beings. I think one of the things, if I look across the world—and I've traveled a lot—that really differentiates America in a very positive way is that we've always realized that because we're immigrants, and someone stepped up to help us when they didn't need to, that we need to give back. We need to pass it on."

If there's a common theme that unites all twelve of the people's stories in this book, it is this sentiment, reflected throughout Mustafa's story: Americans respect hard work. Americans respect effort, industry, ambition. I found this over and over in the immigrant stories I researched for this project. Despite whatever racism and xenophobia Americans may have harbored toward immigrants—and may still harbor today—individual acts of kindness abound. And economic mobility is available for those who most diligently work for it. This is a basic belief that the American economic system, at its best, is neutral: that it's oppressive to everyone, that it's resistant to everyone, and that individual will is what matters most, far more than race, religion, or place of birth. Whether you're a Jew from Russia or Germany, an Arab from Syria, a Roman Catholic from Ireland, a Chinese family from Paris, Mexicans in Texas, Haitians in Boston, or Jamaicans in New York, what matters most is how hard you work and how much you defer gratification. Those who embrace this belief have the possibility, at least, of thriving here.

There is, of course, a psychological cost to devoting your life to work in this manner. "My father is a hard dude," Mehmet observed, with a smile. "But that's how he survived. For him, being the best was the only way to go. It was a very tough environment that he came from, and he tried to pass along the fear he had that I would be complacent in my life. For my father the big issue was not being good enough; it was being the best. That was the only way he had ever lived his life, and to me it's the story of all immigrant families in America: we came with a gusto for competition, for seeking out merit, and expecting to be paid emotionally, physically, monetarily, for doing a good job. That's my father's background, so it was not always easy to be with him. It wasn't really a question about whether I was doing well; it was a question of whether I was doing the best. My father never asked me when I gave him my grades whether I was satisfied. He didn't care. What he wanted to know was, 'Did anyone do better?' For example, *Time* magazine has this once-a-year event where they pick a hundred influential people. So I told my father that I was elected, and the first question he asked me was, what number was I? It's out of six billion people."

Mehmet and I both laughed hard at his father's question—understanding both the drive behind it and the difficulty of relaxing that drive. First-generation immigrants often battle with their children, for this reason and many others. I was actually quite impressed by how little conflict seems to have occurred between Mehmet and his father and how strong the bond is between the two. In our interview, Mehmet repeatedly told me that he has immense respect and love for his father—and that he is intensely grateful and indeed awed by the way Mustafa overcame the obstacles in his path. "It was all just a challenge," said Mehmet. "It was just an opportunity to go in a different direction. When someone tells you no, it means you have to ask differently. And I think often about what my life would be like if my dad had not taken that fateful trip to Cleveland with zero understanding of the English language or the country. I would be a very different human being and quite certainly would not be sitting here in front of you, if my father had not made that trip."

We then began to explore Mehmet's mother's family, by looking at one other trip that his father took—a trip that was just as significant to Mehmet's existence as the journey to Cleveland. In 1959, after almost four years in America, Mustafa returned to Turkey for a ten-day visit. His family had moved to Istanbul, a historic, cultured city with great extremes of wealth and poverty. Mustafa's life and outlook were now very different. He had been transformed by his experience in the United States. He had money and status. He wanted to marry—and he was able to find a bride who would have been completely inaccessible to him just half a decade before.

"My mother," said Mehmet, "was not someone he could possibly have thought of marrying before he left for the United States. She was from a very affluent family. And they only met because my father's sister was a seamstress, who made very pretty dresses. She made dresses for my mother, and in the course of one of her fittings she said, 'My brother is in America. You should really meet him.' And they arranged a meeting, which again goes against all tradition. And they married, with a little bit of resentment from my mother's family. But he was a surgeon now."

Mehmet's mother is Suna Atabay, born September 4, 1938, in Istanbul, the daughter of Kemalettin and Iffet Atabay. The contrast between the Atabays and the Ozes cannot be overstated. "My mother's family," Mehmet told me, "was one of the most influential and affluent families in Turkey, and they had a very different approach to life. My mother is very different in how she thinks through problems than my father. My father wants to know, 'How can I work harder to fix the problem?' My mother wants to know, 'How can I work smarter?' She's much more diplomatic, much more thoughtful in how she gives advice, much more reserved in speaking at all. And I thought at the time it was just male versus female, but as I've gotten older I've begun to appreciate much more how the things that she wants to happen, happen—whereas my father will often get himself into a dither thinking that what needs to happen is not happening. They represent a kind of duality of cultures within Turkey, which I think exists in many countries."

I asked Mehmet how he delineated his parents in his mind. He replied immediately, without pausing to reflect. "My mom," he said, "completely encapsulated the concept of love to me. And it was unconditional. As much as I applaud and appreciate my father as a parent, I think I am who I am because of my mom. I've been able to do things emotionally that I probably wouldn't have been able to do, except that I knew that I was loved. I think for many of us, we do things to be loved. So if your mom loves you unconditionally, then you're more comfortable losing what you've got because your mother still loves you. I say that because I've always found that the major driver of a child's happiness, and probably an adult's happiness, is how much they think they were loved—not how much they were actually loved, how much they *think* they were loved. I thought I was loved all the time. I never doubted it for a moment."

Looking at a photograph of his mother taken more than fifty years ago, Mehmet lowered his voice reverently. "She was a very wise woman," he said. "Very quiet. She would never challenge my father on issues publicly. Anything within the family, publicly I wouldn't know there was an issue. She was remarkably adept at getting what needs to happen to happen. My father wanted to come to America and conquer medicine and change the world. And my mother wanted to live in the world, to experience the world for what it was, to celebrate it where it was."

Suna's mother, Iffet, was born in 1910 in Istanbul. Her father, Kemalettin, was born in 1908 in the province of Duzce, in northwestern Turkey. He came from a family of pharmacists and moved to Istanbul in the 1920s to study pharmacy himself. Supported by his family back in Duzce, he proved monumentally successful, working his way up in the industry and eventually opening his own drug factory in 1950, the same year that Mustafa Oz, an impoverished student, left a government boarding school in Konya to study medicine, carrying all his belongings in a box.

"I recognized," said Mehmet, "very early in my life that my mother's family was prosperous and my father's was not. It was reflected in every single interaction I had with the family. Expectations from life, ways of dealing with problems, the ability to envision yourself making a difference in the world, whether you thought the system works for you or against you—all that was reflected in the fairly substantial differences between the two family sides. I understood why my father's side felt that only hard work would pay off and that there was no reason for trusting the system to help you. But I also could see my mother's side saying, listen, the system works well. If you can just understand it and play to it, then it will help you prosper. And in many ways these ideas colored the way I see the world and how I try to balance two perspectives, not just culturally but economically."

Kemalettin's father, Mehmet's great-grandfather, was named Esat Sezai Sunbulluk. He was born in 1885 in Istanbul. A writer and a very devout Muslim, Esat wrote a number of books about Islam, including interpretations of religious poetry. He was also an artist of Islamic calligraphy. It is interesting to note that Esat and his son Kemalettin had different surnames. Mehmet's aunt told us that when Turkish law required its citizens to adopt surnames in 1934, Esat chose the name of the Islamic sect to which he belonged, "Sunbulluk," while Kemalettin chose "Atabay" in honor of Mustafa Kemal Ataturk, the founder of the Turkish Republic. The difference in these surnames signifies a tremendous generational gap between the two men. Ataturk, one of the great leaders of the twentieth century, had taken control of Turkey after the collapse of the Ottoman Empire at the end of World War I. A singularly brilliant man, committed to modernization at almost all costs, Ataturk completely remade Turkish society—restructuring the government, changing the written language, and secularizing what had for centuries been an Islamic state. The results proved deeply polarizing to the Turkish people (Ataturk's policies are still a source of tension today)—and one can see this in the choice of surnames in Mehmet's family. Mehmet's great-grandfather Esat showed himself to be a traditional Ottoman, looking to the Islamic past, while his grandfather Kemalettin embraced Ataturk's secular Turkish Republic, looking to the future.

"I never thought of that before," said Mehmet, when I asked about these diverging worldviews. "Absolutely they had different last names. There must have been a big divide there. As a devout Muslim, Esat probably was very conflicted about Ataturk. He spent fifty years of his life before Ataturk brought a republic to the country. Whereas my grandfather was of the modern generation: he had been educated to be a pharmacist, he believed in Western medicine. Ataturk was showing him the future, and he was going to rebel against the old school. The names make perfect sense, and I think reflect their personalities." He considered further: "I don't know if it's quite as clear as that. I didn't know much about my great-grandfather. But I know there was some scandal around this, because he was an artist and a writer. So he lived in Istanbul, which was the cosmopolitan hub of the world, in his opinion. And my great-grandmother, his wife, wanted to go back to Duzce, where her family was from, and live a more humble life. And so they ended up living apart from each other for a good part of their existence, which of course was unheard of back then."

I showed Mehmet a photograph of his great-grandfather—the first he'd ever seen. And suddenly the whole story made more sense. In the photo, Esat Sezai was walking along the Bosporus, dressed in an overcoat and a top hat. He looked so elegant, so refined. Neither of us could imagine him moving back to a rural village. "He wanted to be there," said Mehmet, smiling. "I can't say I blame him."

Esat's wife, Mehmet's great-grandmother, was a woman named Zekiye Kuyumcu who was born in Duzce in 1888. Her ancestry contains some fascinating stories suggesting that her line may have been largely responsible for the wealth and success of Mehmet's maternal ancestors. *Kuyumcu* means either "jeweler" or "goldsmith," and Zekiye's father, Mehmet's great-great-grandfather, was a goldsmith named Hadji Ali Bey. He was born around 1840 in Krasnodar, which is part of the Circassian region of what is now southern Russia. He and his family were leaders of the Shapsugh tribe, one of the dominant Islamic tribes in the region. In 1864, the Russian army swept through this area, taking possession of the land. The "mountain dwellers," as the Russians referred to Mehmet's ancestors, were pushed out. They were given the choice of resettling in another part of Russia or moving south to the Ottoman Empire. Hadji Ali Bey, like many of his Islamic brethren, chose to go south. The event is known today as the Great Circassian Exile, and it resulted in large areas of northern Turkey, such as the Duzce Province, becoming populated by Islamic tribespeople from Russia.

"I'm fascinated by that," Mehmet admitted. "Isn't it amazing how these huge shifts happen, and then they're forgotten and swept away by the sands of time? Can you imagine if the Cossacks came gallivanting down the street, and we had to move right now? You forget that existed. These are all the shadows of our past. There had been family lore that one of our ancestors had come from the Circassian Mountains. They had some wealth, because they had actually bought land in Jehunger, which is an old part of Istanbul where my family had some property, but no one ever knew why we lived there. Imagine if you discovered that you have a lot of property in Midtown Manhattan—you know you can't buy property in Midtown now, so someone must have moved in a long time ago and happened to settle there. The rumor was that he had come with some families, and because he was a tribal leader, he had a role in picking where they were going to live, and they pooled their resources to buy it."

The documentary record more or less confirmed this piece of Mehmet's family lore. It also uncovered an amazing story about his ancestor Hadji Ali Bey. I showed Mehmet a letter that we found in the Ottoman archives dated January 1, 1864. Translated, it reads, in part, "To the chairman of the Immigration Committee, The Resolution of the Canik counsel is attached. It states that some houses for the retinue and relatives of Hadji Ali Bey of the Shapsugh tribe from the Circassian refugees have been built, and the rest is also gradually being built. The construction costs of the houses have been covered by the government." This, as I explained, shows that the Ottoman government actually built homes for Mehmet's great-great-grandfather and his family and that he was, almost certainly, a leader of his people. And it provides rare documentary evidence not only of his family's immigration from Russia to Turkey but also of the Ottoman government's willingness to accept fellow Muslims and help them resettle and build a new life. Mehmet noted, "That's probably how they ended up in Jehunger, that part of Istanbul."

This, however, was not the end to Hadji Ali Bey's journey. According to Mehmet's family's oral history, when Hadji fled Russia, he went first to the province of Canik and then moved to the Jehunger neighborhood of Istanbul with help from the Ottoman government. But Jehunger did not yet possess the economy of Midtown Manhattan, and Hadji struggled to support his family there. We learned through documents we found that Hadji ended up traveling to Cairo, Egypt—leaving his family behind—looking for work as a goldsmith. After several years, he returned home, only to find that his entire family had died of illness. He was devastated and moved north to the Duzce Province, where so many of his fellow tribesmen had gathered. And there he started another family, which included Mehmet's great-great-grandmother. That's how Mehmet's mother's family came to the region where they prospered so well over the next century.

"This is fascinating!" Mehmet exclaimed. "That you lose your whole life and start over again. What a different world. Traveling from Russia to Istanbul to Cairo in 1860s is a big deal. This guy is like Marco Polo."

Hadji Ali Bey was the earliest person that we could document in Mehmet's maternal grandfather's family. Looking at his maternal grandmother's line, we were able to go back only a few generations—from his grandmother Iffet to her parents, Ahmet Bedri and Neyire Kiyangan, born in Istanbul in 1867 and sometime around 1890, respectively. We learned that Ahmet Bedri was a railroad engineer inspector for the Ottoman government. His father was also named Ahmet and was an interior minister. We also learned that Neyire's mother was a woman named Ayshe, but beyond her, the documentary record was nonexistent.

Mehmet recalled hearing many stories about this side of his maternal family. "I was only a little kid," he said, "but I remember stories that the circumstances under which Ayshe was born were supposedly suspicious. Her mother apparently was in a harem. Around 1800, one of the sultans was being deposed. He was still a young boy, and there was a Circassian servant girl who protected him. His uncle was trying to seize the throne, and she hid him. His allies came back, reestablished the throne, and put him back as sultan. From then on, the Ottoman court would always have Circassian women in it. They were light-skinned. They were big women. They were felt to be beautiful. And so the Ottomans were always going up into Russia and capturing Circassian women and bringing them back into the harem. Apparently one of those women was my maternal ancestor, and she had one child in the harem, whose father is unclear. And of course the lore is that it was some noble person in the court. It could also have been the doorman. Who knows? And then in the mid-1860s, just before Ayshe was born, this sultan was deposed, and the harem was cleared out. So my ancestor who was in the harem was allowed to go free. She married, and that led to this lineage."

We were not able to verify this story, although elements of it do correspond to historical events surrounding the murder of Sultan Selim III in 1807 and the ascension of his son, Sultan Mahmud II. A version of these events by the nineteenth-century Ottoman historian Cevdet Pasha claims that Mahmud was saved by the machinations of a Circassian slave girl named Cevri and that thereafter, Circassian girls were popular within the harem. We also found some evidence suggesting that Ayshe may have actually been freed from the harem during the reign of Murad V, sometime around 1875, and married to a low-level member of the Muslim clergy. But the records are so sketchy that it is simply impossible to make any definitive claims about Ayshe, her life, or any earlier members of her family.

By this point, we had been able to trace Mehmet back four generations on both his paternal and maternal sides—and he was thrilled. "This is fabulous," said Mehmet. "I didn't even realize these names were in my family."

Before we began to consider his DNA testing results, I asked him if what we had learned about his family changed the way he felt about his identity as a Turk. After all, the research had shown that on his oldest maternal line that we were able to identify, he was Circassian. The family of Hadji Ali Bey stretched back to a Muslim minority in Russia, not Turkey. Indeed, his line only goes back three generations in Turkey on his mother's side.

"I don't know if it changes my feeling as a Turk," he replied. "What it does is spread my horizon a bit. It opens the vista of who I think I am. And I guess in a very healthy way it emphasizes that we all came from everywhere. At the end of the day there are so many different parts of the puzzle—in my case, spread among Russia, Turkey, and I suspect other parts of the world as well. But, you know, I treasure my heritage very much, and

I'm not prouder that I'm Turkish or Turkish American or even American. I think it's just spectacular that I have had the opportunity to marry different cultures together, because when you can see the world from two different perspectives—as I think I've been blessed to have an ability to do because of my upbringing—you're better off."

I agree with this completely. And when I showed Mehmet his admixture DNA test results, I was pleased to see that he got very excited when he realized that he had a tiny amount of Asian heritage: 3 percent, as compared to his 97 percent European background. "Oh, I have Asian blood," he said, delighted. "That's great—I was always thinking that, because one of my sisters looks very Asian. Her face just has that beautiful broad appearance. And her eyes are much more oval than the round ones that my mom has."

I then told him that his maternal haplogroup was H2a1, which arose in the Near East about fourteen thousand years ago, when the Ice Age was drawing to a close. Members of this group migrated through the Caucasus and Ural regions, into Central Asia, and along the Baltic Sea. Today H2a1 is most prevalent in eastern Slavic-speaking populations such as those in Russia and the Ukraine. They carry this haplogroup at levels of about 8 percent.

The Family Tree DNA database that we consulted revealed that Mehmet shares mitochondrial DNA with twenty-one people living in Poland today, twenty-two in England, thirty-one in Germany, and thirty-two in Ireland. These are what are called low-resolution matches, which indicate a 50 percent chance that he shares a common ancestor within the past fifty-two generations, or approximately thirteen hundred years.

Turning to his father's line, I told him that his paternal haplogroup is J2a1b, which is also referred to as J2a4b. Everyone in this haplogroup shares a particular mutation on his Y chromosome known as M67, which can be traced back to a single male who lived twelve thousand years ago in the Middle East. "You're kidding me," said Mehmet, enthralled. "Can you imagine knowing who that was? He had a lot of kids."

I told him that based on archaeological evidence, scientists believe that some members of his haplogroup moved from the Middle East into the Mediterranean Basin between seven thousand and eighty-five hundred years ago with the spread of agriculture. Because of this migration, we find his haplogroup today in northern Italy and Greece, Turkey, Albania, and most frequently in Georgia, where it comprises 15 percent of the male population. It is also common in the Middle East, particularly in Yemen,

Lebanon, Kurdistan, and Syria—and it is common, interestingly enough, among Jews, Muslims, and Christians. In fact, one database we consulted shows that the J2a1b is almost evenly divided among Jews and Muslims, with 44 percent of Muslim men in this database and 55 percent of Jewish men having exactly the same haplogroup. This finding was also echoed within this project: Mehmet, a Muslim, has the same Y-DNA haplogroup signature as Mike Nichols, an Ashkenazi Jew, meaning that both descend from a common male ancestor, affirming through their Y-DNA the biblical story of Abraham's sons founding the Arabic people and the Jewish people. "I know Mike very well," said Mehmet. "I'm honored. I'm going to call him right now! You know, this is thrilling."

I had one further surprise for Mehmet. I told him that the Broad Institute's analysis of his autosomal DNA had revealed that he shared an exact band of DNA, three million base pairs on chromosome 18, with the Jamaican-English writer Malcolm Gladwell, with whom I also share several million base pairs.

"Are you serious?" he asked. "I would never have guessed. It would never have crossed my mind. I'm in good company—absolutely blown away. I love his work. If we met on the street, he'd be the last person I'd think I was related to. It just reflects how simplistic we are in our thought process: he's got curly hair, and mine's straight; his skin's darker; he's from a different part of the world. How many Jamaicans can be related to Turks? Can't be too many. But however many years ago we obviously were in the same place on the planet. If you look how peripatetic the species is, we're probably related to everybody. Obviously, we are."

As our meeting wound down, I wanted to thank Mehmet for the amount of time he had spent with me, explaining the nuances of Turkish history and culture. I felt he had been so generous—transporting me into a culture and country that I had known little about. It had been a fascinating learning experience for me, and I hoped it had been for him as well. Before I left, I asked him what had been the most meaningful part for him. He stopped for a moment and thought before answering. His reply, when it finally came, pleased me, because it articulated so well one of the great hopes I have for this work: to alter the way people think about ethnicity.

"The most compelling of all," he said, "was this statistic you shared with me about how commonly related Muslims and Jews are. This information to me is world changing, because now you're using hardcore science, not belief systems, to say, 'You know what? We are related in ways you could never have imagined.' For Christians and Jews and Muslims to begin to realize how interrelated they are—particularly in the Middle East, where you have warring factions which seem to be based on longstanding genetic differences—for these to be absolutely disproved would undermine a lot of the rhetoric behind these arguments. If folks in the Middle East, in particular, but in all cultures, all societies, recognized how interrelated we really are, that will change things. If we all knew that our mother's mother's mother's mothers and our father's father's father's fathers were playing together, that we were a mixed mishmash, and that our artificial tribal distinctions are not based on any true genetic fact, it would change the way people think about what peace really means."

He grew even more animated. "Can you imagine artificially walling off my sisters from me, arguing that we are genetically different? Because if you remove that idea, then I have to admit to myself—and it takes some honesty to do this, but it's the truth—that the only thing separating us is how we think about things. It's not really the genes that make us up." I have to confess that when I conceived of filming this documentary series, I secretly hoped that a DNA test would confirm the common paternal descent through a shared haplogroup of a Jew and a Muslim. And the kinship between Mehmet Oz and Mike Nichols had realized this important goal.

7

Mario Batali

1960

MARIO BATALI IS one of America's most colorful and celebrated chefs. He owns six highly successful restaurants in New York City, along with a distinctive winery. He has written best-selling cookbooks, hosted a Food Network show, and won countless accolades for his enduring contributions to American and Italian cuisine. I happen to be addicted to his restaurant Babbo. I eat there whenever I can. Babbo's entire menu is a feast for the eyes and palate, but my favorites are the grilled calamari appetizer, the gnocchi with oxtail, the rock shrimp with chorizo and spaghetti, and the huge grilled double pork chop. This is "good-eating" food, food for your stomach and soul, not eye food like that found in so many highly rated American restaurants; no, Mario's restaurants serve comfort food like your mother or grandmother cooked. I asked Mario to be part of the *Faces of America* documentary series because I was interested that his career, his life's passion, is so directly connected to his ancestry. He has built his culinary empire on a foundation of recipes handed down by his Italian grandmother. And, frankly, I also wanted to learn, through his DNA, where that red hair of his had come from; it's not exactly what we think of when we think "Italian," is it?

When we first met, I described the project to Mario by telling him that I was trying to explore the American immigrant experience—to gauge how it affected people of all races and nationalities and to attempt to explain, at a very personal level, how it has shaped the fabric and character of our country. Mario replied that he is deeply engaged with his Italian roots, both professionally and personally, and, in fact, loves traditions of all sorts. He was eager to participate. But he had a question, he said, that might make the whole venture a bit problematic. Though he respects this country and is a proud American, he told me that he is truly perplexed as to why his ancestors would have ever chosen to come here.

"I guess I'm kind of confused," he said. "Why did they leave the idyllic world of Italy? I mean, why would you leave what was perfect? What was the dream of America? Although there's poor in Italy, nobody is wanting. Even poor Italians always have something to eat, they always live somewhere relatively nice. But everyone is excited about being an American. Italians still get excited about the musical *Oklahoma!* They sing the songs, they ride around. Guys, Oklahoma is not so great. It's not a bad place, but it's certainly not worth getting excited about while we're sitting in Florence. And I just always wonder, why they would leave what they have?"

I assured him that his was a most valid question and by no means disqualified him from the project. To the contrary, I said, I was hoping we could provide him with some answers. Truth be told, I always wonder what makes people leave everything they know and love and head to another country. And the answers are as different as the family trees of each of the twelve people I write about in this book. With that, we began to explore Mario Batali's family's past.

Mario Francesco Batali was born on September 19, 1960, in Seattle, Washington, one of three children of Marilyn Laframboise and Armandino Batali. His mother is of French Canadian descent, and his father's roots stretch back to Italy on both sides of his family. Mario is intensely proud of this heritage. He says that he has shaped his own identity around his father's lineage but that both of his parents were extremely important to him and gave him a strong sense of himself as a person.

Marilyn and Armandino, he told me, were very young when they had their children—and as a result, the family has always been very close-knit and supportive. His parents even encouraged him to follow his passion for cooking at a time, in the mid-1970s, when being a chef was not at all the glamorous occupation it is today, especially for men. "Cooking was kind of the last thing you did when you got out of the military before you went to jail," said Mario. "Because it was the lowest common denominator job —everybody could peel potatoes. But even then, even when I was seventeen, my parents said, 'Maybe you should explore this.' And I said, 'Agh, I'd rather go to college.'"

Despite his initial reaction, his parents, of course, were right. Mario was born to cook—and he realized that while he was in college. It's been his sole focus since he graduated, and whenever he talks about food, he comes to life in a way that is infectious and that makes me hungry. Among his earliest memories, he told me, his face lighting up, are his first cooking experiences at home with his family. "I remember making breakfast on the weekends with Dad," he said, "and baking with my mom. We were very

Mario as a teenager (*standing at left*), with his siblings and parents, Marilyn Laframboise and Armandino Batali. (Used by permission of the Batali family)

involved in food all the time. Our family makes something called antipasto. At the end of the summer you go buy all these vegetables, and then you bring them home, and everyone peels the little baby onions or cuts the little mushrooms. Everyone had a job. And then we'd can it all with some tomato sauce and tuna and make this kind of jarred dip that you put on crackers or bread. And that memory of eating that and making that is one of my most visceral memories."

Mario credits both his parents for helping him become a chef. Nonetheless, he says, the single most important person in his professional development was his father's mother, his paternal grandmother, a constant presence in his childhood and a constant presence still today as he shapes his various restaurants' menus. "We always went to Grandma's house for dinner," he recalled. "She lived in Seattle, and we always were at her house for Sunday supper. I'll never forget the amazement that after all the antipasti and all of the pasta—which would have been a dinner at our house, with just Mom and Dad—all of a sudden, Grandma Batali would break out the roast meats and the giblets. 'Grandma, what's going on? Is there dinner still?' We knew that side of the family very well, and we knew that they were very Italian. And that was very, very important to me."

Grandma Batali, as Mario calls her, was Leonetta Merlino, born on March 21, 1902, in Black Diamond, Washington, the child of Italian immigrants. "She was spectacular," Mario recalled, beaming. "She was at the same time nurturing and all over you, and yet also it was great to go to her house. She was a huge collector of knick-knacky, junky stuff and had all kinds of things around, as well as photos and memorabilia from the family. But there was one thing that everyone would remember, all of the cousins, everyone: her ravioli were amongst the greatest single things ever experienced in our lives. She would count them out. It's legendary among my entire family. Every time she served them there was an exact number. That was all you got. And it was the best thing you ever ate."

In the course of this entire project, I am not sure that any of my subjects was as excited about anything—including the revelation that they were related to kings, queens, or Albert Einstein—as Mario was discussing his grandmother's ravioli. "What was so amazing about it?" he asked.

The Batali family at Easter 1946. Mario's grandmother Leonetta Merlino Batali is wearing the floral dress, to the right of center. (Used by permission of the Batali family)

"What was a madeleine to Proust? A thousand things! It had calf's brain, Swiss chard, and sausage in it. And it was served in a *tomato sauce,* sometimes with oxtails. When our neighborhood friends in Washington State would come over and hear what we were having, they thought we were the weirdest people in the world—they were still at that point buying sliced turkey and putting it on white bread. So that Grandma would create these meals is amongst the most intense memories I have."

Mario told me that he has a video of his grandmother, now deceased, making this ravioli. It is one of his prized possessions. And, not surprisingly, he claims that his career flows directly out of his experiences in his grandmother's kitchen. "My first true inspiration of understanding the joy of the table was at her house," he said. "If I had to select one familial influence, one member of my family who influenced me the most, it would be Grandma Batali. No question about it. We were always in the kitchen. That was where we lived."

Mario believes his growth as a chef directly paralleled an ever more intimate engagement with his Italian roots. The process, he said, began with his grandmother and continued after college when, while working at a number of restaurants in America (including the prestigious Four Seasons Hotel in San Francisco), he realized that truly to hone his skills he had to live in Italy. "I discovered that I needed to understand Italian food not from the Italian American perspective but to go see how it was made where it was born and learn at the hands of a really good cook. So I wrote a bunch of letters to my dad's contacts, and one family responded. So I went to live in a town between Bologna and Florence, Borgo Capanne. This was an hour and a half from Segromigno, in Tuscany, where my family was from in the old days. I remember thinking that it was a risky move. I didn't speak Italian yet. But within a month after getting over the shock of being in a new place, I was immediately enamored with the culture and the people. It was just a natural fit."

When Mario returned to the United States, after three and a half years of working at a trattoria in Borgo Capanne, he took the New York restaurant world by storm. In some ways, his story echoes that of Queen Noor. Both can be seen as stories of return and reinvention: young, contemporary Americans, generations removed from their immigrant ancestors, discovering their identities in the lands from which their immigrant ancestors first set sail, in cultures foreign to their childhoods yet deeply woven into their cumulative cultural heritage. "I am very happy to have been born in the States," Mario told me, "to have been able to have the opportunities to travel back and understand things in a different way. But, still, I am romantic and nostalgic about Italy all the way."

Looking at the branches of his Italian family tree, I realized that Mario's passion for cooking had been inherited through generations of family members. His grandmother Leonetta's parents, Mario's great-grandparents, were Angelo Sabatino Merlino and Antoinetta Elisabetha Mascitelli. Both were born in the Abruzzo region of Italy, in a small village called Taranta Peligna, about thirty miles from the Adriatic coast, on February 17, 1865, and September 26, 1871, respectively.

Mario remembers his grandmother Leonetta talking a great deal about her father, Angelo. He believes that Angelo owned the first Italian food import store in the Seattle area and that he was an entrepreneurial, charismatic community leader. Our research showed that Angelo was, in fact, a very enterprising individual—and that his journey from Taranta Peligna toward that store in Seattle was neither direct nor easy. Born into a farming community in Italy, he came to the United States when he was thirty-one years old, in 1896, and found work as a miner at the Black Diamond Coal Mine in Black Diamond, Washington.

"That's a nasty job," said Mario. "I can't imagine anything more frightening. I'm a little squeezy about small rooms, so being underground is just not where I would be. It's amazing. These guys worked so hard so that they could give something to their children."

Angelo didn't stay in the mine for long. After just a few years, he had saved enough money to move to Seattle and become an entrepreneur. In 1903, he and his wife opened their a store in Seattle and, after years of missing their favorite Italian foods, began importing a wide variety of products that they sold to their fellow countrymen—including an extra-virgin olive oil that they bottled and named "Leonetta," after their daughter.

All evidence suggests that Angelo did quite well in the food business. We found a book entitled *Seattle and Environs, 1852–1925* that includes lists and brief biographies of prominent members of the Seattle community, including Mario's great-grandfather. His biography reads, in part, "Angelo Merlino, one of the foremost representatives of Seattle's Italian Colony, is at the head of a large wholesale grocery house and has become widely known as the pioneer importer of the genuine Italian olive oil on the Pacific Coast. He is loyal to the adopted country and the strength that he manifests in business affairs has its root in an upright, honorable manhood that commands for him the respect, admiration, and esteem of all with whom he is brought into contact."

Mario was thrilled to see tangible evidence of his great-grandfather's success. His father, he told me, after working as an engineer for Boeing for thirty years, opened a meat-curing shop in Seattle in 1999 as a retirement project, attempting to re-create something of the store that his grandparents opened in 1903. "I think for our family, this whole gastronomic thing was always on our minds," said Mario. "And for him to get back into that, he did it to create a legacy from his family down to my children, his grandchildren. He wanted them to have a train of continuity. It gives me, and my dad, great satisfaction. He became one of the great leaders, the godfathers, of the cured-meat movement in the last ten years."

Our researchers in Italy were able to trace the Merlino family all the way back to Mario's ninth-great-grandfather, a man named Baldassarro Merlino, who was born in the year 1625 in Taranta Peligna. This is the same town that Angelo left when he immigrated to the United States—meaning that Mario's ancestors lived in one small town in Italy for almost four hundred years. "That's my big question," said Mario, "after so long there, why leave? Imagine how great it must have been. I remember when I moved to Italy for the first time in the late '80s, and I told people there was this really old church I'd seen in Boston. They said, 'Really, how old?' 'Oh,' I said, 'it must have been from the 1750s.' And they cracked up: 'The house over there is from the 1560s, and we're not making a big deal about that.'"

We were unable to discover exactly why the Merlinos left Italy, but they were part of a massive wave of Italian immigration to America. Turning to the Batali line of Mario's family tree, we were able to shed some light on the motivations and aspirations of them all.

Mario's father, Armandino Batali, was born on October 11, 1937, in Seattle, Washington. His father, Mario's paternal grandfather, was Armando John Batali, born on October 9, 1903, in Silver Bow, Montana, to Italian immigrants. In the 1930 federal census, Armando; his wife, Leonetta; and their daughter, Isolina (Mario's aunt), are listed as living in Seattle. According to the record, Armando was twenty-seven years old and was working as a grocery salesman. Tracing his journey backward from Seattle to his birthplace in Montana, we found the 1910 census records for the city of Butte, Montana. These show Armando living with his parents, Sebastian and Maria Isola Batali. At this time, Mario's great-grandfather Sebastian Batali is listed as a mine worker in Butte—the same occupation pursued by Mario's other Italian great-grandfather, Angelo Merlino, in the early 1890s in Washington State.

Mario's great-grandparents Sebastian and Maria Isola Batali with their family around 1920. Mario's grandfather Armando John Batali is the young man standing to the left. (Used by permission of the Batali family)

Today, when we think of Montana, we think of beautiful natural vistas, mountains, streams, and even buffalo. It's an idyllic part of America, Big Sky Country, an icon of the West, serene and largely unpopulated. But at the turn of the twentieth century, when the Batalis arrived, the little town of Butte was something altogether different. It was a mining boom town, gaining international renown as "the richest hill on earth." That was its motto—and that's how it was known to immigrants across Italy. The town had mushroomed in the mid-1880s with the discovery of silver and copper in the surrounding hills. Well over twenty-two billion pounds of rock and ore were ultimately extracted from its mines. It was an entire city devoted to mining. And it was filled with Italians.

The 1900 census record for Butte indicates that almost the entire town had been born in Italy. "My God," said Mario, amazed, as he looked over column after column of Italian names. "They must have gotten a boat together and brought them all over at one time. There must have been posters in their hometown that said, 'Hey! Come to America, and you can live in Butte!'"

I told Mario that there were at least two possibilities. Either an individual Italian immigrant (or a handful of them) arrived in Butte by chance and sent word back to their countrymen, or recruiters from Butte reached their village in Italy. We could find no evidence to support either possibility, although it seems most likely that one person or a few people sent word back. But regardless of how the news got out, it clearly traveled like wildfire. Everyone knows about New York's Little Italy and Boston's North End. But it turns out that there was a Little Italy in the rugged hills of Butte, Montana, too. It was called Meaderville. This defies our stereotypes of the traditional Italian American narrative. We tend to think that every Italian came to the East Coast and opened a shop or worked on the docks. But many went west and into the mines, the Batalis among them.

Why did they leave Italy in the first place? We found the birth certificate of Mario's great-grandfather Giovanni Lorenzo Sebastiano Batali, or Sebastian Batali, as he was called in America. He was born in 1876 in the Lucca region of Italy, in a small village called Segromigno in Piano. Finding this record led us to the names of Sebastian's parents, Mario's great-great-grandparents: Marco Batali, born in 1849, and Maria Matteucci, born in 1855. This, in turn, led to the discovery of their marriage record and baptismal certificates. All were filled with compelling information that provided clues to their decision to emigrate. Their marriage record did not tell us exactly what the social class of his family was, but it noted that all the witnesses to the wedding were "tenant farmers." We can reasonably assume that the Batalis were tenant farmers as well. This means that they did not own land and were most likely scratching out a living farming for the aristocracy. What's more, the baptismal certificate of Marco Batali indicates that he was an orphan, living at the time of his baptism in a church orphanage in the local parish. Our researchers in Italy believe that this means Marco was an illegitimate child, taken to the orphanage right after his birth. This was not uncommon in Italy in that era. The Catholic Church, of course, was and is very strict about premarital sex and forbids abortion, so

Italian orphanages were crowded. After his baptism, Marco, our research-ers believe, was probably given to a local family who were paid to take care of him—something like today's foster-care system.

Because of the circumstances of Marco's birth, his parents are un-known. But his life is most likely reflective of all Mario's Italian ancestors. He was at the bottom of a rigid social ladder and owned next to nothing. In the mid-nineteenth century, Italian nobles ruled over and exploited land-less peasants, as they had for hundreds of years. The tenant farming system provided no security and no means of accruing wealth. A farmer depended on each season's harvest and on the whims of the nobles. The scarcity of land in the Italian countryside and the burgeoning population left many without the means to survive. In the face of tremendous poverty, many had no choice but to migrate.

Mario's great-grandfather Sebastian most likely heard about the great opportunities for immigrants in the United States from others in his family and his town. American records show that many of his brothers, cousins, and neighbors immigrated as well—and that, indeed, he came here during the absolute peak of Italian immigration. But regardless of how he learned about the possibilities in America, in 1899, at just twenty-four years old, Sebastian boarded a ship with his new wife to seek his fortune in the New World.

We showed Mario the passenger list from the SS *La Champagne,* which docked in New York in December 1899. It includes the names of Mario's great-grandparents, as well as their final destination of Butte, Montana, showing that they already knew where they were headed when they left Italy. Five years later, we found Sebastian Batali listed as a resident of Butte in the 1905 city directory. (Before people had phones, they were listed alphabetically in city directories.) The directory indicates that Sebastian was employed as a miner in the Leonard Mine, a copper mine located in Meaderville that employed Italians almost exclusively.

Mining in this period was very, very dangerous. Sebastian was risking his life every day that he went to work. His daily routine required that he be lowered into the Leonard Mine in a steel cage, descending thousands of feet in a stomach-churning drop. The temperatures below ground were sweltering, often over one hundred degrees, and, in this heat, Sebastian and his fellow workers extracted ore from the rock in backbreaking twelve-hour shifts. I imagine it had to feel as close to being in hell as one pos-sibly could feel on this earth. Moreover, while the work itself was gruel-ing and sometimes deadly, the secondary effects of the labor were just as

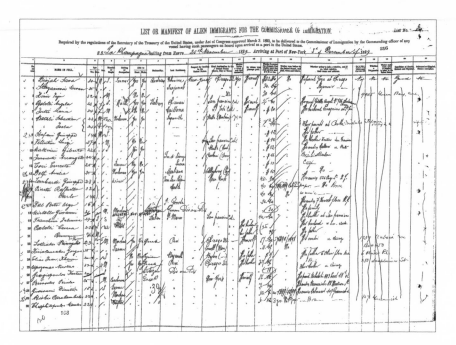

Passenger list of the ship *La Champagne,* which arrived in New York in December 1899, carrying Mario's great-grandparents Sebastian and Maria Isola Batali. (Public domain)

bad. We found the death certificates of two of Sebastian's brothers, Luigi and Angelo Batali, Mario's great-great-uncles. They died in 1909 and 1911, respectively, at the ages of twenty-seven and twenty-four. According to Luigi Batali's death certificate, he died of "La Grippe"—a euphemism for miner's consumption, also known as black lung. It is the result of inhaling toxic dust. Angelo's cause of death, at age twenty-four, is listed as cirrhosis of the liver, which was probably connected to the heavy drinking that was so common among Butte laborers as a way to unwind from their horrible workday.

These tragic records give us a glimpse of how difficult Mario's immigrant ancestors' daily lives could be. He was visibly shaken as he looked at them. And unfortunately, it got worse. Even more disturbing than his uncles' death records were the many death certificates that we found for infants in the Batali family in the early 1900s. Between 1901 and 1911, four Batali babies died of illness or malnutrition before they reached the age of six months. Butte, Montana, was not an environment for the weak.

When our researchers first discovered these records, they noticed that by 1914 there was no trace of Sebastian or his family in Butte. They simply disappeared, to surface later in Washington State. We could not determine what had happened until we started interviewing members of Mario's extended family. One of his cousins told us that he had heard that the reason Sebastian left was somehow tied to a terrible mining accident. So, as we always do with family stories, we searched for evidence to corroborate this story. We found a newspaper article in the *Butte Miner* indicating that five employees of the Leonard Mine were killed when an engine failure caused the steel cage that was holding them to drop eight hundred feet. This, of course, occurred in the very mine in which Sebastian worked, and it is likely that he witnessed the accident. Even if he did not witness it directly, he was on a crew that entered the mine after the accident to recover the dead bodies.

According to the family story, Sebastian was so disturbed by this experience that he quit his job that very day. He left the mine, and he never went back, moving his family out of Butte and ultimately benefiting from a new federal policy that parceled out land grants to immigrants willing to venture west and become farmers. He ended up in Washington State and

Immigrants in a saloon in Meaderville, the Italian neighborhood of Butte, Montana, during the early twentieth century, when many Batalis lived in the town. (Used by permission of Jim Matteucci)

was apparently quite a successful farmer, eventually opening a tavern and small store in the tiny town of Harrah, Washington.

"I always wondered why they left Italy," said Mario solemnly. "It makes a lot of sense in retrospect. I understand it now. These people must have been *very* poor in Italy. Because it's not like they were in a great world in the mines here, that's for sure. How they stayed for fifteen years in Butte —they must have really had no other option. I would have given them the advice at this point to go back to Lucca. But I'm weak stock. We're twentieth-century guys—a torn nail is a bad day for us. So I don't have any idea of the kind of tenacity and intensity for survival that people in this era must have had."

This was, I agree, the answer to his question. The Batalis came here seeking things that were not available to them in Italy: land, status, wealth, opportunity. They were to endure almost unimaginably challenging conditions in their quest for a better life. Many died along the way—but none went back to Italy. And, within one generation, they had reached their goals. Theirs is a tremendously impressive immigrant success story—an iconic story.

Turning to the maternal side of Mario's family tree, we began to trace the roots of his mother's French Canadian ancestors. Again, we found people who came to the western United States and showed great strength and determination. Indeed, the tenacity, as Mario so well puts it, on both sides of his family is as powerful as is his love of Italian food.

Mario's mother, Marilyn Laframboise, was born on May 29, 1937, in Yakima, Washington. Her parents were Leon Louis LaFramboise and Mary Hardman, both born in Yakima, on July 4, 1914, and January 16, 1913, respectively. Mary's parents were Richard Hardman and Elizabeth Critchley. They were immigrants, both born in Lancashire, England. They came to America in the early 1900s, and Mario's great-grandfather Richard found work in the coal mines of Roslyn, Washington. "I've got coal dust in my veins," said Mario, shivering.

Marilyn's father, Leon Louis LaFramboise, was the son of a man named Antoine LaFramboise, born in Montreal in the year 1877 and the descendant of a long line of Canadian fur traders. Records show that at the end of the nineteenth century, Antoine was living in northern Minnesota. He was engaged to a woman named Eugenie Labissoniere when a group of real-estate developers known as the Moxee Company recruited him to be their blacksmith. Moxee was created by wealthy East Coast investors, including Alexander Graham Bell, to develop farmland in the western United States.

They paid for Antoine to move to Yakima, Washington, leaving Eugenie behind. It must have been a difficult decision. But at the end of his five-year contract, Antoine had earned enough money to buy land in Yakima. He purchased the fields near his blacksmith shop to farm his own crops and began building a house. When it was finished, sometime around 1902, he returned to Minnesota, fetched his fiancée, and brought her back to live in Washington. This house still stands today—it is a landmark of sorts and part of the National Historic Register.

"I've been to the house," said Mario. "We call that affectionately 'the ranch.' Grandpa and Grandma, Leon and Mary, lived there for as long as I can remember. They eventually sold it or gave it to my aunt, who lives there now. My mother and my uncles all grew up there. It's a great place."

Antoine's wife, Eugenie Labissoniere, was born in 1882 in Red Lake Falls, Minnesota. (Red Lake Falls is not far from where Louise Erdrich's Native American ancestors lived just thirty years earlier—on lands that they had owned and then been cheated out of by the U.S. government.) Eugenie's family was also French Canadian. Her grandfather, Mario's third-great-grandfather, François Hubert Labissoniere, was her immigrant ancestor. He seems to have been yet another very determined individual on Mario's family tree.

François was born in 1812 in Quebec. According to family tradition, he was a hardworking farmer who was unable to make a living in Canada. This is no surprise, as the historical record shows that the rural economy in Quebec stagnated throughout the first half of the nineteenth century, while just below the border in the United States, urban industrialization was providing a massive number of new jobs. As a result, between 1850 and 1890, almost one million Canadians migrated to America seeking new economic opportunities. François was at the very forefront of this immigrant wave. In 1849, he decided to move his family south to the rapidly growing city of St. Louis. Unfortunately, the Labissonieres arrived in St. Louis just as a massive cholera epidemic was sweeping the city. One-tenth of the population died that very summer; corpses were literally piled in the street. François and his family arrived, looked around, and immediately returned to Canada, settling in Lafontaine, Ontario. "Think about the risk," said Mario. "We complain about taking our shoes and belts off at the airport. Cholera —just think about traveling into that."

This, however, was just a temporary setback. François eventually tried his luck in America again, moving to Minnesota, searching not for industrial work but for better farmland. And this time, François succeeded.

By the 1880s, thirty years after first leaving Quebec, the Labissoniere family appears in the census records, farming in Red Lake Falls, which was then a community largely composed of former French Canadians like themselves.

Beginning in the early 1900s, one by one, the next generation of Labissonieres moved westward to Washington State. The family's journey, over the course of fifty years, had taken them from Quebec south to St. Louis, then north to Ontario, south to Minnesota, and then west to Yakima. They traveled all this by wagon, carrying everything that they owned. It's an amazing journey. I wonder if anyone walking into Mario's restaurants in New York would guess that he is the grandchild of such frontier people, the progeny of Western pioneers on both sides of his family?

Reflecting on his family's hardships, Mario said, "I never put it in that perspective, but the idea of living in any part of America in the mid-nineteenth century just doesn't really filter in. Growing up in the suburbs of Washington State, you would never think of such an epic struggle to just continue. It's really fascinating."

At this point, we had traced Mario's paternal ancestors back to the early 1600s in Italy and his maternal ancestors back to French colonists who began exploring their northern territories around the same time. I now wanted to go further and see what we could find about his earliest ancestors who migrated to the New World. We were able to trace Marilyn Eugenie Labissoniere's genealogy back to Mario's eighth-great-grandfather, a man named Marin Boucher who was among the first colonists in Quebec. He came on a ship from France in June 1634, fourteen years after the *Mayflower*, as part of a group of mainly single men who were charged with claiming the land for France and defending it from the Native Americans.

Marin interacted with one of the most notable figures of his era: Samuel Champlain, the founder of Quebec City and the discoverer of Lake Champlain, sometimes called "The Father of New France." The exact nature of the relationship between Boucher and Champlain is unclear, but when Champlain died in the year 1635, his last will and testament includes the line, "I give Marin Boucher, a mason, the last suit that I had made from the fabric that I got at the store." So Mario's tenth-great-grandfather was mentioned in the will of a legendary explorer!

We don't know what happened to the suit, but Marin Boucher led a long and productive life. We found a French census from 1667—one of the first North American census documents in existence—indicating that Marin, who was at this point eighty years old, was a land and livestock owner in Côte-de-Beaupré, Quebec. According to the document, he lived with his family and a domestic servant, owned eight head of cattle, and had about seventeen acres of land under cultivation. Mario looked at the record in awe. It was tangible proof that his family had been feeding people in North America for more than 350 years.

There was one more story in Mario's family tree. Moving along a different branch of his mother's line, we came to a man named Jean Fafard, who was born around 1598 in Normandy, France, and was, like Marin Boucher, one of Mario's tenth-great-grandfathers. Jean Fafard never came to the New World. He lived in France during the reign of King Louis XIV. The most notable thing about Jean Fafard, at least for this book's purposes, is that he is also an ancestor of Louise Erdrich. As I explained to Mario, this means that the world-renowned Native American writer and the Italian chef are ninth cousins once removed—both descended from a Frenchman!

"I'm overwhelmed," said Mario. "It really gives perspective to the finiteness of the human race throughout time. It kind of ties it all together in a way that makes it really interesting to think about. Everything comes from one place. That's what is the most evident, I think. And now that I have a cousin that I'm very aware of, I'm going to go look her up."

Turning to his DNA testing, I told Mario that our admixture tests reveal that he is 100 percent European: no Asian, no African, no Native American, nothing but white people sleeping with white people. He seemed genuinely disappointed. "Damn it," said Mario. "I was hoping for more depth here—but I'm going to be all right with that."

I told him that he need not worry, there was plenty of depth in his European roots. Indeed, it would be hard to go much deeper. His mitochondrial DNA falls into haplogroup J1a, which is a branch of haplogroup J. This haplogroup originated about forty-five thousand years ago on the Arabian Peninsula. Over time, its descendants, including Mario's distant maternal ancestors, began to move north and east. The expansion of agriculture, about seven thousand years ago, finally carried them into Europe. It is one of the first haplogroups to appear in Europe. And although we found no evidence of Italian ancestry on his mother's line, his maternal haplogroup is fairly common in Italy: as many as 15 percent of all Italians carry it. In addition, the Family Tree DNA databases show that he has exact mitochondrial DNA matches with people who live today all over Europe—including 121 people in Ireland, 79 in Scotland, 29 in Norway, 24 in Sweden, 211 in the United Kingdom, 29 in France, 111 in Germany, and 25 in Italy.

Looking at his Y-DNA, our testing revealed that Mario's paternal line carries a subbranch of haplogroup R1 called R1b1b2a1a2d. This branch originated in southwestern Asia about thirty thousand years ago. Members of it eventually migrated across Eurasia, and their descendants, including Mario's distant paternal ancestors, were part of the many migrations that populated and shaped Europe from the arrival of farmers between about ten and seven thousand years ago to the movements of the Anglo-Saxons and the Vikings.

We found exact Y-DNA matches for him with people living today in Ireland, in the United Kingdom, and in Italy, including one in the small town of Forli, not far from Florence. We also found more than forty lower-resolution matches throughout Italy, including two in Ravenna and one each in Val Marecchia and Modena. All told, it appears that his roots are deepest in northeastern Italy, but on both Mario's lines, his mother's and father's, his DNA tells us that his ancestors were some of the original Europeans. "That feels great," said Mario, laughing. "It's funny. Agriculture— food and the growing of food—determined them? I'm not surprised."

Mario was also very excited to learn that autosomal DNA testing at the Broad Institute revealed that he and Queen Noor share segments of DNA on chromosome 2, matching from base pair 213 to base pair 221, which translates into eight million base pairs of DNA. "That's killer," he said. "Wow, I would have never guessed that. She's beautiful. And she's really smart. I just got lucky!"

Mario and Queen Noor share a common ancestor as recently as the past 250 years. But our testing also revealed that, much more distantly, he is also related to Stephen Colbert, Malcolm Gladwell, and to me. We three share an ancestor who lived at the end of the Ice Age. I joked that looking at the four of us, who in the world could guess that we're descended from anybody in common? An Italian, two black guys, and an Irishman.

"This is spectacular," he said, poring over his charts. "It's so unifying to be part of one race, not a giant group of a thousand different disparate races."

Our time together was now up, but I wanted to know one more thing. I was curious whether the process of learning about his family's past had changed the way Mario thought of his Italian identity. His answer, I thought, beautifully summed up our country's great capacity for self-invention.

"Italian is my root," he said, unwavering. "That is where I'm from. I'm French Canadian and Italian, as everyone in my family will tell you. But what America represents is opportunity, freedom, the greatest possible extension of all of the things that we've learned together—because we're part of a melting pot and not just one race of people from Lucca or Segromigno or from Canada or from France. What we represent is the best possible expression of all of the good parts of our genetic stuff, and some of the bad ones, becoming part of something completely new. And for me that is the greatness of America: people here don't look back two generations to find out whether your family has a pedigree. You're as good as your last lasagna. And if my lasagna wasn't good, I'd be worth nothing here, too."

8

Elizabeth Alexander

1962

DR. ELIZABETH ALEXANDER is a poet, professor, and chair of the African American Studies Department at Yale University. She is the author of five books of poems (including *American Sublime,* a finalist for the Pulitzer Prize) and two collections of essays. Among her many honors, she has been awarded a National Endowment for the Arts Fellowship, two Pushcart Prizes, a Guggenheim Fellowship, and the inaugural Alphonse Fletcher, Sr. Fellowship for work that "contributes to improving race relations in American society." In 2008, Barack Obama selected her to compose and read a poem at his inauguration as president of the United States.

Elizabeth was my student at Yale and since then has become a dear friend, someone whom I have relied on for advice and inspiration time and time again. I asked her to be in the series for the same reason that I asked Malcolm Gladwell: because both can trace their ancestry, in part, to the West Indies. I also invited her because over the years I thought I had come to know part of her family story, and I was fascinated by the way in which it embodies the complex nature of racial identity in America. She and her parents, like countless other African Americans, forged strong identities for themselves despite knowing very little about their deep ancestors. Her mother has written two excellent books on her family's past, but there are profound questions that she has been unable to answer. I wanted to take a try at these questions myself. And I must say, the results truly surprised her and me. Elizabeth, as we shall see, has one of the largest documented family trees of any African American on record—with ancestors whose lives, it turns out, stretch from Jamaica to Wales, from the heart of Africa to the heart of Europe.

Her story begins in one of my favorite places on earth: New York City. Elizabeth Alexander was born on May 30, 1962, in Harlem. Her parents were Clifford Leopold Alexander, Jr., and Adele Logan, both also born in New York, he on September 21, 1933, and she on January 26, 1938. Theirs

Elizabeth Alexander, chair of the African American Studies Department at Yale University. (Used by permission of Elizabeth Alexander)

was an exceptionally close family with a clear sense of what it meant to black and what it took to succeed in 1960s America. Elizabeth's father was a pioneer in the civil rights movement and a very significant person in African American history. A trailblazer in the truest sense, Clifford attended Harvard University in the 1950s, where he was elected the first African American student-body president. He graduated with an A.B. in government and then went on to study law at Yale, one of the first black people to earn degrees from both those universities. Among his many accomplishments, he was one of President Lyndon Johnson's closest advisers on civil rights, and he played a major role in the passage of the Civil Rights Act of 1964. He was also, under President Carter, the first African American secretary of the army. In this capacity, he promoted Colin Powell to the rank of brigadier general.

Elizabeth says that even as a very young child she was aware that her father was engaged in a something important—and that it was deeply related to race. "We had a sense of being in the midst of a historical time," she told me. "We were race people—that was always plain and clear. That was part of the language. It was the primary lens. I wouldn't say that my

Elizabeth's father, Clifford Alexander, with President Jimmy Carter. (Used by permission of the Jimmy Carter Library and Museum)

parents were race obsessed in any way, but they saw the world in large part along the lines of those struggles."

The Alexanders moved from Harlem to Washington, DC, when Elizabeth was two years old, because her father was offered a job in the Johnson administration. So Elizabeth grew up in the nation's capital, during one of the most tumultuous times in our history, immersed in the civil rights movement. "One of my most powerful memories," she said, "was when Martin Luther King was killed, and Washington erupted in riots and fires. I remember my father couldn't come home. I'm not sure what President Johnson sent him to do to help, but as the city was burning maybe ten blocks away from our house, I knew that Daddy was doing something helpful—but also that he wasn't there, and we were waiting for him to come back. And then when he came back, he told us about flying over the city and watching it burning. We knew at that point already who Dr. King was and what he was trying to do. We knew about Medgar Evers. Somehow it all seemed tied together."

As we began to explore her genealogy, Elizabeth told me that she knew much more about the great sociopolitical events of her youth than she did about her ancestry. Politics, culture, and race, she said, were constant subjects in the Alexander home. The past was not. "I had my whole child-hood with my maternal grandmother and my paternal grandfather," Eliza-beth said. "Both of my grandparents were only children. We spent a great deal of time with these grandparents. But they didn't tell us much of any-thing about where they came from."

Her paternal grandfather, Clifford Alexander, Sr., was particularly reti-cent. He had immigrated to America from Jamaica as a young man, leav-ing behind a mother whom he never saw again and rumors that he was the illegitimate son of a Jewish merchant. Perhaps unsurprisingly, he rarely discussed these matters. "He gave a few tantalizing details," said Elizabeth. "He told me that his father died in the great earthquake in Jamaica in 1907, but that was about it. When he was a few days away from passing, in the middle of the night I realized we don't know his parents' names. And so I asked him and received no last names, just Emma and James, and that was pretty much all that we knew."

This is a rather sad story, and the telling of it clearly gripped Elizabeth. She said to me that she was especially eager to learn more about her grand-father and that, indeed, she had peppered him with questions as a child. Everything about his life was interesting to her. "I remember," she said, "I asked my grandfather once, 'Did you know anybody in America when you came?' And he said no. I couldn't imagine going somewhere and not be-ing met, so I asked, 'What happened when you got off the boat?' 'Well,' he said, 'there were always people there. There were chaps.' That was the way he talked: he was from Jamaica, his English was different. His vocabulary was not the same as ours. So he said, 'There were chaps who would show you where you could live and where you could work.' And you needed these chaps, because this was a segregated country that he was coming into. He said these chaps took him to Harlem and showed him a boarding house and where you could get a job."

Harlem, at the time, was a melting pot of comparatively well-educated West Indian immigrants and many more poor, less-educated African Americans migrants from the South who transformed Harlem from a com-munity that was 67 percent white in 1920 to a community that was 70 percent black just ten years later. Class tension, racial tension, and cultural tension between the groups abounded. But Elizabeth does not recall that her grandfather suffered from these things. They certainly did not limit his career. Clifford ended up overseeing a YMCA and managing the branch of a bank. He was a community leader in every sense of the term and an enduring inspiration to his activist son.

Elizabeth's paternal grandfather, Clifford Alexander, Sr., soon after he emigrated from Jamaica to New York. (Used by permission of the Alexander family)

"The sense that I got from my grandfather was of an incredibly vibrant Harlem," Elizabeth said, "with a whole lot of different kinds of black people in it. That was always my sense of that world. And he became someone who was a very helpful figure in Harlem. When he passed away, I can't tell you how many people at his funeral came up and said, 'Your grandfather gave me advice about starting a patty stand,' 'Your grandfather gave me help with this.' He really was a community person in the present, and he just didn't talk about the past. Maybe there are sadnesses, too. You leave your mother, and you never see her again. So who knows if that was part of it? Maybe he just didn't want to discuss that."

I asked Elizabeth if she thought her grandfather was embarrassed about his immigrant status. I kept thinking of him getting off that boat and looking around for a "chap" to show him where to stay. I can imagine African Americans making fun of a Jamaican like that.

Elizabeth told me that she didn't think so. Her grandfather, she believed, was simply someone who had reinvented himself and did not want to look backward. As evidence, she told me that she had once asked him to tell her the story of his journey from Jamaica to New York. He turned the whole thing into a kind of shaggy-dog story for his grandchildren.

She remembered him chuckling as he spun his yarn: "He started out by saying that he was born on the road between Spanishtown and Kingston, and we loved that, because we were these urban children, and we couldn't imagine being born on the road. And then he said he stowed away on a banana boat, and I didn't know what to think. But when I cleaned out his apartment after he died I found sort of a passage document from a United Fruit Company boat. So maybe he stowed away, but with papers? He chuckled when he told us the stowaway part, so I don't know if he was trying to give us an adventure tale, but that's all we ever knew. We knew that there was something funny but couldn't quite discern what it was."

It turns out that Elizabeth's grandfather's story about being a stowaway on a banana boat was a riddle of sorts. We found the actual records of her grandfather's immigration to America. They show that his story was an interesting mix of fantasy and fact—leaning heavily toward the side of fantasy. The SS *Turrialba*—owned by the United Fruit Company (in a way, a "banana boat")—arrived at Ellis Island, New York, from Jamaica on August 31, 1918, and its manifest lists twenty-one-year-old Clifford Alexander not only as a paying passenger but as a first-class passenger as well. His race is listed as "West Indian," and his home is Kingston, Jamaica.

We were also able to find his birth certificate in Jamaica. It indicates that Clifford was born in Kingston to a woman named Emma Honeywell, a seamstress living at 4 Wildman Street. No father is named on the birth certificate, but Emma's address gave us a starting point for some theorizing. Wildman Street is in the oldest part of Kingston, a very poor neighborhood. Number 4, where Clifford was born, is today an alley running behind the street. Some of the oldest residents of the neighborhood told us that, for the past century at least, the alley has been filled with one-room rental apartments. So Clifford Alexander was born into intense poverty.

The fact that no father is named on Clifford's birth certificate indicates that the family legend about his being illegitimate is almost certainly correct. I wanted to find out if the stories about his Jewish father were also true. According to Elizabeth, Clifford had told her, at the end of his life, that his parents were named Emma and James. The Emma part had checked out. What about the James part? Could we locate a Jewish merchant named James Alexander?

If you do enough genealogical research, you will be forced to face the sad fact that family stories are often pure invention. In my own family, we cherished the idea that we were all related to Horatio Gates, the Revolutionary War general. Research showed there wasn't a shred of truth to the story. For many African Americans, whose ancestry is hidden by slavery, myths of Native American roots or Igbo princesses from Africa abound. Very few are true. Another, less common but nonetheless persistent mythology in some West Indian families is the existence of a male Jewish ancestor; Malcolm Gladwell's family, as we shall see, shared the same belief. (As a matter of fact, about 35 percent of all African American males are descended from a white male ancestor, according to their Y-DNA.) Of course, there are often kernels of truth in family lore, and sometimes family stories turn out to be true. From our research, it seems that it might be possible that Clifford Alexander's father was a Jewish merchant. We don't know for certain, but there is significant evidence to support it.

First is the surname: Alexander. Alexander in Jamaica is thought of as a "Jewish" name, and it's not uncommon for a woman to give her illegitimate child the father's name to create a connection to the father, even if they're not legally associated. This was, indeed, quite a common practice at the time when Elizabeth's grandfather was born. There are other factors that led us to think that he might have been Jewish as well. Jamaica in the nineteenth century was a very complex society with regard to race and class. Everyone had a place, everyone knew that place, and that place was signified by color. The white ruling elite, of course, was at the top. Jewish people and free people of color were at the same social level one tier down (and both groups, curiously enough, won the right to vote in the same year, 1831). Below them was the bulk of the population: black slaves of all different skin tones but predominantly pure, unmixed black people. So in spite of the second-class status of Jews, claiming a Jewish ancestor for a black person meant that you had white ancestry. And in Jamaica that was a very good thing. For a black woman, slave or free, a relationship with a white man, even a Jewish man, could be a dramatic step up in the world. Emma may have been willing to engage in a relationship for this reason alone.

Unfortunately, this is all speculation. With the records available to us we were not able either to prove or to disprove the existence of a Jewish merchant in Elizabeth's family or to document a connection between Emma Honeywell and any man who might have been the father of her son Clifford. There are no records of a man named James Alexander living in Jamaica at that time, nor is there any evidence that a man fitting his description might have died in the 1907 earthquake, as Elizabeth's family story says. (DNA, however, has something to say about this story, as we later found out.)

Our research, however, was not entirely fruitless. It did yield more information about Elizabeth's great-grandmother Emma Honeywell. We found her baptismal record, dated May 6, 1859. It shows that she was born in Kingston, in the parish of St. Elizabeth, sometime in March 1859. Her parents are listed as Edward and Esther Honeywell, and her mother's occupation is listed as "servant." We also found the marriage certificate of Edward Honeywell and Esther Elisabeth Powell. They were married on July 15, 1857, by the Reverend R. D. Lynch in St. Elizabeth Parish. We wanted to see if Esther Powell was related to Colin Powell, whose family is also from Jamaica, but unfortunately we found no connection at all.

Further searching uncovered Emma's father's baptismal record. It shows that Edward Honeywell, "a Domestic of Northampton," aged twenty-one years old, was baptized on September 17, 1852. This record also contains a very telling omission. It does not state Edward's complexion, which in the Jamaica of this era means that he was black (white people and those with mixed blood made this known because it was a badge of honor). So, based on his profession as a "domestic" and the absence of recorded information about his race, I told Elizabeth that it was almost certain that her great-great-grandfather was black and a former slave.

"That's amazing," said Elizabeth. "It doesn't surprise me, but I also never even allowed myself to speculate beyond the one person that we knew. We had heard of Emma, but I never thought about her parents."

Elizabeth and I were both intrigued by the fact that Edward was baptized at age twenty-one. This means that he was born about 1831. And although the British act abolishing slavery in Jamaica passed in 1833, and became effective in 1834, slaves were still held in apprenticeships until 1838. So Edward most likely spent the first years of his childhood as a slave and then, when he was about seven, received his freedom. But he was free for fourteen years before he was baptized. Why did he wait so long? There's no way of knowing. It is possible that he came under the sway of religion at this point—possibly through another person such as his wife, Esther, or via the influence of a preacher. Records show that he was baptized on the same day as many of his neighbors, so it seems entirely possible that some kind of a hell-fire preacher came into his community distributing the fear of God en masse. There is no way to know for sure, but it seems a very likely explanation.

Elizabeth and I both wanted to know more about Edward's slave past. His baptismal record notes that he was a domestic servant and that he lived in Northampton. This was not a familiar place name to us, so our researchers began searching and found hand-drawn maps from the early nineteenth century of St. Elizabeth Parish. They showed that the parish contained something called "Northampton Pen." The word *pen* was the Jamaican term at that time for a cattle farm, and Northampton Pen was one of the largest pens in the country—including a plantation house and an estate of over fifteen hundred acres. This is where Elizabeth's great-great-grandfather and most likely his parents were slaves.

The farm is a ruin today, just some walls, the bare remains of some kind of entrance gate, open fields crossed by a single road, and lots of goats. But in the first decades of the 1800s, it was a very significant operation, owned by an Englishman named John Chambers. Records show that in 1826 Chambers owned 299 slaves. That's a large number of slaves for Jamaica and is much larger than most plantations in the United States held, even at the height of slavery here. When Chambers died in 1832, the inventory of his estate listed all his slaves. On the list is a boy named Edward, age two and a half years, valued at forty pounds (which would be about forty-five hundred dollars today). Incredibly, this two-and-a-half-year-old boy is Elizabeth's great-great-grandfather.

"My God," said Elizabeth, looking at the record. "When you see in black and white what it is to be valued as property when you're a toddler —I'm sorry, but these are all babies. That's hard to take."

This inventory told us more about the lives of Edward and the other slaves. It appears that Chambers did not treat his property as badly as many Jamaican slave owners did. Jamaica, like the rest of the Caribbean islands and much of South and Latin America, was a death camp for African slaves, a far worse place to be than the United States in terms of life expectancy. As a matter of fact, of a total of about 10.8 million slaves who survived the Middle Passage, only 450,000 or so Africans arrived in the United States between 1619 and 1865. The common practice in many parts of the Caribbean and South America was for owners simply to work their slaves until they died and then replace them, devoting little or no effort to maintaining their health or adequately feeding them. In America, by contrast, the importation of Africans was abolished in 1808, so slaves could not be easily replaced through importation. They were thus bred for generations of work and, while clearly mistreated, were not primarily viewed as replaceable parts. As a result, although there were only 450,000 Africans brought to the United States in the slave trade, the African American population today numbers over thirty-five million people. Far more slaves went to the Caribbean and to South America—and the vast majority of them died, leaving no descendants. But the Northampton Pen was an exception. Chambers's records show a large number of births on his estate and many slaves who seem to have lived into their seventies and eighties—which in the 1830s was a very long time. So they must have been fed decently and received some kind of medical care. This, of course, does not make Edward and his family's slavery acceptable in any way. Elizabeth and I simply find it interesting to know that it could have been much worse.

Unfortunately, we could learn nothing more about Edward—and nothing at all about his parents. But, as I told Elizabeth, I think this scarcity of detail in itself tells us something about the Honeywells and illuminates her grandfather's silence about his past. Genealogies reflect a family's history in many different ways. They are so much more than a list of names. And when you find lives as elusive as these, it is because, for whatever reasons, our ancestors could not, or did not, record key facts about their existence. They were too poor to have access to records or for records to have access to them; they didn't own property or pay taxes on property. Often, births of the poor were not recorded; some churches kept records of baptisms, marriages, and funerals; others did not. And even when these sorts of records were kept, sometimes they have been lost, destroyed, or discarded. Frankly, if you think about it, most of our ancestors, on any branch of our family trees, were regular people who lived on the lower levels of society, most often beneath literacy. The only records that we were able to locate across two generations of Honeywells were a baptismal certificate, a marriage license, and the estate records of the white man who owned them. These were not prosperous people. I am always astonished by how much we can find out about anyone's ancestors, to tell you the truth, given the small percentages of literacy in Europe and America and in any country until very recently and given that the overwhelming percentage of our ancestors were, at best, members of the working poor.

"But there they are," said Elizabeth, pointing to her great-great-grandparents' marriage license. "It's hard to imagine. I mean, what you can know is that the kind of work they had to do wouldn't have left much time for imagination, but what we also know about people under all kinds of difficult conditions and what we know about black people is that creativity and beauty comes out of that privation. So we have the spirituals, and we have folk tales, and we have aphorisms—we have so much production that comes out of people under very, very extreme circumstances. And I imagine in that regard they were like so many others. But it's all imagining, isn't it? Even with what we know as scholars about the sorrow songs—we have some records, but really, really trying to understand the circumstances from which those arise you have to use imagination."

Elizabeth is right, of course. It's a stirring fact that our slave ancestors left behind not documents or property but an incredible amount of cultural wealth. It is a tragedy that we are only able to imagine their individual contributions to that collective wealth—and the worlds they might have made had they been free.

Moving back down Elizabeth's paternal line, we looked at the ancestry of Clifford Alexander's wife, Elizabeth's grandmother, Edith MacAlister. Edith was born in 1902, in Yonkers, New York, just a few miles north of the Harlem neighborhood where she spent most of her adult life. She died when Elizabeth was a baby, and Elizabeth has no memory of her. Fortunately, her life is well documented. Her mother was a woman named Harriet, who was born sometime around 1880 in Pennsylvania, and her father was Walter Nathan MacAlister, born in July 1880 in Cumberland County, North Carolina. Harriet and Walter were almost certainly the children of freed slaves. And though we could not identify Harriet's last name or the identity of her parents, we were able to trace Walter back two generations into slavery using plantation records and census data. His parents were Nathan MacAlister, born in 1840 in Cumberland County, and a woman named Margaret, who was born a slave in Virginia in January 1854 and died a free woman sometime in 1900. We even found Nathan MacAlister's mother: a woman named Maryanne MacAlister who was born in 1816 in North Carolina.

This meant that on Elizabeth's father's side, we were able to trace her ancestry into slavery back to 1816 in America and 1831 in Jamaica—which is quite extraordinary for any African American.

Turning to Elizabeth's maternal line, we started with her mother, Adele Logan, born in 1938 in New York City. She has an impressive family as well. Adele's mother was Wenonah Bond, born in Birmingham, Alabama, on December 18, 1906. Her father, Elizabeth's great-grandfather, was Robert Percy Bond, born on June 18, 1868, in Norfolk, Virginia. His father was a remarkable man named John Robert Bond, born on May 24, 1843, in Mold, a town in Wales. John is Elizabeth's immigrant ancestor on her maternal line. According to her family's lore—and to some very impressive research done by her mother, a highly regarded historian—John was the son of a white woman from England and a black ship's cook named Robert Bond. According to the family, John came to America as a young man to join the fight against slavery. It's a wild story, more like a Hollywood movie than what we tend to find in the historical record, and I was eager to see what portion of it might be true. Much to my surprise, records suggest that the family account is substantially true, but with a few surprising twists.

Census records from Liverpool, England (which is about twenty miles from Mold) show that in 1851, an eight-year-old boy named John Robert Bond was living with his thirty-five-year-old father, Robert Bond, and his thirty-year-old mother, Ann Evans. In the records, Robert Bond lists his occupation as "cook on a ship" and states that he was from Bermuda. These are, undoubtedly, Elizabeth's ancestors.

"That's a total shock," said Elizabeth, ecstatic. "It was a big unknown, and again I didn't know enough about the history to be able to even speculate on whether he would have been in Liverpool for some time, for another generation, or come from Africa as a slave or come from the West Indies. That's fascinating. Bermuda was never in the equation."

Records also show that John Robert Bond left England and journeyed to New Bedford, Massachusetts, around the time of the Civil War (we could not identify the precise date of his arrival, but records definitely place him there by 1863). In that era, New Bedford was a center of the shipping and whaling industries, the latter of which was perhaps the most open occupation in the entire American economy for black men. Shortly after escaping to freedom in the North, Frederick Douglass had moved there for this very reason. We don't know exactly what drew Elizabeth's ancestor to New Bedford or what he did there, but we do know that John made a very unusual decision for a foreign-born black person. In May 1863, as the Civil War entered its third long year, he enlisted in the Union navy. He was twenty-one years old and had lived almost all his life in England. But he clearly believed in the Union cause, and he served with honor. On February 1, 1864, he was wounded in action when a bullet pierced his chest. It could have been a fatal wound, but he survived, was honorably discharged, and was granted an invalid's pension of eight dollars a month. He was just twenty-two years old. And around this time, he met an African American woman named Emma Thomas. We weren't able to track down records of where Emma was born or who her parents were, but she and John Robert Bond married in June 1865, just weeks after the end of the Civil War. They eventually headed north to New England and settled in Hyde Park, Massachusetts, where they raised a family of four children, one of whom was Elizabeth's great-grandfather Robert Percy Bond.

John Robert Bond died peacefully in Hyde Park in 1905, never returning to England. I wanted to find out more about the family that produced this remarkable individual. Unfortunately, this proved very difficult. We knew that his mother, Ann Evans, had moved from her home town of Mold to the nearby city of Liverpool sometime in the late 1840s or early 1850s. The 1851 census records for Mold list her father, John's maternal grandfather, as a man named John Evans. At the time, John was sixty-eight years old, and according to the census, he was a former farmer turned pauper. We were able to trace John Evans back three more generations to Elizabeth's seventh-great-grandfather Edward Evans, born in nearby Northop, Wales, in January 1706. But we couldn't find out much about any of the people along this line. They most likely lived in the same region for generations, earning a subsistence living as farmers and miners like virtually everyone around them.

We were also unable to determine why Ann Evans left Mold for Liverpool. Maybe her reasons were economic; maybe there was some kind of conflict with her family. There is no way to tell. But in Liverpool, she met and married the ship's cook from Bermuda, Robert Bond, and this may have made it impossible to return to her family. Neither Elizabeth nor I can imagine this white girl from a small village coming to the big city and marrying this mulatto, then returning to her hometown.

"That's a story," said Elizabeth. "Even a hundred years later that story is seen as a novelty. Think about that confrontation. Even now when people talk about our president's parents, that's seen as a novelty. Of course, we know these comings together aren't so novel after all. But it had to be traumatic—it couldn't have been just 'Oh, a negro; come, sit down, take tea.' "

We then tried to learn more about the ship's cook, Robert Bond. This search proved frustrating as well. Census data indicated that he and Ann lived on Leeds Street, in the dock area of Liverpool, one of the busiest ports in the world at that time, with a well-established black community. The census indicated Robert had come from Bermuda—and this conforms to what we know of nineteenth-century Liverpool. Many sailors from the Caribbean settled there because of the shipping industry and married local women and had families. But we could learn nothing more about Robert or his ancestors. We could not even figure out what happened to Robert and Ann after 1851. They simply disappear from the historical record. The fact that Robert was a cook on a ship offers a clue as to why there's no further trace of him or his family. Perhaps he and Ann died, or perhaps they went back to Robert's home in Bermuda. But we just don't know. We do know that their son did not disappear. John Robert Bond made his mark on history. He was a half-English, half-Caribbean freedom fighter. I wish we could have learned more about him—but the little glimpse we have is nonetheless wonderful and inspiring.

I asked Elizabeth how she felt knowing that so much of her ancestry —on both her parents' lines—was white or at least racially mixed. "Well, you know," she replied, "blackness is not a monolith. It never has been. We were always already mixed in a million different ways. Even as our family stories and our family trees differ, things are much less black and white, if you will, than rigid categorizations would have us think. At the same time, that doesn't mean that our social identities are not very defining in many ways. I care about all my ancestry, but I'm still black—always have been. I just have always seen it as something that's a complicated weave."

Moving back down Elizabeth's maternal family tree, we traced the ancestors of her mother's father, Arthur Courtney Logan. Arthur was born in 1909 in Tuskegee, Alabama. His mother, Adella Hunt, was born in 1863 in Sparta, Georgia, and her ancestors stretch back six generations to a man named John Batte, who was born in 1606 in Yorkshire, England. He is Elizabeth's eighth-great-grandfather. He is also her oldest immigrant ancestor —and he was a wealthy white Englishman. It is unclear when the African and Anglo populations mixed in Elizabeth's maternal line, but there is no question about John Batte's ethnicity. He was as English as can be. His former home in England, Oakwell, is today a museum, and he lived the life of a gentleman of his time and class.

The story of John Batte's journey to the New World illuminates the diverse economic and cultural systems that shaped early America. Virginia was settled with a very different attitude and ethic than New England was. The original settlers of New England were fleeing religious persecution;

the people who went to Virginia, primarily, were there to make money. In 1606, the year when John Batte was born in Yorkshire, King James I of England gave a charter to what was known as the Virginia Company of London which allowed its shareholders to establish a colony on the coast of America. Almost as soon as the first settlers arrived, they realized that there was money to be made in farming and land development, the colony's most basic resource and the major resource that Europe lacked (Europe's poor and middle classes had almost no access to land ownership—it was all controlled by the nobility). But while there was plenty of land in Virginia, there was a shortage of people to clear it and work it. So the Virginia Company came up with a plan which they called the "head rights system." Businessmen would pay the cost of transporting indentured servants from Europe to Virginia. The servants would arrive and work off their indenture for a fixed period of time (usually seven years) and then become freemen, qualified to own land. This plan supplied the colony with labor. The reward for the businessmen who paid for the transport was significant: for every individual they brought over they received fifty acres.

Elizabeth's ancestor John Batte saw a pot of gold in this system. In the year 1628, when he was just twenty-two years old, he set sail for Virginia with a business partner and thirteen indentured servants. In exchange, he received a land grant of 750 acres in Charles River County, Virginia. John, however, did not remain long in America. Records show that he returned to England and then, for more than a decade, traveled back and forth from the colony to his homeland for business. In the year 1643, he received a second grant of 526 acres in James City County, Virginia, for transporting another eleven people from England to the colony. This meant that he and his business partners owned more than a thousand acres of land in Virginia in 1643, all farmed by indentured servants and, possibly, by African slaves (the first slaves came to Virginia in 1619, but the slave system did not come to dominate the colony's economy until almost a century later). In 1651, John moved his family to the colony, after fighting on the losing side in the English Civil War. He died sometime around the year 1653, a founding settler of Virginia and a wealthy man.

"He was entrepreneurial," said Elizabeth, looking at the many records we had of her eighth-great-grandfather's business deals. "But it also makes me think about what enables you to make your mark as a person like this. Well, one thing is that a whole lot of other people have to do the laboring for you. I think about all of those indentured servants and eventually the slaves who did that work. That's a question mark. He exploited people.

And it's impossible for me to not read that against all that it takes for non-white people to make their way."

I then told Elizabeth that however she felt about him, John Batte was by no means the end of this line of her family. He was from the English upper class, and his well-documented roots stretch back generations to John I, King of England, and his titled mistress, Clemence. John I was born in 1167 and is a crucial figure in world history. The youngest son of Henry II and Eleanor of Aquitaine, he engaged in a long power struggle with his brother, King Richard II, also known as Richard the Lionhearted. The rivalry between these brothers is a focal point of the Robin Hood legend, and it has been treated, with varying degrees of accuracy, in countless films, poems, and novels. As a child, I remember thinking it was just a fairy tale. But it was, in fact, a very real rivalry, and when Richard died childless in 1199, John inherited the crown—and a divided nation. From the beginning of his rule, the barons of England and Scotland blamed him for a multitude of social problems as well as for heavy taxes, the loss of English territories in France, and abuse of power. After years of conflict, the barons finally drew up a list of demands and threatened civil war if John didn't agree to meet them. This led to one of the most significant events of the past two thousand years: in June 1215, John and the barons met at Runnymede, outside London, and drew up a document which came to be known as Magna Carta.

Magna Carta was a milestone in the history of world government. It limited the king's powers and led to what we now call English common law —and it forms the basis of the constitutions of many countries, including our own. It was, in essence, the first document to declare that no man is above the law.

Elizabeth's ancestor John was forced to sign Magna Carta, which is not exactly inspiring. But among the barons who forced him to do it was another relative of Elizabeth's: her twenty-second-great-grandfather Saher De Quincy, the Earl of Winchester.

"That is completely mind-blowing," said Elizabeth. "How about that? It stretches me completely beyond anything I could have imagined. I thought I had some English ancestry, but I just wouldn't have thought to take it there. It never occurred to me—again, in part because of my own devotion to African American history and culture and bringing out the voices that haven't been heard—to think that there are volumes and volumes about these people. I could spend years in the library reading about them. It's amazing."

Moving back even further from King John, I showed Elizabeth that her family is deeply intertwined with the royalty of almost every medieval European nation—from France to Italy to Germany, including a figure even more important than John: Charlemagne, Emperor of the Holy Roman Empire. Born in the year 742, Charlemagne is called "the Father of Europe" and was the greatest ruler of his age—a legendary warrior and statesman who was one of the people who wrested Europe out of the Dark Ages. The power base and center of his court was in Aachen, in the western part of Germany, on the border of Belgium and the Netherlands. In the year 770, Charlemagne inherited the title King of the Franks and went on to accumulate titles and territory by waging war all over the continent. He ventured as far east as Hungary and south to Lombardy in northern Italy. In 774, he became King of Lombardy and, in 800, Holy Roman Emperor —crowned by Pope Leo III himself.

Charlemagne was a man of war and conquest, of course, but he was also respected as a man of learning. His reign ushered in what is known as the Carolingian Renaissance, which included a revival of art, religion, and culture—in an era when almost all these things were on the verge of being lost to Western civilization. Most of the surviving works of classical Latin were copied and preserved by Carolingian scholars. And through internal reforms and foreign conquests, Charlemagne helped to define what we now think of as Europe. We also know what he looked like. His biographer, who was his servant, described his appearance: "Charles was large and strong, and lofty of stature, though not disproportionately tall, his height is well known to have been seven times the length of his foot; the upper part of his head was round, his eyes very large and animated, nose a little long, hair fair, and face laughing and merry."

Charlemagne is Elizabeth's thirty-seventh-great-grandfather. He had good reason to be smiling all the time, to be laughing and merry. He had twenty children that we know about, thirteen with his five wives and seven others with his five acknowledged mistresses. Elizabeth is descended from his second wife, Hildegard, born sometime around the year 757 in what was then called Rhineland.

I told Elizabeth that her family tree is more radically mixed than any African American I have ever studied. She laughed, but we both know this kind of knowledge can be somewhat confusing. Most African Americans have some white ancestry; according to geneticists, 58 percent of the African American people have at least 12.5 percent European ancestry, the equivalent of one great-grandparent. And we have already discussed the

Charlemagne, the first Holy Roman Emperor. Born in the year 742 and one the most significant figures in European history, Charlemagne is Elizabeth's thirty-seventh-great-grandfather. (Used by permission of Getty Images)

fact that fully three out of ten black men trace their ancestry to a white male, most probably during slavery. At some point in our lives, we almost all realize that one side of our family profited enormously by exploiting the labor of another side. Elizabeth is unusual, in my experience, in that she can put names and faces for quite a distance in time on both sides. I have white ancestors whom I cannot name, starting with my great-great-grandfather on my father's side. Elizabeth, on the other hand, can point to John Batte and say, "I descend from this man who owned a manor in England in 1640, a man who helped settle Virginia." And Elizabeth, like Quincy Jones, can point much further back than that—to legendary kings and queens of Europe. Very few African Americans can do that. And it is, I think, a very complicated thing to know about oneself.

Asked how she feels about these people, she replied, "I have ambivalence about them, not because they're white but because of how they built what they had. All of this stops when it gets to the black people—that generationally amassed wealth doesn't make it all the way down. It's hard to feel that connection. And I can't look at the aristocrats on the European side without thinking about that moment where they start to mix in the United States with people of African descent. What happens to those lines? I keep going back to the case of Captain Batte. What is privilege if it's tied to exploitation? Unto itself, it's not just a beautiful coat, right? This is a complicated, thorny history that's not just about beautiful things but also about the human cost of beautiful things."

I reminded her that one of the most important facts about African American history is that our ancestors who came to this country as slaves almost invariably came because they were captured, in Africa, by their fellow Africans, carried to a port, and sold to Europeans. Africans were not innocent in the slave trade. Our African ancestors fought and captured and sold other Africans into the slave trade to the New World. And if we could trace our roots back to African nobility, as someone like Elizabeth can do directly to European nobility, we would most probably realize that we are related to dark-skinned kings and queens whose privilege was built on the same kind of exploitation that white men like Captain Batte employed. It's just a fact. There are no innocents on our family trees. The sad truth is that the only reason most of our poor ancestors didn't exploit other people is that they couldn't.

"That's true," said Elizabeth. "And in a funny way, you know, it takes me back to my little teeny-tiny nuclear family and the two grandparents that I knew. I've made a life for myself essentially knowing about only two generations, drawing on what I respected and was proud of in those generations. I'm so proud of the grounding and sense of self that my parents and grandparents gave me. That sense of identity wasn't so much about being able to go far back but about connecting to a history of struggle and commitment to issues of justice—the ethics with which you live your life. So the micro matters—that's what's important, that's what you can get your teeth into. But then what do you do with the centuries?"

I told her I had no answer to this question. She has millennia of documented ancestors, stretching back farther than any African American I know. But only she can decide what they mean to her, how the knowledge of their names and stories will shape her identity over time.

Turning to our DNA testing, I told Elizabeth that her admixture results revealed that she is 66 percent European, 27 percent African, and 7 percent Native American. She told me that she had more or less expected this result, given what she knew from the genealogy. She had even heard stories, she said, that her maternal grandmother, Edith MacAlister, was part Native American—and though we could not verify these stories, they could well be true. She certainly does have a fairly significant amount of Native American ancestry, unlike most African Americans.

We then began to look at some of the most interesting DNA results that I have ever seen. Elizabeth's mitochondrial DNA belongs to a haplogroup called L0a. This is a subgroup of the most ancient haplogroup of all, L0, which arose about 150,000 years ago in Africa, probably in what is now Ethiopia. Over the millennia, offshoots of L0 arose in many different parts of the African continent. Elizabeth's originated about 55,000 years ago, and, ultimately, its members were very likely part of the Bantu migration just a few thousand years ago, one of the greatest migrations in human history. Between three and four thousand years ago, a small group of Bantu-speaking Africans migrated out of a core area in what we think is southern Cameroon and basically peopled a huge percentage of the rest of central and southern Africa, bringing a totally new genetic mixture to African populations. They carried their language and their genes west and then to the southeast, all the way to Mozambique.

When geneticists compared Elizabeth's mitochondrial DNA with everyone in the Family Tree DNA database, they found that she shares a genetic signature with thirteen people living today in Guinea-Bissau, eight in Gabon, seventeen in Cameroon, five in Ethiopia, and four in Angola. These are her genetic cousins. They all share a common ancestor in the past few thousand years. Another testing company, Roots for Real, which is based in Cambridge, England, also ran the results through their database, and they found that Elizabeth matched people living today in Nubia, Angola, and Guinea-Bissau. The vast geographic spread in the distribution of these findings—she has matches all over Africa through her maternal line —shows just how far the Bantu migration went, how radically it changed Africa just a few thousand years ago.

I showed Elizabeth's results to two prominent slave historians at Boston University, John Thornton and Linda Heywood. They worked with me on *African American Lives,* and I asked them to review Elizabeth's data to see if they could narrow down the African origins of the first slave ancestor on her maternal line—the woman in her family who was first brought to the New World. They were able to rule out her matches in Nubia, Ethiopia, and Gabon because none of these countries was involved in the slave trade to Jamaica or to the United States. There was some slave trade with Cameroon, but it was insignificant. So that left us with either Angola or Guinea-Bissau. Elizabeth has more exact matches in Guinea-Bissau, but her haplogroup tends to be more common in Angola. Also, her oldest known ancestor on her maternal grandmother's line was from Virginia, which, along with other southern states, received a high percentage of slaves from Angola. So based on our genealogical research on her mother's side and her genetic analysis, Thornton and Heywood concluded that Elizabeth's original female African ancestor most probably came from Angola, along with 24 percent of the ancestors of all the African American people. In addition, based on the history of the slave trade, Thornton and Heywood also concluded that Elizabeth's ancestors probably lived near the Angolan coast, in part of what was known as the Lunda Empire, which sold large numbers of slaves, captured in wars with neighboring African tribes, to the Dutch and Portuguese.

Through DNA, we had therefore unlocked a crucial piece of Elizabeth's heritage. Despite all the white Europeans in her family tree, her mitochondrial DNA goes straight back to Africa.

It was now time for us to solve a few mysteries. Our genealogical research had been able to identify Elizabeth's third-great-grandfather on her mother's line, Robert Bond, the ship's cook from Bermuda who settled in Liverpool. He disappears from the documentary record sometime after 1851, perhaps returning to his home in Bermuda. We had been unable to trace his line back any further using available records. So we turned to DNA in the hope of learning more. But to study Elizabeth's maternal great-great-grandfather's DNA, we needed to test a male directly descended from him in her mother's family, because as a woman, Elizabeth does not carry any Y-DNA at all. One of her male cousins agreed to let us test him, and the results indicated that Elizabeth's maternal grandfather's Y-DNA belonged to the haplogroup called E1b1a. This haplogroup dominates the region south of the Sahara. It's most common among Bantu-speaking Africans, and it reaches levels of up to 90 percent among the Mandinka and the Yoruba people. Its distribution throughout Africa is often used to chart the expansion of the great Bantu migration throughout sub-Saharan Africa. It is also the most common haplogroup among African American males. About 60 percent of African American men can trace their ancestry to this branch of the family tree.

According to John Thornton and Linda Heywood, many of the Bantu speakers who share the E1b1a haplogroup come from Mozambique. But only 2 percent of the slaves who arrived in the New World came from that region of Africa. And none went to Bermuda. So John and Linda focused on another area where this haplogroup is common, one that did contribute greatly to the Bermuda slave trade. And they concluded that the male line of the Bond family hails from the Senegambia region, in the country that is today known as Sierra Leone, which is dominated by the Mende people. Our consultants' databases added credence to this theory when they revealed that Elizabeth's male cousin matches haplogroups with two people living today in Sierra Leone, both of whom are Mende.

There was one further mystery to try and solve. We wanted to see if DNA could tell us anything about the identity of Elizabeth's paternal great-grandfather—Clifford Alexander, Sr.'s father—the man who, according to family lore, was a Jewish merchant named James residing in Jamaica at the turn of the twentieth century. To map the Y-DNA of Elizabeth's paternal ancestors, we collected a sample from her father. It shows that her paternal line belongs to the haplogroup called J1e, which is a subgroup of the haplogroup J, which originated in the Near East about twenty thousand years ago, during the Ice Age. Of special significance, J1 is the most common haplogroup among Ashkenazi Jews. About 40 percent of Ashkenazi men have chromosomes in J1.

Looking at the Family Tree DNA database, we found people matching this Y-DNA in many places today: there were single matches in Spain, Hungary, Poland, Romania, Slovakia, and the Syrian Arab Republic. And all these matches identified themselves as Ashkenazi Jews. This is very strong evidence that Elizabeth's great-grandfather was in fact an Ashkenazi Jew.

Elizabeth was not surprised at this discovery. She had long believed the family stories about her grandfather's being the illegitimate child of a Jewish merchant, and as indicated earlier, there had been some circumstantial evidence to support these stories. Elizabeth was very surprised, however, by what else we learned from her father's DNA. Her father's Y-DNA, I told her, pointed to an Ashkenazi Jewish background, and his mitochondrial DNA also pointed to Europe. This, as Elizabeth and I both knew, was highly unusual. Almost 95 percent of the African American people can trace their mitochondrial DNA straight back to Africa because it is comparatively rare to be descended from a white woman who had children with a black man. Elizabeth's own mitochondrial DNA, for example, show that her mother's line goes to Angola. But her father's DNA reveals that his maternal line doesn't go to Africa at all. He belongs to the haplogroup called U6a, which is European, just like his father's line. And he has exact mitochondrial matches with people living today in the United Kingdom and the Netherlands. There is no doubt he is descended from a white woman. We don't know her name, we don't know the story, but we have incontrovertible genetic evidence that there *is* a story. Clifford Alexander, civil rights pioneer, is descended on both sides from white people. This is true for about 1 percent of the African American people. Anybody who looked solely at his Y-DNA and his mtDNA, in fact, would think he was a European man.

"Well, it just gets curiouser and curiouser," said Elizabeth. "But of course, if all of us were known only by our DNA, we'd have a whole different American history." I told her that truer words were never spoken.

The autosomal DNA testing conducted by the Broad Institute revealed that Elizabeth is a distant cousin of Stephen Colbert. They share eight million identical base pairs on chromosome 2, pairs 160 to 168. Elizabeth was delighted with this news and excitedly told me that she had once been on Stephen's show and felt a connection with him. But she and I, I think, were both still reeling from the amount of information we had gathered and processed together. We had been able to show her that some of her most treasured family stories were true. Some we had verified with a paper trail, some with DNA. And we had uncovered new stories—some wilder than anybody in her family ever could have fantasized.

"I think there's something wonderful about having certain sureties disrupted," she said, looking at her father's DNA test results. "Especially in the middle of one's life, to learn that certain things that you always thought were in place actually are much more entangled and complex and deeper than you ever could have known—that's completely fascinating. I just wish I knew all of the pieces. We happen to know a tremendous amount about Europe in my particular case, but there are still pieces that we don't know. And what does it mean if you grow up not knowing any of this—a culture that teaches you not necessarily to identify with any of that, not to dream that any of that could mean anything, could have any connection to you? There's something fabulously disruptive that shakes up the orders of things, when you draw the line in a different way than others might expect."

She considered further: "But what does that change for me? Well, it gives me a lot more to wonder about and to think about. And it gives me a more complicated way of thinking, not just about black people and blackness but about human questions, human communities, human families—and very, very tangled and fascinating human histories.

"I find myself thinking about Charlemagne," she said, as I rose to leave her home in New Haven. "He was a learned man, able perhaps to prognosticate about the direction of human history. Could he have imagined me, in his wildest, wildest, wildest imaginings into the future?"

My guess, I said, is no.

9

Malcolm Gladwell

1963

MALCOLM GLADWELL IS one of America's most creative journalists. The author of four *New York Times* best-selling books and a staff writer for the *New Yorker,* he has redefined the way we think about an array of subjects large and small—from statistics to cognition to the underlying causes of genius, from the invention of hair dye to the source of Led Zeppelin's guitar riffs. He is a truly eclectic thinker, someone who is constantly challenging conventional wisdom. His is one of the most brilliant minds of our time.

I asked him to participate in this series after reading his thoughts on why our ancestry matters. In his book *Outliers,* he wonders how his Jamaican mother, a descendant of African slaves, had managed to wind up a successful professional in Canada. He discovers that she was the beneficiary of generations of social privilege—and he concludes, in effect, that where we go in life actually depends quite a lot on where our ancestors have been. In so doing, he touches on several ideas that are, obviously, engaging to me and deeply relevant to this project. But more than this, I was very touched by his family's story—and by the very open way he discusses the impact of race and class on his mother's life. I found that he made me think more deeply about some of my own beliefs about these subjects, and I wanted to explore his story further. He generously agreed, and the results of our research and conversation were very exciting to me. We were able to trace Malcolm's mother's "privilege" back more than three centuries, all the way to her fifth-great-grandmother, a free woman of color in eighteenth-century Jamaica. And in so doing, I was given a glimpse into racial dynamics that were totally alien to my experience as an African American, and I was able to give Malcolm an even deeper understanding of the true extent of the social privilege from which he and his ancestors had benefited.

Of all the people involved in this project, Malcolm is the most recent immigrant, having moved to the United States just ten years ago. He was born on September 3, 1963, in Gosport, England, and raised in Ontario, Canada. His father is an English mathematician and a professor of civil engineering; his mother is a Jamaican writer and psychotherapist.

"I think of myself as a Commonwealth baby," he told me, smiling. "It is because of the legacy of British empire that my mom went to college in England and met my father and that my father got a job in Canada."

The Gladwells moved several times in Malcolm's youth, finally settling when he was six years old in Elmira, Ontario, about a hundred miles west of Toronto, in a rural region that was dominated by Mennonites. This is where Malcolm grew up—in an atmosphere of tolerance and, by his accounting, near total color-blindness.

"It was a very specific part of Canada," he said, "the heart of Mennonite country. And the Mennonites are a very wonderful and peculiar group. They're a conservative religious Protestant denomination, but they are the most strikingly open-minded and friendly and accepting of people. Acceptance was much more of an issue for my mother, who, after all, looks black in a way that I don't. But once we moved to Canada, she got as warm a welcome as you can imagine a brown person getting thousands of miles away from her home. That was not her experience in England before we left or in America in the time we spent there. We're talking about a mixed-race couple in rural Bible Belt Ontario in 1969. Yet she was welcomed into the community. And now my parents, by the way, go to that church."

Like Mike Nichols, though under far less stressful circumstances, Malcolm was an immigrant child, arriving in a new country, Canada, when he was just beginning to understand the world around him. He remembers that in the beginning, the experience was quite difficult. "I had an English accent," he said, "and I looked and talked and dressed differently. I had some troubles." Malcolm does not, however, recall being the victim of racism in his new home. "I never thought about race, really," he said, "until I went to college. I thought more about class when I was growing up. My parents were among the very few parents in my elementary school or middle school who had gone to college. Most of my friends' parents did not go to college. So the primary point of difference was that I came from a household where learning was prized and books were taken seriously. Most of my peers were farmers, whose parents were probably not that well educated. And since no one brought up the racial issue, I never thought about it. It wasn't until I came down to the United States that I realized, 'Oh my goodness, it's an issue in the world.' "

I was amazed by this story and questioned Malcolm about it further.

Was it really possible to grow up half black surrounded by a sea of white people and never think about racism? "It just never occurred to me," he said, emphatically. "I remember as a child my mother had a black Jamaican friend named Jo, who had spent some time in Atlanta. In the mid-1970s, I overheard her telling my mother, 'In Atlanta you can cut the racism with a knife.' I remember that phrase. I was ten years old, and I remember being completely baffled. I had no idea what she was talking about."

In almost all African American autobiographies, there is a crucial scene of discovery wherein the author is made to realize that he or she is black—and that being black is a negative thing. In the slave narratives, this scene invariably involves the author's discovering that he or she is a slave, which, of course, has terrible consequences. After the abolition of slavery, these scenes vary in quality and kind, but the realization that you are black is always a deficit in the context of larger white society.

"My mother had that moment," said Malcolm. "She had many of them, but I wasn't aware, mostly because they happened in England when I was too young. I learned about them later when I read her memoir. But it wasn't something that she dwelled on. The key figure in all of this is my father, who is the most genuinely color- and class-blind person I've ever met. My father is as comfortable chatting with the Old Order Mennonite farmer next door, who drives a buggy, as he is chatting with a fellow Ph.D. in math from the university. We went to Jamaica every two years, and we would go off into the hills, and my father would commandeer some large group of kids and organize us all in these games. And it never struck him as odd that a very, very English mathematician should be in the hills of Jamaica organizing games with dozens of barefoot Jamaican boys.

Malcolm added, "He isn't someone who perceives difference, which I think is why it wasn't an issue for him to marry my mother in 1950s England. On some primal level, it never occurred to him that she was a different color. I don't think he sees color. So I was growing up in an environment where my father, who was the dominant person in the home, just didn't see the world that way. It was very easy for me to see the world through his eyes. I realize it was an utterly anomalous experience. Only much later did I realize how remarkable my father's attitudes were for an Englishman of his generation."

Malcolm's parents are Graham Maurice Leslie Gladwell, born February 21, 1934, in Otford, England, and Joyce Eugenie Nation, born on September 9, 1931, in Harewood in the St. Catherine's Parish of Jamaica. They met while Joyce was studying in England in the early 1950s. At the time,

The Gladwell family. Malcolm stands in the back row, next to his parents, Joyce Eugenie Nation and Graham Maurice Leslie Gladwell. His paternal grandparents, Basil Morris Gladwell and Doris Alexandra New, are seated in the center. (Used by permission of the Gladwell family)

interracial marriage was illegal in many American states. And although it was legal in England, it was quite rare. Malcolm believes that his English grandparents were initially shocked by his parents' relationship.

"I think that they were a little bit taken aback by it," he said. "As I understand it, they didn't bar the door, but I think they had grave reservations about what it would be like to be a mixed-race couple in England in the fifties. I recall my mother telling me one of the things that my grandmother said to her was, 'Think about the children.' They were thinking about the prospect of having mixed-race kids and what they would have to go through in school. But also, my grandparents were born at the beginning of the twentieth century, a very different generation with very different attitudes about race. So this would have been a shock. But to their credit, they got over it."

By contrast, Malcolm believes his Jamaican grandparents were delighted by the marriage. "They had a very different attitude," he said. "In Jamaica, the idea of a mixed-race couple is nothing new. It's been going on for

Malcolm's parents, Graham Maurice Leslie Gladwell and Joyce Eugenie Nation, on their wedding day. (Used by permission of the Gladwell family)

hundreds of years. If anything, given the prevailing attitudes about color, it's an upgrade, right? If you can bring in a little whiteness into the family line, it's all good. Also, one of the arguments that my parents both made explicitly was that they had much more in common than not. If you forget color for a moment, their backgrounds are astonishingly similar. They come from these deeply religious, educated, middle-class parents who had very similar attitudes about the world and who were quiet, thoughtful people. Absent color, they were a very highly compatible couple. And that's what they told everyone who was willing to listen."

Malcolm's parents are still happily married today, and in his view, the two sides of his family long ago realized just how highly compatible they are. As an American, when I heard Malcolm's parents' story for the first time, I thought, how could that be possible in that time? But the more I learned about the family, the more I realized that his account, though rare, is true. Moreover, I also came to realize that Malcolm's parents' story disrupts many conventional American notions of race. In his mother's excellent memoir, *Brown Face, Big Master,* Joyce describes her painful realization that people in England saw her as "black." Why was this so upsetting to her? Not for the reasons I expected. British antiblack racism, no doubt, stung. But Joyce was also upset, she says, because as someone who in Jamaica was considered "middle-class brown," she had grown up enjoying the privileges that came with her fair skin color. In her book, after a racist landlady forces her and her husband to move from their apartment, Joyce imagines an angry conversation with God that ends with a surprising insight: "As far as God was concerned, we were equally guilty and guilty of the same wrong. We were both children of our background caught in the deceitfulness of false values and emphases." It is remarkable to me that she could use what had to be deeply painful experience to reflect upon her own prejudices and sense of privilege.

"I think what she's reflecting," said Malcolm, "is that she is acutely aware that the same kind of racist standard that was being held against her in England worked to her benefit in Jamaica. The brown-skinned person got all of the advantages and held her brownness over the blackness of people further down the scale. So she was honest and wise enough to know that she had no standing to cry racism or to point the finger at someone else's bigotry."

He continued, "What that attitude has meant for me is from the very beginning I've understood that the racial question in my case is very complex. And I've also always felt very strongly that I cannot use my own success as a yardstick—I can't extrapolate from my own experience to those of other people of color. I've had an anomalous experience, where skin color has not been for the most part associated with negative consequences. I've been lucky. Part of the reason my mother talks about that incident so passionately and clearly is that it was a rarity. She came from a society where she wasn't looked down on; she was looked up to."

Malcolm's mother, Joyce Nation, with her sister, Faith, in Jamaica in the late 1930s. (Used by permission of the Gladwell family)

He thought further about the cultural difference: "The shock of racism to a West Indian like my mother is profoundly different than the shock of racism to an African American who was born and raised here. In the American case, it is the repeated body blows that you never escape. But in the West Indian, it's this shock at something that you would never have experienced back home. It always begins with, 'What on earth are you calling me black for? I'm not black.' That's the West Indian attitude—because they have a much, much lighter cross to bear. I think it's very important for people to understand, particularly when they look at how successful West Indians have been in this country, that their success is not proof that racism doesn't exist. It's proof that West Indians come from a completely different environment. And that immigrants do better."

Turning to his Jamaican ancestors, we focused first on Malcolm's mother's parents, Donald and Daisy Ford Nation, both born in St. Elizabeth Parish in 1902 and 1899, respectively. In Malcolm's book *Outliers*, he writes about how his mother's path to success had been blazed by her

Malcolm's maternal grandparents, Daisy and Donald Nation, in 1940. (Used by permission of the Gladwell family)

mother, Daisy. He also shows how her grandmother's determination and ambition for her children was the legacy of her own ancestors, the Fords.

"According to oral history in my family," Malcolm said, "when we go back to the late eighteenth century, there is an Irishman named William Ford. I don't know who he was, but the family says at one point he owned a coffee plantation or something like that. And he takes an African slave as a concubine. They have a son who is a preacher, a brown-skinned preacher who marries an Arawak Indian. That's the claim. And that starts in motion this line of brown-skinned Fords, my mom's people. Many of them have some kind of profession: they're merchants or preachers, or they're doing something more than simply being slaves or descendants of slaves. So because of the special privileges accorded to brown-skinned children of white people in Jamaica, the Fords have a leg up. So that's the story. And it begins with this decision by William Ford to take as his consort this slave."

To explore this story, our researchers went to Jamaica and interviewed Malcolm's relatives who still live there. They told many of the same stories that he did, tracing the family back to an Irishman named William Ford and an unnamed Ibo slave. They talked a great deal, especially, about William Ford's son, John Ford, who was Malcolm's great-great-grandfather. By all accounts, he was quite a remarkable person. Everything we heard about John Ford suggested that he made the most of a special status in Jamaican society as the mixed-race child of an Irish immigrant. A lay preacher and a businessman, John is reported to have owned land around St. Elizabeth and in Manchester Parish in southwest Jamaica, where many of his descendants live today. And according to some relatives, he came to the aid of an oppressed indigenous community, helping them to defend their land and building them a church. He used his privilege not just for personal gain but also to help others, and that's an admirable thing.

The problem is that we could find no record of his father, William Ford, arriving in Jamaica from Ireland in the late eighteenth century and buying or operating a coffee plantation, or any other kind of plantation, which is the initial part of the family story. So we were stumped. Then we found something surprising: a baptismal record of a child named William Ford, dated 1788. It states that this child was the "reputed son of Mr. John Ford by Hannah Burton, born November 27th, 1786." It also indicates that the child was "not white." Now this was the only William Ford on the whole island of Jamaica who was the right age and in the right place to be Malcolm's third-great-grandfather. And this William Ford clearly was not an Irishman. He was a mulatto. What's more, the phrase "reputed son" indicates that his parents were not married. Also the fact that his father is referred to as Mr. John Ford suggests that his father was white, whereas his mother, Hannah Burton, must have been colored or black. "The plot thickens," said Malcolm, genuinely surprised.

I told Malcolm that our researchers had initially believed that perhaps his white Ford ancestry came to Jamaica a generation or two earlier than the oral tradition of his family held. Maybe the rest of the story was essentially true. So we searched for the first Fords in this part of Jamaica to see when his ancestor may have arrived. We found a land patent for a woman named Mrs. Ann Ford, who received 360 acres in St. Elizabeth Parish in 1672. The timing of this patent is significant. It appears that the Ford family arrived in Jamaica during what is known as the third Anglo-Dutch war. At this time, England and the Netherlands were struggling for control of their colonies in the New World. As a result of the war, the English ceded control of the colony of Surinam to the Dutch in exchange for the colony of New Netherland (which, of course, we know today as New York, New Jersey, Pennsylvania, and Delaware). This meant that the English settlers on Surinam were resettled on the island of Jamaica, in St. Elizabeth's Parish, right where Malcolm's ancestors have lived ever since. The process of resettlement began around 1667 and concluded around 1674. So the Fords came right in the middle of it, and we wondered, was Mrs. Ann Ford the great-grandmother or great-great-grandmother of William Ford? Is this where his original white Jamaican ancestor came from? After months of searching, unfortunately, there was no way we could confirm this theory through the records.

Luckily we had another tool at our disposal, DNA testing. We asked Malcolm's mother's cousin, also named John Ford, if he would take a DNA test. As we know, his Y chromosome was passed down directly from the original Ford progenitor. And as it turned out, John Ford's Y-DNA is indeed European. We found three high-resolution matches in the Family Tree DNA database with people living today in England, not Ireland, as the Ford stories claimed. And we found eight lower-resolution matches —again, all in England. This strongly suggests that William Ford's white ancestors were English, and they may well have included Mrs. Ann Ford.

I asked Malcolm if he had any idea why his family has so long believed that their original European ancestor was Irish rather than English. This might seem like a small distinction, but the English in Jamaica were the colonial masters, and there was a significant advantage to being of English descent—much more so than being Irish. Malcolm had no idea. And neither did other members of the Ford family who we spoke to in Jamaica. It seems that at some time in the distant past, someone in the family decided he or she preferred the myth of an Irish ancestor from the eighteenth century to the reality of an English ancestor from the seventeenth.

At this point, I wondered whether the discrepancies between the story as the family told it and the story we found really mattered. A family who enjoyed a privilege of being mixed race in Jamaican society and who used that privilege to educate their children and to help those less fortunate than themselves did create, as Malcolm has written, the legacy that empowered Daisy Ford Nation and Joyce Nation Gladwell, even if the details do not match at every point.

"It's sobering, though," said Malcolm, "because, in fact, they were anxious to delete the black part of the heritage and pretend that this ancestor was all white when in fact he was not. It's a little depressing, isn't it? It's one thing to observe racist attitudes in the world we live in now, but it gets depressing when you go back—what, seven generations?—and you see the same thing. It just makes you wonder whether this stuff will ever stop."

The Fords' identity as mixed-race people in colonial Jamaica gave them a different social status from other people of African descent. White slaveholders often conferred freedom, property, and education on the mixed-race children that they had with their slave mistresses. Jamaica's British governors encouraged this hierarchy of color privilege; indeed, it worked well for them all throughout the Commonwealth. The British, essentially, saw the free people of color as a buffer between themselves and the great mass of black slaves. I wanted to figure out when Malcolm's ancestors first crossed over the line from slavery to freedom. But our research was unable to find the original slave ancestor in the Ford family. So we began to look at other branches of Malcolm's Jamaican family tree.

We found a baptismal record for a woman named Martha Levy dated 1842. Martha is Malcolm's great-great-grandmother, the grandmother of Donald Nation. She was born in 1841 in St. Elizabeth Parish. Although the act that abolished slavery passed in 1833, slaves were still held in apprenticeships until the year 1838. We wondered whether Martha's parents had been slaves. Research suggested otherwise. We found the marriage record of her parents, Benjamin Samuel Levy and Frances Powell Dare, from 1819, which clearly states that they were free persons of color. And as we went back on the Levy line, we kept finding more free people of color. For example, Malcolm's fourth-great-grandfather Eliezer Levy was born and baptized in 1775. And he was the "reputed son" of another Mr. Eliezer Levy and Margaret Mullings, a free woman of color.

In the end, we failed to find a slave in Malcolm's Jamaican ancestry. What's more, we found a stunning instance of the opposite: black slave owners on Malcolm's family tree. Margaret Mullings left a will which reads, in part, "My desire is that all my funeral expenses and my just and lawful debts should be discharged and satisfied as soon after my death as possible out of any money I may die possessed of or may be due my estate. And if that should not be sufficient, then the Negroes I may die possessed of shall work in jobbing or otherwise and the money arising from such labor shall be applied for the purposes already mentioned."

This means that Malcolm's fifth-great-grandmother, a free woman of color, owned slaves. She even spelled one of them out by name, leaving her slave "Ruthie" to her grandson, Malcolm's third-great-grandfather Benjamin Samuel Levy, another free man of color.

"Oh my goodness," said Malcolm, stunned. "The kind of mental jujitsu you have to go through is quite remarkable. It was a class-based society, and so color was class, class was color. There it is. How far back in her history do we have to go to find a slave? Her mother or maybe her grandmother?"

I told Malcolm that we didn't know. Margaret Mullings is as far back along that line of his family as we could go. Her mother, most likely, was not a slave. But beyond that, it is unclear. Obviously, Malcolm descends from slaves at some point in his family tree: almost every black person in the New World, except for recent immigrants from Africa, did. But his ancestors did not stay slaves for very long. And as soon as they were free and could afford to do so, it appears that they began to buy slaves themselves.

Malcolm quite correctly perceived Margaret's decision to own slaves as a class issue. "I'm assuming it's a way of underscoring your new status," he said. "If you are a member of this special privileged class and you would like to heighten your position and assert your whiteness, having a slave is certainly one sign of doing that, isn't it?"

The answer to that question is, of course, yes. But I also I tend to think the issue was perhaps simpler, more crudely economic. Margaret Mullings had a farm; she needed workers, and the workers were slaves. That was the system. Does that let her off the moral hook? No. But it was the system.

"You could have multiple motives," said Malcolm in agreement. "But we're seeing a fascinating and slightly heartbreaking aspect of Jamaican history. I don't know how to describe it. But get this little glimmer, the door opens a crack, and you run towards the light—literally. And you embrace it and replicate it. You don't transform the system; you become part of it."

Aside from two pieces of land in St. Elizabeth Parish, which she left to her sons, the total value of Margaret Mullings's estate was £1,180. Almost all of it came from the value of eleven enslaved human beings. By Jamaica's standards, Margaret Mullings was not a rich woman. Elizabeth Alexander's ancestors, as we have seen, were slaves on a plantation that contained almost three hundred Africans. But owning eleven slaves indicates that Margaret was probably staunchly middle class, even if she was not legally married to the father of her children.

We were able to determine what happened to one of Margaret's slaves. The twenty-year-old "Ruthie" who was willed to her grandson Benjamin Samuel Levy in 1823 appears in a slave return filed by Levy later that same year. By this time, she has a four-month-old daughter, "Margaret Sambo." (A Sambo was a racial classification for the child of a black parent and a mulatto parent.) Tragically, Benjamin Samuel Levy's slave return from the year 1826 indicates that both Margaret and Ruthie had died, the child at sixteen months and her mother at age twenty-three. So Margaret and Ruthie, two of Malcolm's ancestor's slaves, did not live to see emancipation.

"This strengthens the feeling that I always had," said Malcolm, "the feeling that was expressed by my mother in her book—that our privilege had a pretty rickety foundation morally. In her case it meant that she couldn't in good conscience turn her wrath on someone who treated her with bigotry because she knew that there was bigotry in her own past as well. And this strengthens it. The foundations of this privilege were slaves. So it doesn't permit any easy moral judgments about my family's accomplishments, does it?"

I did not know how to answer this question except, of course, to agree with Malcolm. There is no way fully to understand the decisions our ancestors made, and there is no reason to worry about excusing the moral shortcomings of our ancestors, white or black—and to my mind, no point in trying.

Extraordinarily, we could not identify one slave ancestor on any line of Malcolm's family tree. All we found were free people of color—many of whom owned slaves. I've done research on nineteen other black people before Malcolm Gladwell; in every case, we were able to identify their slave ancestors, and in three instances, we identified the individuals on their family tree who became free, long before the Civil War.

We then turned our attention to the question of how Margaret Mullings, a free woman of color, came to own land in St. Elizabeth Parish as well as eleven slaves by 1820. Could this property have come from the reputed father of her five children, Eliezer Levy? Who was this man? He did not leave a will, and he was never baptized in an Anglican church. Much as we saw in the case of Elizabeth Alexander, Malcolm believes this mysterious white ancestor was Jewish.

"I'm guessing he's a Sephardic trader," he told me. "There were many traders who came through the West Indies, and there's a Jewish community in Jamaica going back to the eighteenth century. So I'm assuming that with the name Eliezer Levy, he's probably part of the Jewish population of Jamaica."

Although Levy is certainly a Jewish surname, it is actually quite common in Jamaica among people who are non-Jews. And it doesn't necessarily indicate that a person with that surname embraced the Jewish faith. However, if Malcolm's fifth-great-grandfather Eliezer Levy was Jewish, it would explain why Margaret Mullings and Eliezer Levy could live together only in common law. Despite her free status and comparative wealth, his religion would have prevented him from marrying her legally.

We sent researchers out to where Margaret Mullings once owned land, around Wally Wash Great Pond in St. Elizabeth. It's not far from a town called Black River. And in Black River we found an old house decorated with Stars of David; it was once the meeting house for the town's Jewish community. The house is about an hour's horseback ride away from Margaret Mullings's land. So if Eliezer Levy lived there with her, it would have been easy to ride into town to practice his faith. There's also an old Jewish cemetery nearby in a place called Lacovia. The tombstones there, engraved in Hebrew, date from the 1740s and the 1750s, but we couldn't, unfortunately, find any Levys among them.

But there was general historical evidence to tie Eliezer and Margaret. Jews and free people of color were both second-class citizens in Jamaica. Marginalized by the British colonial system, they couldn't even vote until 1831, at which time both groups were simultaneously given suffrage rights. And as with the many English men who took either slaves or mulattos as mistresses, because there were so few English women around, the Jewish community was overwhelmingly male. It was a matter of numbers. Given all the circumstantial evidence, the world's leading scholarly expert on Jamaican Jews, Ainsley Henriques, told us that Malcolm's ancestor Eliezer

Levy was almost certainly Jewish—meaning that in the 1770s, Malcolm's fifth-great-grandparents were a mixed-race couple having children at the time Thomas Jefferson was writing the Declaration of Independence.

I asked Malcolm what he thought about the fact that his ancestors, not just his parents but his ancestors all up and down his tree, have been crossing racial and cultural lines for so many generations—and his parents were, in effect, just living out something that was part of their family's DNA.

"You don't want to fall into the trap of historical determinism," said Malcolm, "but it is also a reminder of what a weird polyglot place colonial Jamaica was—the original melting pot. It was the wild genetic west, wonderfully open with a fluidity which didn't exist in the United States at the same time, where there were laws prohibiting this kind of interbreeding. And think about, who is the most famous Jamaican? Bob Marley. What is Bob Marley? His father was Scottish. That's just one generation. Lord knows what we'd find with him if we went back as far as we did here. So maybe that's Jamaica's unique contribution to the world: we broke down a whole lot of barriers in advance of everybody else."

I then asked Malcolm if the things we'd learned about his family had changed his feeling about their privileged social position that he described so well in *Outliers*. He replied that, if anything, his new knowledge had only deepened his understanding of that privilege and its impact on his life.

"Sociologists," said Malcolm, "use the phrase 'cumulative advantage' to describe the way advantages grow over time and are built on from one generation to the next. I remember having this conversation about Jewish lawyers that I recount in *Outliers*. Why are all the top lawyers in New York Jewish? I was talking to this really fascinating guy who had done a lot of the research in this area. And he said the striking thing when you look at these patterns of Jewish achievement in New York is how long it took. People usually think that when Jewish immigrants came here, next thing you know they're attaining professional success. He said actually there was a whole generation of Jewish lawyers in New York who struggled and made almost no money, who were almost wiped out by the Depression. From getting off the boat to founding Skadden, Arps is three long difficult generations. And he said, thinking about this with respect to women or people of color, we have to understand that taking a group from the bottom to the top takes a lot of time. When I look at my family history, you had seven and eight generations here. It's the same story."

Malcolm is absolutely right. His family tree shows a long steady march toward, well, toward Malcolm Gladwell, the best-selling author and brilliant thinker.

"That's the thing that's so sobering," he said, nodding. "It is this incredibly powerful reminder that when we deal with the underprivileged, the first thing we need to bring to that fight is patience. So much of the opposition to attempts to help people up is based on impatience, on an expectation that if it didn't work in ten years, it's never going to work. There's another thing, which is a reminder of how tenacious the advantages of privilege are. Three hundred years ago these ancestors of mine got a break, and through every conceivable economic, cultural, political upheaval that the West Indies went through, they clung to their middle-class status and didn't give it up."

I told Malcolm that I agreed with him but that it was also important to note that his ancestors knew that their grasp on privilege was tenuous, too. They knew that if they didn't cling to it assiduously, it would be gone. Many did lose it. The research I've done on this project, I told him, traces dozens of families into decline. A family tree is not a record of upward progress, necessarily.

Malcolm's family, however, undeniably did make steady progress. Using genealogy, we were able to trace his origins back to the seventeenth century in both England and Jamaica. And on his father's side, in England, we saw the same kinds of hardworking values maintaining status over time. Aside from moving closer to London during the Industrial Revolution, the Gladwell family seems to have stayed in one place—Suffolk County in East Anglia—as far back as records can tell us. Indeed, Malcolm's paternal grandparents, Basil Morris Gladwell and Doris Alexandra New, spent their entire lives in England, primarily in Kent. The farthest they ever traveled was to Devon. Their stable lives and prosperity had been fueled, in part, by some real risk-taking along the line of Malcolm's grandmother Doris New. Her parents were Frederick William New and Jane Mary Adams. Both were real characters, by all accounts. Born on December 6, 1866, in London, Frederick took off for Australia on his own at age fourteen to seek his fortune. His wife, Jane Mary Adams, was born on June 24, 1870, in Balleret, Australia, to parents who had emigrated from the United Kingdom. Her father, Malcolm's great-great-grandfather Thomas Adams, went to Victoria, Australia, from Liverpool with his parents around the year 1850 as part of what became known as the Castlemaine gold rush. The Adams family went there to open stores, cleverly providing supplies to the miners.

The wedding of Malcolm's paternal grandparents, Basil Morris Gladwell and Doris Alexandra New. (Used by permission of the Gladwell family)

"I've heard of these people," said Malcolm, smiling. "I remember stories that there was a group of ancestors who went off to Australia and had adventures—one of them lived in a tree. It was all pretty vague."

They certainly were adventurers. Thomas Adams married a girl named Jane Wilson, who came to Australia from Ireland on her own in about 1854 in the charge of a family named Taylor. According to a family history, "It was intended that [Jane] should go to [Taylor's] brother and his wife to help with the children. But she had a will of her own and stayed in Melbourne with a minister and his wife. Jane was quite fearless and although only five feet tall, would stand up to men who were stealing in the gold fields."

A young woman who would go to Australia on her own at that time must have been quite unusual. "I can't imagine," said Malcolm. "Either things were really bad where she came from, or she was powerfully curious. I suspect it's a bit of both."

I asked Malcolm if he felt any kinship with these people. He laughed. "Well," he said, "I feel like I'm a curious person. And I think I share my father's attitude towards travel, which is that it's an adventure. I never step on a plane without a sense of excitement. But all this was a long time ago, and I know nothing, really, about Australia."

Turning to Malcolm's DNA testing, I told him that his admixture test revealed that he is somewhere between 70 and 77 percent European and between 20 and 30 percent African. Although his family lore had suggested that he had a native Arawak ancestor, the DNA says that that's just a myth.

"That seems just about right," said Malcolm. "If you just did the math, if your father's white and your mom's half white, then you should be about 75-25, right? So there I am."

Malcolm told me that he had taken a DNA test several years ago to try and pinpoint the origin of his mother's roots in Africa. The results, he said, were very vague: "I'm not sure I was completely understanding it; it looked like basically East Africa."

Before I tried to give him some clearer results, I wanted to know why this knowledge was important to him. "When I went to Africa for the first time," he said, "I was in South Africa, and I went to one of those caves where so many of the fossilized remains of early man have been found. And I found it incredibly moving. I think it was part of the same idea of uncovering where we're all from. It's some sort of primal thing. There is a kind of emotional power to it."

I know the feeling Malcolm describes. You can say it's irrational, you can say it's essentialist, and it doesn't matter; it still has power. We all want to go back to the motherland. "It just matters," he said, nodding. "It forces you to contemplate your own history. And I think it's so powerful."

To find out more about his slave ancestors' origins we needed to examine his maternal haplogroup: L3f1. Haplogroup L3 has played a pivotal role in the history of the human species. Soon after it arose in eastern Africa, about sixty thousand years ago, a relatively small band carried it across the Red Sea to Arabia, inaugurating the intercontinental migration that eventually settled every major land mass on earth except Antarctica.

L3 has also been mobile within Africa, spreading south with migrations of Bantu-speaking populations over the past few thousand years. And the Atlantic slave trade carried it to the Americas as well—as various branches of L3 are found today among more than 25 percent of the African American population.

Malcolm's subgroup, L3f1, split off as a subset of L3 sometime between twenty and thirty thousand years ago, arising in eastern Africa and moving westward before the peak of the Ice Age, when the Sahara Desert expanded and rendered much of the northern part of the continent uninhabitable.

"It's astonishing," said Malcolm, "that you can just spit in a cup and detect the passage of your ancestors across the Sahara so many millennia ago."

Malcolm's mitochondrial DNA yielded no exact matches in Africa with anyone in the Family Tree DNA database. However, we did find distant matches with people alive today on the African continent in Ethiopia, Cameroon, and Gabon.

The Ethiopian result, as Malcolm and I both know, is highly unusual. "They are the best-looking people in the world," said Malcolm. "I would like to think I had some Ethiopian."

I told him that I was sorry to disappoint him, but the result had to be a fluke—an aberration in the data. No slaves came to the New World from Ethiopia. A possible explanation for this result is that a person with Malcolm's genetic signature moved recently to Ethiopia from a country in west or central Africa, where African Americans' ancestors originate. However, I did have some ideas about where his ancestors may actually have come from. After examining his results, our slave-trade historians, John Thornton and Linda Heywood, suggested that his maternal ancestor may have originated in the Deshava Province of the Democratic Republic of Congo. This area was part of the Lunda Empire, which sold large numbers of slaves to the New World as a result of conquests. Slaves from the Lunda Empire would have been purchased by merchants and brought to the Luanda coast, which is now Angola, where the British were participating in the central-African slave trade in the eighteenth century.

This narrative reflects the history of Malcolm's mitochondrial DNA, which goes back directly along his mother's line, passed from mother to daughter across generation after generation. The farthest we could go back on this line using the historical record was Malcolm's great-grandmother Ann Elizabeth Forrester, who was born in Jamaica around 1864. But Malcolm has more than one African ancestor, obviously. And to learn about the others, we consulted what I consider to be one of the most valuable and impressive historical research tools ever created: the Trans-Atlantic Slave Database. This database is a compilation of the records kept by shipping companies involved in the slave trade. It offers detailed information on almost thirty-five thousand transatlantic slave-trading voyages that occurred between 1514 and 1867. Compiled under the direction of David Eltis, with the collaboration of Stephen D. Behrendt and David Richardson, it is in the largest uniform, consolidated database of its kind in the world. The authors estimate that the assembled data cover at least two-thirds of the slaving voyages that crossed the Atlantic Ocean to the New World.

We knew from our research that Margaret Mullings, Malcolm's slave-owning free ancestor, was most likely the granddaughter or great-granddaughter of an African slave. Given that she was already freed by the 1770s, the Trans-Atlantic Slave Database suggests that she was most likely an Ibo or an Akan person, two ethnicities from today's Ghana and eastern Nigeria, respectively, which were especially prevalent in Jamaica at that time. Interestingly, Malcolm's family lore had long maintained that William Ford, the putative Irish coffee-plantation owner, had taken an Ibo slave as his wife. The story, research had shown, was false. But it is quite likely that that Ibo detail was based on fact, an echo of an accurate description of another ancestor.

I asked Malcolm if he felt connected to these African ancestors. "'Connected' is too strong a word," he said. "A lot of time has passed, but I feel it's fascinating. And it take a little while to sink in. It isn't until you go to Africa that you appreciate what it means. This notion that we're all from there is totally abstract until you go there. You get a sense of the ancientness of it and the primacy of it. It's just fascinating. And it's so bizarre that this can be reconstructed in 2009."

Malcolm and I then began to consider what DNA could tells us about his paternal ancestry. We were able to trace his father's line all the way back to his eighth-great-grandfather Joseph Gladwell, who was born in 1660 in Suffolk, England. That's already quite far back in time, but DNA was able to tell us more. Malcolm has identical matches of his Y-DNA with people who live today in England, Ireland, Scotland, Spain, and Germany. "The Spain thing is really interesting," he said. "How were people from England dispersed into Spain?" I told him that we don't know. We have no sense of the trajectory. But these are his genetic cousins.

His father's haplogroup and that of the entire Gladwell line is R1b1b2a1a, which is a branch of haplogroup R. This particular haplogroup is a widespread and diverse branch of the Y chromosome tree that is extremely common in Europe, where it spread after the end of the Ice Age, about twelve thousand years ago. It appears to have originated in southwestern Asia about thirty thousand years ago when it split into two main branches. Malcolm's branch, R1, is the dominant haplogroup in Europe today. (Mario Batali, as we saw, belongs to this branch, by way of its subset R1b1b2a1a2d.) Various branches of R1 testify to the many migrations that have shaped the continent from the arrival of farmers between about ten and seven thousand years ago to the movements of ethnic groups such as the Anglo-Saxons and the Vikings. The variation R1b was confined during the Ice Age to pockets of territory in Mediterranean Europe. The largest was in the Iberian Peninsula and southern France, where men bearing the haplogroup hunted mammoth, bison, and other large game and the climate was more like present-day Siberia's than the mild climate prevailing there now.

These men, Malcolm's ancestors, were among the first to record depictions of their lives in the famous cave paintings at Lascaux and at Altamira. As it turns out, his R1b subgroup, R1b1b2, is actually the most common in western Europe, where it is found in more than 50 percent of the men. In fact, three other men in our series belong to this exact same paternal haplogroup: Stephen Colbert, Mario Batali, and me. "So we're all white in the same way?" asked Malcolm, grinning.

I told him that we are. And we both reveled in the idea that the four of us share a paternal ancestor who lived in the distant past, sometime around the height of the last Ice Age, about seventeen or eighteen thousand years ago. "He would have been an interesting guy, I'm guessing," said Malcolm with a smile.

I then told Malcolm that when we submitted his data to the Broad Institute in Cambridge, Massachusetts, autosomal DNA testing revealed that he shares a common ancestor as recently as five to ten generations ago with Dr. Mehmet Oz and with me.

The relationship between Malcolm and me is a particularly close one. We share several long segments of DNA not on one chromosome but on two: number 7 and number 11. Malcolm and I are therefore distant cousins, and according to the Broad Institute, it's not on the African side; it's on the European side, which only makes sense. I'm 56 percent European, 37 percent African, and 7 percent Asian. Malcolm is about three-quarters European and a quarter African. I descend from seven sets of black ancestors who were free well before the Civil War, the latest by 1823. Our admixtures are fairly similar. We both have ancestors who were brought from Africa to the Americas as slaves, as well as ancestors who came from the British Isles. Because of our skin color, family history, and where we grew up, we've had different experiences of race. But in the grand scheme of things, our families' stories are not of the standard "up from slavery" variety. They are tales of light-skinned privilege within the larger black community, one in Jamaica, one in the hills of western Virginia.

Malcolm was delighted, "I always think that the more ways you can define yourself, the better off you are," he said, "and the less likely you are to get trapped by a definition or to judge someone very narrowly. What's lovely about all of this is that it adds a whole other way for me to think about myself. It doesn't cancel out anything I've known about myself in the past; it just adds an entirely new dimension. And it's such a humbling way of defining oneself. The process of self-definition is very much a function of the knowledge about ourselves that we choose to expose ourselves to. I say 'choose to' because I think it has to be a kind of active process. If you sit passively by, you get trapped by a small number of narrow definitions. Now that I know I'm related to you, my world is suddenly richer. It offers a different way to define who we are. What people have come to understand is how extraordinarily liberating it is to have another way of thinking about yourself, of knowing who you are and where you come from. It is just an impossibly enriching experience."

Before we parted, I wanted to ask Malcolm once more about his ancestors who owned slaves. This fact is much more common in African American history than even scholars want to admit; one of the cousins on my Redman line is listed as a slave owner in the 1850 census in Virginia. And I wanted to know how he felt about finding this in his family's past.

"Well," he said after a long pause, "we're not sitting in judgment of our ancestors. We're sitting in judgment of ourselves, right? The importance of that fact is not what it says about them; it's the way it informs our self-perceptions and our own attitudes towards race and history and disadvantage. Like I say, it's a humbling fact, humbling for us. And I feel that as humans, we need more humbling facts. It reminds us, when we look around at what we have accomplished, that some of it was a little bit ill gotten along the way. That is an important thing to keep in mind when the world asks things of you—that what is yours did not all come to you honestly. And that little bit of self-realization can go a long way in making this world a better place."

10

Stephen Colbert

1964

STEPHEN COLBERT IS one of the most original political satirists in the United States today. I adore *The Colbert Report,* his Emmy and Peabody Award–winning series on Comedy Central. I love the way in which his character—a conservative talk-show host who revels in his Irish American identity and basically claims he's more American than apple pie—is so carefully and affectionately drawn. You feel for the guy, in a strange way, even as he acts like a crazy monster version of Sean Hannity. I was not at all surprised to learn that the character is, in fact, a product of Stephen's own deep Irish roots and the singular circumstances under which he was raised.

I asked Stephen to participate in this project because I wanted to include an Irish American family, and I relished the idea of spending some time with him. I've been a guest on his show three times, and he's one of the funniest, most engaging people I've ever met. I was hoping to see how his perspective emerged from his family's past. But as I researched his ancestry, I realized that for all his good humor, Stephen's family story is a story of resilience, a story of generation after generation enduring calamity, oppression, and persecution yet ultimately transcending even the most personal tragedies. That his family's history, primarily in Ireland, produced a comic genius in this generation is perhaps not so very surprising given the great Irish storytelling tradition to which Stephen is heir.

Stephen's ancestors, like most Irish Catholics, were tenant farmers. English laws prevented them from buying land, practicing their faith, holding public office, or even owning a horse. They could not—or would not —record the details of their lives in church or civil records. So they often left Ireland without leaving behind a trace. Trying to trace their family lines was often frustratingly difficult, yet their collective story offers a glimpse into an absolutely essential element of the American immigrant experience. It may not explain the peculiar contours of *The Colbert Report,* but

Stephen's family tree taught me a great deal about our shared history, the shared history between Ireland and the United States.

Stephen Tyrone Colbert was born in Washington, DC, on May 13, 1964, the youngest of the eleven children of Dr. James William Colbert, Jr., and Lorna Tuck Colbert. His father was a prominent doctor and an academic. In the early 1960s, he served as the president of Physicians for President Kennedy and was the nation's youngest dean of a medical school—heading St. Louis University, a Jesuit institution. When Stephen was born, his father was working for the National Institutes of Health in Washington, DC, but in 1969, he changed jobs yet again and moved his family to South Carolina. This had a profound effect on his five-year-old son.

"It was like moving to the moon," said Stephen. "We moved to a place called James Island, which is just across the harbor from Charleston. It was very sleepy, you know, dogs sleeping in the street. When I read *To Kill a Mockingbird*, I picture that town where I grew up. It had dirt roads and some really ramshackle neighborhoods where the black people still lived, essentially—if not literally—in the houses where their ancestors had been slaves. And there were cotton fields and peanut fields and tomato sheds, and—that's South Carolina."

Stephen spent the rest of his childhood in and around Charleston and has repeatedly told interviewers that he felt alienated by southern culture. He claims that his well-educated Irish Catholic parents seemed to disdain the anti-Catholic, anti-intellectual sentiments that surrounded them. Stephen says he even tried to avoid developing any kind of southern accent and, in fact, tried to mimic the accents of television news reporters. As I listened to him, it was evident that he is the product of a tightly bonded family. Tragically, in 1974, the family confronted any family's worst nightmare: on their way to enroll the boys in a private school in Connecticut, Stephen's father and the two brothers who were closest to him in age were killed in a plane crash. Stephen was just ten years old. I showed Stephen the newspaper headline and asked him to tell me about that day.

"I was at school," said Stephen, "and I got picked up by my brother Billy, so I knew something was wrong. But he didn't say anything. We went home, and everybody was there in the house, so I knew something was up. I went upstairs, and my mom told me there'd been an accident. I knew that my father and my brothers were going off to boarding school—and I immediately made the connection. It wasn't a long conversation—it was a very short one, actually. And then after that I remember the house filled with people and food. There are huge gaps in my memory around then."

Stephen (*second row, next to his mother*) at home in South Carolina with his family, several years before the death of his father and two closest brothers. (Used by permission of the Colbert family)

I asked Stephen how he coped with the sudden loss of his father and brothers at such a young age. He told me that he is not sure that he ever really dealt with it, that it still pains him today, that sometimes he halfway expects them all to come walking back through the front door of their home, but that he and his mother definitely took solace in their family bond and their Roman Catholic faith. "We became daily communicants at church," he said. "My mother found great strength—I don't know about peace—by going to Mass. Because it was just the two of us at home, I was often there with her. And that made a powerful impression on me."

Stephen says that his mother, Lorna Tuck Colbert, held the family together in the face of her sadness and allowed him to grow up in a deeply nurturing and loving environment to become the person he is today. Lorna is still alive, and Stephen speaks of her with intense warmth. "She's bright," he told me, "not just intelligent but bright: she shines. Hopeful, indefatigable, great faith. Tough—she raised eleven kids, and she raised me after my father and two of my brothers died. And she's Irish, *so* Irish."

The last lines of this statement are, I think, quite telling. There is no central narrative to the Colbert family tree, no dichotomy between differing races, no strong distinctions of wealth and poverty among the different branches, no villains or scoundrels, no famous people. Instead, with only one notable exception, there is a shared story spread among all his lines: the story of ancestor after ancestor struggling to get out of Ireland and build a life in America. That so many of them succeeded, despite extremely humble beginnings, is a great testament to their collective resilience. When Stephen said that his mother was "*so* Irish," it was a very meaningful compliment.

Seven out Stephen's eight great-grandparents are of documented Irish descent. Many of their family stories are similar—or follow similar patterns. And, as already noted, all are clouded by a lack of records. I could have begun our journey along almost any of these lines. I chose to start with his paternal heritage because it seemed, somehow, logical. James Colbert's father, Stephen's paternal grandfather, was James William Colbert, Sr., born in Chesterfield, Illinois, on February 10, 1894. He died when Stephen was only seven years old, but he is the only grandparent Stephen has any memory of at all.

"I remember that he was quite old. And I remember him sitting in my father's chair, which no one did. And I remember sitting across the dining room table and him teaching me a card trick. I still remember the card trick. I did it for some of my daughter's friends the other day. He evidently had a misspent youth, because he was very good at cards and very good at pool. He was a traveling salesman, and he knew some dicey characters."

Records show that James was a glass-bottle salesman for a successful company called the Owens Illinois Glassworks (which later became part of Owens Corning) and that his parents were George William Colbert, born in 1863, and Angeline Garin, born in 1871. Angeline came from an Irish immigrant family. George's ancestry is less clear. The family story is that Angeline was Catholic, but George was not—and that the name Colbert actually comes from France. "He married a Catholic girl," said Stephen. "And he may have converted—probably did—and the story is that there was a cross burned on his lawn, and she said, 'George, what are we going to do?' And he said, 'Let it burn. It sheds a lovely light'—which is a great story. We'll still tell it in my family."

There is no evidence to support this story, as evocative as it may be. There is also nothing in the documentary record to suggest George was French. In fact, according to our Irish researchers, Colbert is an Irish name linked to a few quite specific places in Ireland. Furthermore, we found the marriage license for George and Angeline, dated January 13, 1894. It indicates that George William Colbert was a thirty-one-year-old farmer and that his "race" was "Irish." Today, we don't think of Irish as a race, but in the nineteenth century, amid massive waves of Irish immigration, it was, in the same way that Elizabeth Alexander's grandfather's "race" could be listed as "West Indian." And I can think of no good reason why George Colbert would have listed himself as Irish on his marriage license unless he was, in fact, Irish.

Nonetheless, we cannot prove it. George Colbert is the only one of Stephen's eight great-grandparents on this side of his family tree who could not be definitively traced back to Ireland. He was born in Virginia, as was his father, a man named John J. Colbert (born between 1820 and 1828), and so, most likely, was his grandfather, a man named Anthony Colbert who was born sometime in the 1790s. Irish people, of course, have been coming to America since the mid-1600s, but most of us think of them as arriving in the 1850s and the 1860s. Not this branch of Stephen's family. They had a deep purchase on the American experience. They arrived in the eighteenth century, perhaps earlier, and they were so proud of their heritage that they were still identifying themselves as Irish in the late nineteenth century. "I knew nothing about that," said Stephen, surprised.

We could not identify Anthony Colbert's father, and we assume this is because he was born in Ireland. But when we went there to look for documents related to him and his family, we were unable to discover even the slightest trace of them. This was just one of many dead ends we encountered in researching Stephen's ancestry—all caused by the centuries-long British oppression of Irish Catholics. As I explained to Stephen as we prepared to go forward, he was going to need to prepare himself for a lot of loose ends, unanswered questions, and outrage against England.

"That's a big part of being Irish in America," he said, nodding his head. "The English are bastards. And that was what I was raised with, absolutely no doubt. When I met my wife, who is Presbyterian, we went to visit her sister, who was living at the Oliver Cromwell, a building on 72nd Street in New York. And I thought, 'I can't tell my mom that anyone in their family lives at the Oliver Cromwell,' because Cromwell is Satan. He drove our family west of the River Shannon to farm rocks, 350 years ago maybe? And yet I was raised with that story. It has not gone away. Part of being Irish, even to this day, is not liking the English."

I told Stephen that I was well familiar with this attitude and the history behind it. Even though more than 80 percent of Ireland's population was Catholic, Catholics there were a largely powerless, oppressed majority under Protestant British domination from 1652, when the country was conquered by the Puritan Oliver Cromwell, through 1921, when the Irish Republic was finally granted independence. As Stephen had intimated, the oppression of Catholics began the moment Cromwell took power. Learning about it was shocking to me. Cromwell ruthlessly reconfigured the country, replacing the native-born Irish gentry with absentee landlords from England, seizing and shutting Catholic churches, and denying Catholics almost all rights to property and civil liberties. This situation persisted, with some slight modifications, for centuries. As a result, Irish Catholics were, for the purposes of genealogy, almost total nonentities. The only records left behind by most of them are the parish registers of their local churches during the periods of time when these churches were not outlawed. To find these records, however, you have to know exactly where a particular ancestor lived. And you have to hope that the church in which they worshiped was not seized or destroyed by the British overlords. In other words, good luck successfully conducting deep research into an Irish person's history. Researching an Irish family tree can be deeply frustrating. Our head genealogist, Johni Cerny, sent us a message, which read, "Colbert's ancestry has been the most difficult to search of anyone I've worked on in over thirty years. I can say that without reservation."

"I'm a mysterious person," said Stephen, with a grin. Nonetheless, our researchers kept trying. And they managed to uncover a great number of stories, fragmentary though some of them might be.

Moving back down Stephen's paternal line, I told him that we had found some interesting information about the family of his father's mother, Mary Margaret Tormey. She was born on November 22, 1894, in the Bronx, New York. Her parents were Henry John Tormey, born on February 17, 1866, in the Bronx, and Margaret Ann McCrory, born in 1864 either in Ireland or in New York City.

According to Colbert family lore, the McCrory line is the source of Stephen's middle name, Tyrone. "On my father's side," he said, "the McCrorys were O'Neills way back. And the story was that one of the O'Neills had been the Earl of Tyrone, and so they named me Tyrone after him."

We looked into this story as best we could. According to our researchers, almost every Irish person believes that he or she is descended from Irish royalty. And the Second Earl of Tyrone—a.k.a. Hugh O'Neill—is especially popular for a number of reasons. He was known to recognize his illegitimate children and leave them property, and, perhaps more important, he is a famous Irish patriot. In the year 1607, the Earls of Tyrone and Tyrconnell chose permanent exile from Ireland over cooperation with the English. This marked the end of the Gaelic aristocracy that had ruled Ireland since the fourth century AD. It was a defining moment of Irish history, a part of the failed Irish resistance to England that culminated in Cromwell's invasion, and it helps to explain why the Irish have been bitter against the English crown ever since.

Given this history, it is easy to see why so many Irish people name their sons Tyrone. African Americans, of course, have similar beliefs. Many of us think we're descended from Thomas Jefferson or George Washington or James Madison. Among Stephen's people, it's the Earl of Tyrone. Unfortunately, however, there is absolutely no evidence of any connection between Stephen's family and the O'Neill family that once held that title. "The nice thing is, that just makes me more Irish," said Stephen. "If I have a stereotypical delusion about my Irish ancestry, that just makes me more Irish than Joyce."

The Tyrone family legend did prove somewhat useful to our researchers. County Tyrone is in the province of Ulster, and today it's one of the six counties that make up Northern Ireland. As it turns out, County Tyrone was full of McCrorys and McCreashes, the surnames of Stephen's great-great-grandparents. A record collection known "Griffith's Valuations," the first public accounting of landlords and tenants in Ireland, conducted from 1848 to 1864, incredibly shows 381 listings for McCrorys alone. Unfortunately, there were no surviving parish registers for any of the towns where a Margaret Ann McCrory was listed, so we could never know for sure. But it does seem this could be where Stephen's family's Tyrone myth was born.

We then tried looking for the family of Margaret Ann McCrory's husband, Stephen's great-grandfather Henry John Tormey. Henry's death certificate indicates that he was born in the Bronx around the year 1866, and it includes the names of his parents: John Tormey and Honora Manning, both born in Ireland. At first, this seemed to be yet another dead end. The Tormey family never appears in any records in either America or Ireland. However, as we were searching for them, we came across something intriguing: a passenger list of the SS *Kangaroo*, which landed in New York Harbor on July 11, 1863. The list includes the name Honora Manning, age twenty-three. She boarded the ship in Liverpool, like many other Irish immigrants of the era, and she traveled in the steerage class, unaccompanied by any family members. Her occupation is given as "spinster." That occupation, of course, did not last. She is Stephen's great-great-grandmother.

The *Kangaroo* was an Australian steamer. Honora's journey in steerage took several weeks. And I was struck by the date that she arrived: July 11, 1863. At the time, America was in the midst of the Civil War. President Lincoln's Emancipation Proclamation had taken effect on January 1, 1863, and since Lincoln had become president, the New York Democrats, who were proslavery, had been warning immigrants, especially the city's many Irish immigrants, that if the Union armies were successful in the South, they would free all the slaves, who would then come north and take the jobs on the bottom of the socioeconomic scale, jobs that were currently held by the Irish.

"She's coming in for hell, isn't she?" said Stephen. "The scene of her arrival is in *Gangs of New York* by Scorsese. People meeting them at the ship, indoctrinating them into a political philosophy of 'Don't fight for the black people.'"

Stephen is right. His great-great-grandmother walked off her ship into a hornet's nest of racial tension. In March 1863, just months before she arrived, a new draft law had been passed that widened the pool of men subject to military duty. Every able-bodied man had to submit to a conscription lottery—except for those who could afford to hire a substitute. The cost of a substitute was generally three hundred dollars (roughly five thousand dollars today). So this was a system that allowed relatively comfortable people to buy their way out of military service. But the new Irish immigrants, of course, weren't in that position, and they were at risk of being conscripted into the Union army in droves. As a result, New York was full of poor, white workers totally outraged by the conscription law. Their line of thought was simple: why should they risk their lives to liberate people who were only going to take their jobs—and colored people at that?

On Saturday, July 11, 1863, the very day that Honora Manning stepped off that boat, the first draft lottery took place. For twenty-four hours all was quiet. Then on Monday morning, July 13, New York City exploded into five days of mayhem and bloodshed that we know today as the Draft Riots. Thousands of men and boys—a great majority of whom happened to have been Irish—started attacking military and government buildings. Soon their anger and rage turned toward black people and anything that represented black political, social, or economic power. Eleven black men were lynched; hundreds were forced to flee. Even the Colored Orphan Asylum, home to hundreds of children, was attacked and burned to the ground. "She spent weeks in steerage, down among the pigs, got off the boat, and that's what she saw?" asked Stephen, incredulous.

The riots resulted in at least 120 deaths, two thousand injuries and over a million dollars of property damage. It was a terrible, shameful event. But as I explained to Stephen, in my view, it clearly reflected a very complicated situation in which people in power used economics, fear, and xenophobia to manipulate two disadvantaged groups into hating each other. In newspapers of the day, the Irish were frequently caricatured as apes, often interchangeably with blacks. The two groups were thought to be at the lowest rungs of American society and were often pitted against each other as economic rivals. These practices continued into the twentieth century.

"During my childhood," Stephen said, "my mother would tell me about how 'Irish Need Not Apply' signs were everywhere. It's hard to believe today. It doesn't feel personal. Two of those stereotypes live on—that the Irish fight and the Irish drink—but those are jokes. They're not weapons against the Irish. But this is so far removed from my experience of what it is to be Irish; it's purely historical. John Kennedy was BC and AD for the image of the Irish in America. The deification of Kennedy buried this prejudice forever. But this was the image that made it hard for him to get elected."

Honora Manning witnessed the riots firsthand. She must have been absolutely terrified and may have considered returning to Ireland. She remained, however, and became the matriarch of this line of Stephen's family. It is fascinating to imagine what she must have thought on her first nights in America—a single woman, alone, amid a burning city. "I don't know what Ireland was like back then," said Stephen. "She might have said, 'This is better.'"

Unfortunately, we were unable to trace Honora's family back any further into Ireland and find out. For the purposes of Stephen's genealogy, the Manning family was yet another stunted branch on his family tree.

We then moved back down the branches of Stephen's family tree to look at the line of his paternal great-grandmother Angeline Garin, his grandfather James Colbert's mother. She was born January 1, 1871, in Greene County, Illinois. She was the wife of George William Colbert, Stephen's one great-grandparent who may or may not have been Irish. George Colbert died when he was only forty-four years old. Several years later, Angeline remarried another Irish American, named Thomas Kelley. The name on her death certificate is "Angela A. Kelley." Her birthplace, as written on her death certificate, appears to have been a town or county in Ireland—but the handwriting on the certificate is illegible. None of us could decipher it. However, according to Angeline's death record, her parents were named Michael Garin and Bridget Caffery. And this was a valuable clue, because while our researchers were searching for Garins in Ireland, a distant cousin of Stephen's told them that the family was from Limerick. So we focused our attention on the parish records of County Limerick. And we got lucky. Many people in Ireland at this time had similar surnames, and since few of them were literate, these names could be spelled in countless ways. But we finally found the baptismal certificate of a child named Michael Garin. This, we believe, is Stephen's great-great-grandfather. He was baptized in St. Mary's Roman Catholic Church in Limerick City on June 9, 1840.

Michael's baptismal record lists his parents as "Michael Gearon and Johanna Nicholson." We found their marriage notice, which led us to the baptismal record of Michael Gearon, son to "Thomas Gearon and Bridget Connors," born January 28, 1805, in Limerick. We were then able to find the marriage license of Thomas Gearon and Bridget Connors, dated 1800. This was as far back into Ireland as we were able to go along any line of Stephen's family tree.

Stephen knew absolutely nothing about this line of his family. But their story is quite fascinating. The Gearons left Limerick at a crucial moment in Irish history—in the early 1850s—the years of what we call the Great Potato Famine (the Irish call it the Great Hunger). Their immigrant experience, like that of many other Irish families, is intertwined with the terrible story of this famine.

By the early 1800s, the potato had become the main and, in many areas, the only form of sustenance for the Irish underclass. Historians estimate that as much as a third of the country lived on little more than potatoes and water. When a blight decimated the potato crop in 1845, widespread famine ensued and continued for the better part of seven years. Over that time, roughly one million people died of starvation and disease, a figure that amounted to almost a quarter of the entire Irish population. As a result, the number of Irish immigrants who came to America exploded, reaching as many two hundred thousand per year in the years 1849 and 1850. Those who had the means to leave were the lucky ones, and nearly a million fled over the course of the famine—including Stephen's ancestors, the Gearons.

The famine was a natural disaster, but it was exacerbated by the English landlords and the English government, which controlled Ireland. Collectively, they declined to intervene in any manner. Indeed, many historians allege that through their near-systematic neglect, the English were effectively engaged in a quasi-genocidal effort to depopulate Ireland and better control its resources. Though this position is controversial, there is certainly ample evidence that while the Irish Catholic masses were starving, Protestant English merchants and landlords continued to extract rent from the population and to export enormous amounts of food from the Irish farms which they owned. Limerick City, where the Gearons lived, contained a thriving bacon industry, with about six thousand pigs slaughtered per week, and a busy port. Shipping records indicate that continuous cargoes of meat and produce were sent off to England and elsewhere throughout the years of famine, right past the starving people and the mass communal unmarked graves.

This most certainly was a period of almost unimaginable cynicism and cruelty. A prime example was a man named Francis Spaight, a Limerick merchant, landlord, and British magistrate. Among his many businesses, Spaight ran a fleet of ships importing timber from Canada. As the famine mounted, he did nothing to help the Irish people. But he figured out some clever ways to exploit their plight. When his ships arrived from Canada laden with timber, his workers unloaded them, and then, rather than send them back to Canada empty, Spaight began filling the holds with human beings desperate to leave Ireland and willing to pay a fare to do so.

Spaight later made a statement to the British Parliament's committee on the famine, in which he essentially said that if you make a place bad enough, you can make a business out of getting people out of it. His statement reads, in part, "I found so great an advantage of getting rid of the pauper population upon my own property that I made every possible exertion to remove them. I consider the failure of the potato crop to be the greatest possible value in one respect in enabling us to carry out the emigrations system."

"That is the British version of the Final Solution," said Stephen. " 'What a great advantage all this suffering is for us.' It makes Swift's 'Modest Proposal' seem less like comedy."

I told Stephen that given what we know about his family's history, it seems very likely that his great-great-grandfather Michael Garin, along with his parents and siblings, left Limerick on one of Francis Spaight's

Declaration of intent to become an American citizen, signed
by Stephen's paternal great-great-grandfather Michael Garin
on August 25, 1860. (Public domain)

ships. After centuries of oppression and extreme poverty, they were simply
starved out of their homeland.

"I can't conceive of it," said Stephen, "to reach that point, make that
decision. Everything in my life has just been opportunities. No one has put
a gun to my head."

Although it was a struggle for Stephen's great-great-grandfather Michael Garin to get to America, he did not lack opportunities once he arrived. He appears in the 1860 U.S. federal census, living in a rooming
house in Carrollton, Illinois, and working as a teamster, hauling goods with
a cart. I was able to show Stephen his ancestor's naturalization papers, revealing that on August 25, 1860, he became a citizen of the United States,
renouncing his allegiance to the Queen of Great Britain and Ireland. I was
surprised at how deeply Stephen was moved as he contemplated the significance of this document to his ancestor and to himself. "I bet that wasn't

a hard oath to take. That's one of the greatest documents I've ever seen," Stephen remarked, moved almost to tears.

One of the many interesting facets of this project, in my opinion, has been the comparison it permits between the different paths to citizenship taken by the ancestors of the twelve subjects. Depending on their race and ethnicity, some their ancestors arrived in America and quickly naturalized —like Michael Garin and the Italian ancestors of Mario Batali. Others, like Queen Noor's Syrian ancestors, endured a complex but relatively brief naturalization process, the main obstacle to which was to prove their whiteness. These stories contrast starkly with those of my own African American ancestors, as well as the Native American ancestors of Louise Erdrich and the Japanese ancestors, as we shall see, of Kristi Yamaguchi—all of whom suffered through decades of humiliation, degradation, and abuse before finally obtaining their right to become American citizens or their rights as American citizens. It is a telling comparison, mirroring the larger issues of race that have plagued this country since its inception. The path to citizenship, like so many other paths, has been much easier to travel for ancestors who were European and white.

"I never thought about my ancestors becoming citizens," said Stephen. "It just was sort of a gradual thing, like when does the sun come up? The light's in the sky, and suddenly it's there. I always sort of imagined it was like that for them being here. But to see the moment of decision to be an American citizen is unbelievably moving."

After becoming a citizen, Stephen's great-great-grandfather Michael Garin lived out a familiar narrative of comfortable immigrant success. Sometime around 1868, he married Bridget Caffery, who had emigrated from Ireland in 1856. If the two had stayed in their homeland, they would almost certainly have lived on rented land for their entire lives. Many old Irish songs glorify the idea of freehold, as it was called—land owned free and clear—because for the overwhelming majority of the population, that was an impossible dream because of economic disadvantage and the English laws. Yet in America, land was comparatively easy to come by. We found documentation showing that sometime around 1871, Michael Garin began purchasing farmland in Western Mound township in Macoupin County, Illinois. Later records show that he and Bridget raised their five children on 120 acres. By the late nineteenth century, the St. Louis–Chicago railroad was running through their property. The right of way for the line most likely earned them a goodly sum. They died, after a lifetime of middle-class prosperity in America, on land that they owned free and clear—land they

Stephen's great-great-grandparents Michael Garin and Bridget Caffery, who fled Ireland during the Great Potato Famine. (Used by permission of the Colbert family)

passed on to their children, initiating the kind of generational ascent that Malcolm Gladwell mapped out among his own ancestors in Jamaica.

At this point, we could not go back any further along any of the lines on Stephen's paternal ancestry, so we then turned our attention to his maternal family tree. His remarkable mother, Lorna Tuck, was born on June 11, 1920, in New York City. Her parents were Andrew Edward Tuck and Marie Elizabeth Fee, both born in Rochester, New York—on May 11, 1874, and July 15, 1885, respectively. Her paternal grandfather, Stephen's great-grandfather, was a man named Andrew Tuck, born on November 9, 1833, in the small community of Lisbon, which is part of St. Lawrence County, New York.

"I know his face," said Stephen, eyeing a photograph of his great-grandfather. "He was a farmer. He raised apples, I believe. And I believe he developed something called the Tuck apple—I always heard that story."

Andrew was indeed a farmer. He was also a schoolteacher and a prominent member of his community. His parents were immigrants, John Tuck and Judith Dunn, both most likely born in County Queens, Ireland, in the early eighteenth century. Andrew was the first member of their family born in this country. Late in his life, he wrote a personal memoir for his children,

Stephen's paternal great-grandfather Andrew Tuck. Late in his life, Tuck wrote a personal memoir for his children which served as a primary source for research into his family. (Used by permission of the Colbert family)

which contains many fascinating details about the family's experience, including a very telling passage which describes how his neighbors in St. Lawrence County reacted when he began working as a schoolteacher. The passage reads, "I heard some feeling against me when it became known that I was a Roman Catholic. The trustee was severely criticized for hiring me, but he claimed his act was constitutional. I realized it was up to me to teach a school and not discuss religion. Little children would be heard saying amongst themselves, Why he is a good fellow, he is just like us. It would seem that they had been led to think that a Catholic was somewhat malformed, unlike human beings."

I find this passage quite remarkable because, as I explained to Stephen, a black person could have written those same words, in just a slightly different context, in that same era. The prejudice that Irish Catholics experienced at this time is a part of the American experience that has been largely forgotten.

Stephen nodded. "I remember, when my family drove from Washington to Charleston, South Carolina, in 1969, there was a sign on the highway in North Carolina that said, 'Welcome to North Carolina, home of the Ku Klux Klan.' And it had a list of undesirables. And the last item on the list was Catholics. My mother said, 'Where are you taking us?' Because that had all ended up north. But we kept going. And I was raised with the knowledge that Irish Catholic lives were made very hard in Ireland. And as a kid growing up in South Carolina, there were people who would tell me I was going to hell because I was Catholic. So I'm not surprised at all."

Unlike Stephen's paternal ancestors from Ireland, the Tuck family did not immigrate directly to the United States; they went first to Canada. Andrew Tuck describes in his memoir how his father, Stephen's great-great-grandfather John Tuck, journeyed to Montreal in the 1820s, leaving his wife Judith Dunn and their children behind in Ireland. According to Andrew, John Tuck's employer, a Canadian quarry owner named Halpin, promised to hold John's wages so he could save up to bring his family over from Ireland. But when John was ready to collect what was owed him, his employer reneged on the deal. According to Andrew, this was a devastating blow to his father. It was more than seven years before he saw his family again. Finally, in 1832, Judith and their only surviving child managed to come over with an uncle and aunt. According to Andrew's memoir, this produced quite a scene. "On landing in Montreal," the memoir reads, "they soon found the Halpin quarry where a messenger was sent to inform father that there was a woman who wished to see him. As there was no place for mother to wait, she went with the messenger to the quarry. Where father, upon seeing her threw up his hands exclaiming, 'It's Judy!'"

This miraculous reunion, which might seem to have been romanticized in Andrew's memoir, seems to be supported in the main by the historical record. Documents show that by the mid-1830s, the whole Tuck and Dunn clan, including a number of John and Judith's siblings, had settled in New York State, just across the Saint Lawrence River from Canada.

Since Andrew's memoir listed several towns in Ireland where the Tuck family lived, we sent our researchers there to see if we could trace the family further back into the past. They ended up focusing on the towns of Mountmellick and Ballyhorahan, in what was once called Queens County and what, since Irish independence in 1921, has been known as County Laois. The records in the two Catholic parishes there turned out to be full of gaps. But we were lucky enough to discover the marriage certificate of Stephen's great-great-grandparents John Tuck and Judith Dunn, from 1817. There were no records of their births, or those of their children, but based on Andrew's memoir and other circumstantial evidence, we concluded that Stephen's great-great-grandfather John Tuck was born around 1775, the year before Thomas Jefferson wrote the Declaration of Independence. Judith appears to have been born around 1788.

This was yet another very significant time in Irish history—a time when the country was chafing against the constraints of British rule. Although some of the Cromwell-era laws had been relaxed, Catholics still had almost no say in their government and, indeed, were barred from participation in the Irish Parliament. They wanted control of their own affairs. The American Revolution of 1776 and the French Revolution of 1789 inspired them to fight for an independent republic. After years of tension, in 1798, violence exploded throughout Ireland, including in Queens County, where John Tuck lived. For a brief moment, the rebels seemed to have the upper hand. Within a few months, however, the English crushed them. Ironically, the most tangible result of the rebellion, in which some thirty thousand people died, was the dissolution of the Irish Parliament and something called the Act of Union, which tied Ireland even closer to England.

John Tuck was a young man at the time of the rebellion and decided after it failed to take a risk on a new life in North America. Was he or any member of his family actively involved in the fighting? There is no way to tell. But his son, Andrew, said in his memoir that the only person who stayed behind in Queens County was his father's brother, Edward. Andrew describes his uncle Edward cryptically as the person "who seems to be the one in my father's family who received the learning." What did this mean? We found Edward Tuck in the mid-nineteenth-century land records in Ireland. And like most Irish Catholics at that time, he was renting small parcels of farmland from English landlords. So even if he was educated, it didn't improve his situation enough for him to become a landowner. And though we found the tomb of Edward Tuck (he died at age eighty-nine, and he is buried next to the remains of the Camross Catholic Church), this was all we could learn about him and the remnants of the Tuck family in Ireland. Local historians told us that nobody with a Tuck surname remains in that area. It seems likely that Edward's descendants eventually left the parish as well, and perhaps they also immigrated to the United States. But we don't know.

Turning to the other side of Stephen's maternal line, we began to look at his maternal grandmother's family, the Fees. Stephen told me that he believed his mother grew up in a well-to-do family, with money and servants, but that he himself never met or heard very much about them. "My mother," he said, "likes things just so. And I had heard about these people growing up, but because I spent my whole life in the South, these were always just stories to me." Research confirmed that the family was indeed relatively wealthy. And we were able to find one of the sources of that wealth: beverage syrups.

Lorna Tuck's mother, Stephen's grandmother, was a woman named Marie Elizabeth Fee. She was born in New York City in 1885. Her father, John Fee, was born in Rochester, New York, on January 31, 1848, and was one of four Fee brothers who are still the emblem of a thriving beverage-ingredient company in Rochester. In their time, the brothers made syrups, bitters, and flavorings for all kinds of drinks. They had two slogans (both of which I love): "The House of Fee by the Genesee since 1863" and "Don't Squeeze, Use Fee's." The company today is run by a man named John Fee. He is Marie's nephew and Stephen's first cousin once removed.

"I don't know much about the Fees," said Stephen. "I heard that at one point they also either made or distributed liquor but that it got drunk away. But this company survived, and these people are still alive and don't live that far from me. So if I've got that story wrong, I apologize. And I know Marie Fee was educated by the Ladies of Loreto, who are very hoity-toity French Canadian nuns. You had to be of means to be educated by them."

The Fee family company was started by the four sons of an Irish immigrant named Owen Fee. Owen was Stephen's great-great-grandfather. And according to the company history, he came to America from County Monaghan, Ireland, in the year 1835. Luckily for him, he got to Rochester at just the right time—and he had a very capable wife. Irish immigrants had begun coming to Rochester soon after the city was founded in 1817. By 1845, a third of the city's population was foreign born, and by 1860, in the wake of the Great Potato Famine, the Irish were the largest ethnic group. The Fees fit right into this growing community. By 1847, within twelve years of landing in America, Owen had started a butcher shop and become an American citizen. He died in 1855, but his wife, Margaret McMahon Fee, was able to keep the business running while raising five children on her own. By 1863, her eldest son, James, turned the butcher shop into a saloon and a delicatessen, making sandwiches and selling them to passengers at the train station. Margaret then mortgaged her house so that James could turn the saloon into a grocery and a liquor store. Stephen and I had talked a lot about the hardworking men in his family who built lives here, but in this case, I think we can attribute the Fees' success to a strong and determined immigrant female who did everything to give her children the best life possible.

Our efforts to find out about the origins of the Fee family in Ireland proved as unsuccessful as most of our other forays into the country. We could not locate any evidence of any Fees or McMahons in County Monaghan. It is a county which seemed very inhospitable to Irish Catholics. In 1834, a year before Owen Fee set off for America, 47 percent of the land was controlled by just ten British landlords, most of whom of course did not live in Ireland but in England. The people struggled to feed their families on tiny rented parcels of two acres or less. The county's only industry was linen weaving, and it had collapsed a few years earlier, leaving the small farmers with virtually no way to supplement their subsistence wages or meager incomes. We found a written account of the county by a visitor at the time. It states, "in no kingdom of the universe did so general an appearance of poverty and destitution prevail." So it's easy to understand why the Fee family left.

At this point, we had traced all Stephen's Irish Catholic lines back as far as we could, given the available records. There was, however, a surprise within one of the lines—and as it turns out, this was the line in Stephen's family that we could map out the furthest into the past, but it was neither Irish nor Catholic. Instead, moving back four generations along his paternal grandfather's line, we came to the wife of John J. Colbert, a woman named Susan Ann Fletcher. She was born in Virginia, most likely in 1827, and she came from an extremely old and well-documented family. We were able to trace her ancestry back to Stephen's sixth-great-grandfather Hans Peter Ledermann, who was baptized September 18, 1711, in Mattstall, a small town in the Rhineland, part of a region of Europe known as Alsace-Lorraine. It is French territory today, but over the centuries it's gone back and forth between France and various German states—and the Ledermanns were clearly German in language and culture. The baptismal record for Hans Peter shows that he was baptized as part of a German service in the Lutheran Church.

"Not only were they German; they were heretics!" joked Stephen. "Lutherans! I had no idea, no idea whatsoever. I thought if anything, you'd find French Huguenot at some point. No idea that there were any German Protestants back there." Ethnic diversity in one's family tree can assume many forms, it turns out.

Records showed that Hans Peter's parents, Stephen's seventh-great-grandparents, were Hans Diebold Ledermann and Anna Maria Engler, born in Alsace in 1685 and 1690, respectively. They are at the center of this family's immigration story. Hans Diebold was a weaver, a skilled artisan. He and his wife had eight children, although five of them didn't survive infancy. They grew up during a difficult time in the Rhineland, which was still recovering from the devastation of the Thirty Years' War—a conflict that began as a regional clash between Protestants and Catholics but turned into a wider war between the era's major European powers. The war had ended in 1648, but the famine and poverty that followed persisted for decades. The Rhineland remained a hotbed of religious and political fanatics in which people like the Ledermanns struggled to get by. Then someone came along, offering them a chance for something better. His name was William Penn, the founder of Pennsylvania, the very same person who played such an important role in the life of Meryl Streep's ancestors.

We found a pamphlet written by Penn in 1681. It was translated into German and Dutch soon after and circulated throughout the Rhineland. It reads, in part, "A plantation seems a fit place for those ingenuous spirits that being low in the world are much clogged and oppressed about a livelihood, for the means of subsisting being easy there, they may have time and opportunity to gratify their inclinations, and thereby improve science and help nurseries of people."

The "plantation" referred to in this pamphlet is, of course, in the Commonwealth of Pennsylvania, forty thousand square miles of land in America that William Penn had just received as payment for a debt that King Charles II owed him. Meryl Streep, as we saw in chapter 2, is descended from a cousin of William Penn's father, and there was a long friendship between her ancestor William Crispin and the Penn family. In fact, the Crispins were among Pennsylvania's first settlers. Stephen's ancestors came just a few years later. They almost certainly knew each other. Who could have imagined that a relative of Meryl Streep and a relative of Stephen Colbert might have known each other, some three hundred years ago? I find this astonishing, actually.

As a Quaker, William Penn declared his new land a haven of religious freedom, and this is how he is generally remembered by historians. Yet in the recruitment pamphlets he circulated throughout Germany, he spoke a very different language, telling prospective immigrants that Pennsylvania was a place where they could make money. The pamphlet is even quite specific about what kind of settlers Penn wanted—and they weren't religious people. They were workers. The pamphlet states, "These persons that providence seems to have most fitted for Plantations are first, industrious husbandmen and day laborers, that are hardly able with extreme labor to maintain their families and portion their children. Second, laborious handicrafts, especially carpenters, masons, smiths, weavers, tailors, shoemakers, shipwrights, et cetera, where they may be spared or are low in the world. And as they shall want no encouragement, so their labor is worth more there than here, and their provision cheaper."

The Ledermanns undoubtedly realized that Penn was offering them civil liberty and the chance of a better life if they moved to his colony, but more important, he was offering them work and the opportunity to own land, which these people had no prayer of ever obtaining in Europe. Pennsylvania had a system of indentured servitude similar to that employed by the colony of Virginia (and exploited by Elizabeth Alexander's ancestor John Batte). People who were unable to pay their own passage to the New World could indenture themselves, usually for a period of seven years. Penn's pamphlets promised that when the indenture was over, each settler would receive fifty acres of land. Given these terms, it's no wonder that by the time of Penn's death in 1718, hundreds of thousands of ethnic Germans had filed into ships bound for Philadelphia.

There was one major obstacle to their success. It is hard to believe today, but anti-immigrant sentiment was already powerful in America, well before it was even a country. And although it's especially difficult to imagine anyone trying to exclude Germans from coming to the United States, Benjamin Franklin himself railed against their settlements in Pennsylvania, writing, "Why should the Palatine Boers be suffered to swarm into our settlements, and by herding together establish their language and manners to the exclusion of ours? Why would Pennsylvania, founded by the English, become a colony of aliens, who will shortly be so numerous as to Germanize us instead of us Anglifying them, and will never adopt our language or customs, any more than they can acquire our complexion?"

Reading this, Stephen laughed. "I don't know why they didn't build a border wall around Pennsylvania to keep the German hombres out."

Franklin's phrase "Palatine Boers" was a reference to immigrants from the Rhine Valley who spoke Palatinate German. Most of the people we now call the Pennsylvania Dutch are descended from these Palatine Germans, including the Amish. Most of us will be quite surprised by this passage. Who could imagine that anyone at this time would be worrying over a supposed difference in the whiteness of the English and the whiteness of the Germans! And I was somewhat surprised that this kind of xenophobia was already prevalent before the Revolutionary War. Freud called nationalism the narcissism of minor differences. And Franklin shows how right Freud was. His words go beyond irrationality. To modern ears, they seem a bit mad.

"I remember," said Stephen, "I was in Vienna once. I was performing at a theater there, and we'd all go to a bar every day to have lunch. And we got to know these guys behind the counter. I was young, so we'd come back at night and drink with the bartenders, and we'd ask about their lives. They were Croats. It was during the Serbo-Croatian wars, and they would tell us the stories of what was happening in this conflict in former Yugoslavia. We'd be all tanked, and they'd say, 'We've got to go back. We've got to fight!' And we'd say, 'Tell us about these Serbs.' And they'd say, 'Well, first of all, they're stupid.' And 'Just look at the color of their skin: it's so dark.' That's when we knew it was time to get the check."

The deep suspicion of non-English-speaking immigrants led to the passage of a law in Pennsylvania in 1727 that required all men over the age of sixteen who were not British subjects to swear allegiance to the English monarchy upon landing in Philadelphia. The second ship to arrive after the passage of this law was a ship called the *James Goodwill,* and it docked in Philadelphia on September 27, 1727. The list of the men from that ship who signed that oath includes Hans Diebold Ledermann, Stephen's seventh-great-grandfather.

Women and children did not have to sign this oath, but from this list, we concluded that Stephen's sixth-great-grandfather Hans Peter didn't come with his parents; he stayed behind in Alsace. His parents and siblings settled in present-day Lancaster County, which is Amish country, about sixty-five miles west of Philadelphia. This was very fertile land, and the area was the destination of a constant stream of German settlers. And once Hans Diebold and Anna settled in, they thrived, despite the feelings of men like Franklin. They even had another child. Their youngest son, Johann Christian Ledermann, was born in the Heidelberg Township, Lancaster County, on August 27, 1730—when the couple must have been about forty years old each. At this point, after four years without his family, Hans Peter could resist no longer. He followed in his parents' footsteps, braving the three-month journey across Holland, England, and then the Atlantic and arriving in Philadelphia on the ship *Britannia* on September 21, 1731. We found his oath of allegiance, too. In it, he anglicized his name to Peter Leatherman. He then moved around the region until he married

Stephen's sixth-great-grandmother, a "Miss Thomas" of Stoney Lick Farm in Frederick County, Maryland.

"We've been here a long time," said Stephen. "It's hard not to respond to this as my character from the show, who wants to be more American than anybody."

Turning to his DNA testing, I passed Stephen a sheet of paper bearing the results of his admixture tests. It showed him to be 100 percent European, with no African or Asian ancestry. He is, as I told him to his amusement, the whitest person we have ever tested. "One hundred percent white man?" he said, laughing. "Okay. I can handle that. Fully committed."

Stephen's mitochondrial haplogroup is called T1a. The Family Tree DNA database shows people with exactly the same mitochondrial DNA living today in Ireland and Germany. In Ireland, these included both low-resolution and high-resolution matches; whereas in Germany, there are only low-resolution matches. This illustrates what we already knew: Stephen is Irish and German. He has strong connections with both those countries, and we could see that from his family tree. His Y-DNA is from the haplogroup called R1b1b2a1a2f, and it yielded both low- and high-resolution matches with people in just one place: Ireland.

When we ran his autosomal test with the Broad Institute, we found, as we saw earlier, that Stephen shares DNA on chromosome 2 with the African American poet Elizabeth Alexander. They match from base pair 160 to base pair 168, which translates into eight million base pairs. "Gosh, that's fantastic," said Stephen. "We are cousins! She was a guest on my show. We had a fantastic time."

I explained to Stephen that Elizabeth is 66 percent European, with English, German, and Irish matches very similar to his own. "That is wonderful news. The woman who read the poem at Barack Obama's inauguration is my cousin?"

Stephen was also excited to learn that he shares DNA on chromosome 5 with Her Majesty, Queen Noor of Jordan, and on chromosome 1 with Meryl Streep. "I had the Queen on my show," he said. "I brought a sword, and she knighted me. And Meryl? Once again, all three of these people have been guests on my show. I've been interviewing family."

As we said goodbye, I asked Stephen if the knowledge he'd gained had altered the way he felt about his identity. He nodded vigorously. "I think of my identity as the people I know," he replied. "And the people who I know were my parents, not their parents and their parents. I didn't have this awareness of the branches of a tree that come down around me. And what's very interesting is that, you know, it's like the branches of a willow tree—they come all the way around me, and I feel surrounded by other people now."

I told him I thought that was a beautiful way to put it. He replied, graciously, "Well, it's a beautiful thing to learn." And I closed by asking him why it mattered. What difference does it make who our ancestors were or what they did? I, of course, have my own thoughts on this matter, but I wanted to hear his.

"I knew so little about all these people," he said. "And it's so great to know what they went through so that I should exist. It changes my view of American history—and my feelings as an American. You look back at your ancestors, and you see their part in American history, or at least their small part in American history, and how they came over. It changes what it means to be an American. The most moving thing to me was to see the certificate of citizenship that we read. It completely took me by surprise. I couldn't get through reading it."

He thought more about why it had affected him so much. "I don't know whether it was because of what the family had gone through to get to that point or what happened to them in the old country, but there was a sense of hope that it conveys. I take my citizenship for granted. I think of myself as an American genetically. But I'm not. I'm those people genetically. To see someone become American by choice . . . Since I never had to make the choice to be an American, I don't know whether I would have taken a risk like these people or whether I would have stayed, like Edward Tuck, and farmed someone else's land my whole life—stayed learned but landless. That chance those people took: that family came here and changed their lives, became Americans, and became a thing which is a huge part of my identity. I didn't expect to be so moved by that."

I didn't expect to be so moved either. But I was. Despite all the dead ends and lost records and question marks—or perhaps because of them —I was deeply moved by Stephen Colbert's family's story and by his reaction to rediscovering these compelling shades from his collective ancestral past.

11

Kristi Yamaguchi

1971

THE FIGURE SKATER Kristi Yamaguchi captured America's imagination in the late 1980s and early 1990s, winning victory after victory on the international stage, culminating in an Olympic gold medal in 1992. Since then, she has had a celebrated professional career and become an active philanthropist. I asked her to participate in this project after learning that her stunning achievements stood in stark contrast to the racial prejudice that had followed her family down through the generations. Both of her parents were imprisoned in Japanese internment camps as children. Three of her four grandparents spent time in the camps as well. It was, I thought, a remarkable American story. And I had barely scratched its surface.

When we first met, I was immediately impressed with the way in which Kristi chose to put her success into historical perspective. She trained countless hours, many of them alone, to win her gold medal. But when she spoke about the experience, she spoke of her pride in winning for all Japanese Americans and of her ancestors who paid a heavy price just to live in this country. She is intensely grateful to them, and as we began to explore their stories, I realized that this gratitude was extremely well deserved.

Kristi Tsuya Yamaguchi was born on July 12, 1971, in Hayward, California, the second daughter of Suyato Jimmie Yamaguchi (called "Jim" by the family) and Carole Doi. Her father, Jim, was born on July 12, 1937, in Santa Clara, California, and was one of nine children raised by Tatsuichi Yamaguchi and Tsuya Ito Tanabe. His parents were hardworking immigrant farmers who were trying to build a life for themselves in an America that was just emerging from the Depression. By early 1941, the family owned and operated a strawberry farm in Gilroy, California. Everyone was involved in the working the fields, even four-year-old Jim, and the days were long and onerous. But the Yamaguchis were gaining a foothold in this country. Unfortunately, their lives were about to take a devastating turn for the worse.

Kristi as a girl in Hayward, California. (Used by permission of the Yamaguchi family)

The attack on Pearl Harbor generated a nearly instantaneous outpour-
ing of anti-Japanese and anti–Japanese American anger, as well as a host of
wild rumors. There were stories about Japanese workers in the Hawaiian
pineapple fields carving arrows into their fields to direct the Japanese pilots
toward Pearl Harbor, stories that some of the planes were actually piloted
by Japanese Americans and that a pilot who was shot down had an American high school ring on his finger. Newspapers and tabloids—always ready
vehicles for anti-immigrant sentiment—filled with crude stereotypes,
showing Japanese Americans as part of a faceless Asian horde, inhumanly
disciplined, unfathomably treacherous. There was no basis to any of these
stories, but America was at war, and panic prevailed. Pearl Harbor was attacked on December 7, 1941. Just two months later, President Franklin
Roosevelt signed Executive Order 9066, which allowed the roundup and
incarceration of people of Japanese descent in the name of "military necessity." Without public hearings or formal charges, the federal government
had reclassified all Japanese Americans as "enemy aliens."

It was one of the most shameful acts in our nation's history. Over
120,000 people of Japanese descent—most of them loyal American citizens
—were detained in makeshift concentration camps known as relocation

Kristi's father, Suyato Jimmie Yamaguchi (*right*), with his mother, Tsuya Ito, and his siblings, on the family's farm in Santa Clara, California, just prior to World War II. (Used by permission of the Yamaguchi family)

centers. Half were children. The Yamaguchis were sent first to a temporary assembly center in Salinas, where families crowded into the stables of a fairground. Then, along with about thirty-five hundred others, they were sent to a camp called Poston, situated on a Native American reservation in the middle of the Arizona desert. When they arrived in July 1942, temperatures were as high as 120 degrees.

Jim was only five years old when he entered Poston. He spent the next three years of his life in the camp but rarely spoke about it with his children. "We really had to pry information out of him," said Kristi. "He just didn't want to talk about it. He'd always use an excuse: 'Oh, I was so young, I don't remember very much, just the dust and being hot a lot.' I do remember him saying how his family shared a horse stall with another family on their way to Poston. But that was about it. And, you know, I think it's kind of surreal for us to imagine that lifestyle."

We spoke with Jim Yamaguchi in the summer of 2009. He told us he has vivid memories of the camp that have never left him. "I remember ants," he said. "They used to hurt when they stung. They were everywhere.

I remember always looking out for scorpions and snakes, rattlesnakes especially. I remember horrific dust storms that got into the barracks, and it was not pleasant. Each barrack was a hundred foot long. We had ten people in our family, so I think we got two sections. There were no internal walls: no modesty, no privacy. The dust would penetrate every nook and crack. It never should have happened. It was not just."

Jim said that he did not often talk about the camp with his children for the obvious reason: it was painful even to think about it. I understand this. A lot of African Americans refused to talk about slavery, even though it was a shared experience. Not talking about all that pain was thought to be a way to erase it, to make it go away. And if you're a member of my generation, born in the 1950s, you most likely grew up, as I did, in a house with parents who *never* talked about it all—because they had a very close connection to slavery, usually to a grandparent who had been a slave. (Both of my father's grandparents were born in slavery, and he knew them well.)

Newspaper headlines in California following the signing of Executive Order 9066, which allowed the roundup and incarceration of people of Japanese descent in the name of "military necessity." (Used by permission of the Library of Congress)

It was as if they thought that by being silent, they could make the past go away, as well as its shame. I think that phenomenon is similar to what many Japanese Americans experienced.

While Kristi's father Jim was growing up in Poston, her mother, Carole Doi, was born in another "relocation center" hundreds of miles north in Granada, Colorado, a place called Camp Amache. Her parents were George Doi and Kathleen Yoshiko Doi. We found an article about her birth in a newspaper called the *Granada Pioneer*, the camp's newspaper. It reads, in part, "To Sergeant and Mrs. George Doi of 11K-8F went the honor of receiving the only visit made by Dr. Stork in Amache on New Year's Day. This well known, long-legged deliverer of bundles of joy presented the Dois with a baby girl. Miss 1945 of Amache."

As the writer of this article indicates, Kristi's mother, Carole, was the first baby born in Camp Amache in 1945. She was also one of almost six thousand children born behind barbed wire during the war. What's truly incredible, however, is something the article only hints at: while Carole's mother, Kathleen, was giving birth to her in the camp, her father, George Doi, was serving as a sergeant in the American military! This was absolutely shocking to me. But it turns out it was not uncommon. During the war, almost thirty thousand Japanese Americans served in the American armed forces—as their wives, parents, siblings, and children languished in internment camps. What's more, these thirty thousand Japanese American soldiers served with great distinction. They were among the most decorated soldiers in the entire war. They won almost ten thousand Purple Hearts, five thousand Bronze Stars, Silver Stars, and Distinguished Service Crosses, and twenty-one Medals of Honor, while 120,000 of their friends and relatives were imprisoned by the nation they were fighting for. As President Bill Clinton said many years later, "Rarely has a nation been so well served by people it has so ill treated."

Kristi's family found itself on all sides of this equation. Her grandfather Sergeant George Doi embodied the bravery and talent shown by so many Japanese American soldiers. "I think it shows their loyalty," said Kristi. "They really wanted to show the country that, despite the fact that their families were basically incarcerated at home, they were willing to go and fight in the war and prove their American citizenship. And, you know, we're so proud of what my grandfather did over there."

I asked Kristi if the facts of her grandparents' lives made her angry. "I think it's hard," she replied, thoughtfully. "The third, fourth generation now say, 'Hey, we need to get the story out there. You don't want to see a repeat

Kristi's maternal grandmother, Kathleen Doi, and grandfather, George Doi, who served in the U.S. Army's 100th Infantry Division, fighting across Europe while his family was interned in a concentration camp in Granada, Colorado. (Used by permission of the Yamaguchi family)

of that history.' I don't think it would happen again, but I think there are a lot of amazing stories in this era of history, and success stories too—things that they should really be proud of."

More than anything, Kristi said, she feels intense love for her grandfather George Doi. She grew up knowing him well, and she considers him a hero. "I used to stand on his feet," she said. "That's how we'd dance around at weddings. They lived in southern California, and we were based in northern California, but we would go down in the summers and every Christmas, and we were very close with them. And he and my grandma were my biggest fans too as I grew up skating."

I showed Kristi a photograph of George in his army uniform. He looks like a very handsome man—with sunglasses, a wry smile, and as Kristi pointed out, an excellent physique. "Look at his biceps!" she said, laughing. "He was always really toned and ripped and could still do pushups and chinups. He was a fun, fun grandpa—I remember him as just being fun and joking, playing around with us. He had the crewcut still, and he liked when we massaged his head. When he had to, he could be tough, and we could see that—but he raised three great children, and we all loved him."

George Doi was, by all accounts, a lively, gregarious man. He lived well into his seventies, surrounded by a loving family. He told a great number of stories and is well remembered by all who knew him. But he never spoke about the war. "I think he saw a lot of things," said Kristi. "As a child we would be at their home, and at night we could hear him having nightmares. And as kids we thought it was funny—'Grandpa's making noise.' As I got older, I realized I can't imagine what he had been through. I'm sure there were a lot of things that he probably didn't want us to know."

Our research showed that George's experience in the army was even more daunting than Kristi or I had thought. Most American-born Japanese served in the segregated all-Japanese American 442nd Regimental Combat Team. George, however, was assigned to the 100th Infantry Division as part of the Quartermasters Company. He was the only Japanese American in his unit. He had dozens of relatives in the relocation centers, and he was on the front lines of Europe, fighting alongside the people who had imprisoned his kin. Kristi and I both marveled at the pressure he must have endured.

"I can't imagine," said Kristi. "During that time there must have been people who were wary about his loyalty and subjected him to prejudice, stereotyping. I'm sure there was a lot of pressure to go above and beyond your duties because you had that obligation. I'm sure he felt it."

Given the powerful anti-Japanese sentiment of those years, I wondered how George ended up in this all-white unit. The story proved to be quite interesting. Kristi's grandfather joined the U.S. Army in September 1941, three months before Pearl Harbor. He did so, curiously enough, only because he was substituting for his brother, Frank. Frank got drafted in September, but he had already scheduled his marriage, ironically, on December 7, 1941, the very day that Pearl Harbor was bombed! So George volunteered with exceptional generosity to take his brother's place in the army and was assigned to the 100th Infantry Division.

George had almost completed his basic training when Japanese Americans were reclassified as enemy aliens. Because of this reclassification, he was sent back through basic training over and over again while the army tried to figure out what to do with him. He spent almost three years in a kind of limbo until finally, in October 1944, he was assigned to Europe with the 100th Infantry. We don't know why the army ultimately chose to act. Whether it realized something about George's character or whether it just desperately needed men for combat—or some combination of the two—there is just no way to tell. Regardless, George was thrown into some of the most brutal fighting in the war. His division penetrated the heavily defended Vosges Mountains in France. They faced Hitler's brutal offensive Operation North Wind in January 1945. They went on to liberate over four hundred cities, towns, and villages on their long, hard march into Germany. And when it was over, George was promoted to lieutenant.

We found an article from the *New York Times* entitled "Nisei Is Promoted." It concerns George. ("Nisei" refers to second-generation immigrants but was used as a general synonym for Japanese Americans.) The writer states that Lieutenant Doi, thirty years old and five feet four, was "unquestionably the company's best soldier." Those words were written just a few months after George's first child, Kristi's mother, was born in the concentration camp in Amache, Colorado. Kristi cried when she read it.

"From what I knew of him," Kristi said, "I don't think he ever wavered in his patriotism. He was a proud man, and I think one thing that probably helped is just having a vision of life in the future for his family. Knowing that hopefully the war wouldn't last much longer and that life after the war would be a lot different for future generations of Japanese Americans —that's probably what kept him going. The sacrifices made by Japanese American soldiers did, I think, lead to greater acceptance."

Kristi is unquestionably correct. But still, it is hard to imagine the inner turmoil George Doi must have endured. We both marveled at the nobility of his actions.

Turning back to Kristi's father's side of the family, the Yamaguchis, we began to explore an equally moving story about another ancestor of hers —a man who died in obscurity long before she was born but who nonetheless did as much as George Doi to lay the groundwork for her success. In a way, Kristi's tale is the tale of two grandfathers.

Jim Yamaguchi's parents were Tatsuichi Yamaguchi, born April 24, 1879, in Ureshino, Japan, and Tsuya Ito Tanabe, born December 28, 1895, in Kumamoto, Japan. When Kristi's father was born, his father, Tatsuichi, was fifty-eight years old. He died in California in 1958 when Jim was just eighteen. Kristi never met him, and her father knew surprisingly little about his origins when we talked to him. But we were able to reconstruct his story—and it is as inspiring as any story I encountered during the course of this project.

We found a passenger list from the Japanese Diplomatic Records Office showing that Tatsuichi Yamaguchi, a twenty-one-year-old farmer, left his hometown in Japan for Hawaii on November 16, 1899, under a labor permit. Tatsuichi had signed a three-year contract with the Onomea Sugar Company on the big island of Hawaii, near Hilo. At that time, Hawaii was about to become a territory of the United States, and it was dominated by vast sugar plantations owned by American companies. These plantations required huge numbers of workers. Most had been running for at least twenty years, and during those years, the indigenous population of Hawaii had been decimated by the diseases introduced by foreigners. Labor had to come from abroad. At first, it was obtained from China, but after the United States passed what is known as the Chinese Exclusion Act in 1882, the Kingdom of Hawaii soon instituted its own restrictions on Chinese immigration. Suddenly, Japanese workers were welcome and desired.

This was a new phenomenon in Japan. Before the mid-nineteenth century, the Japanese government had never allowed its citizens to emigrate for labor and had, in fact, forbidden contact with the West altogether. But starting in 1868, a chain of events called the Meiji Revolution set in motion a process of rapid modernization which led to massive social and political change. From the year 1886 on, Japanese citizens were permitted to seek employment abroad. However, it was often easier said than done. In the Saga prefecture, where Tatsuichi Yamaguchi lived, hundreds applied for the emigration program, but the local government refused them permission to leave, citing reports about the difficulties of Japanese workers abroad and the poor treatment and racism they were often forced to endure.

"Hawaii Fever," as it was called, nonetheless exerted a powerful attraction, especially for younger sons of large families, because they could never expect to inherit their family's farm. And eventually the local government began to relent. In 1899, 130 people from the Saga prefecture applied to emigrate to Hawaii, and 57 were granted permission to go. They set sail in November of that year. Kristi's grandfather was among these pioneers.

"That's crazy," said Kristi, "to leave behind family and your home and everything. It's fascinating to think about what gives immigrants the courage to do it. I feel so lucky, like I've had such a sheltered life."

Tatsuichi was the fourth son in his family. He had no hope of inheriting any land in Japan. It was a calculated risk.

In the 1900 Hawaiian Island census, Tatsuichi is listed as living near Hilo with two other laborers in a ramshackle lodging. He was earning fifteen dollars a month for working twelve-hour days, six days a week, in the blazing sun, cutting and processing sugar cane. Conditions were extremely harsh. The plantations employed thousands of contract laborers, who were stratified and regulated by ethnicity and treated much like slaves. A "luna," or boss, usually a white man, rode through the cane fields on horseback, wielding a whip to keep order.

We found the lyrics to work songs that the Japanese laborers used to sing. One of them pretty much says it all: "Wonderful Hawaii, or so I heard. One look and it seems like Hell. The manager's the Devil, and his luna are demons."

Not surprisingly, many Japanese workers returned home when their contracts ended. But the more adventurous, like Kristi's grandfather, set out for California, where other opportunities beckoned. In the 1910 U.S. census for Sacramento, Tatsuichi is listed as living in a rooming house on a street known as "Japanese Alley," working as a farm laborer.

Conditions were better in California than they had been in Hawaii, but they were by no means ideal. Men like Tatsuichi who came from farming families in southern Japan had experience and skills that were well suited to the labor-intensive farming of Sacramento and Santa Clara counties. They quickly discovered a paradox, however. While their labor was welcome, they themselves were not. Asians as a whole were deemed to be aliens ineligible for citizenship. They were confined to the class of perpetual foreigners and were themselves the target of all forms of racism. Japanese immigrants were new to this scene in the twentieth century, but as they became more numerous, anti-Japanese sentiment spread, and the Unites States and Japan negotiated the so-called Gentlemen's Agreement of 1907, which effectively ended the immigration of Japanese men to the United States. The agreement did allow for the unification of families, however. So from 1908 on, many women came from Japan as the wives of workers who were already here.

Despite this climate of overt racism, by 1917, Kristi's grandfather was doing well enough and felt that his opportunities were sufficiently good that he could travel home and bring back a wife, Tsusa Shimomura. Records show that the following year, the couple was living in Cupertino, California, and had had their first child, a daughter. A second daughter was born in 1920. Because they were born in the United States, these girls were American citizens. The family, it seemed, was following a classic immigrant trajectory. Then, in 1922, tragedy struck. In June, both daughters died within a few days of each other. In October, Tsusa gave birth to another child, a son, who died within days. Tsusa herself passed away in November. They all died from illness—although the records do not indicate what kind of illness. Tatsuichi was now alone, having lost his entire family in just a few months.

"It's amazing," Kristi said. "He had worked so hard to bring them to California. I can't imagine the heartbreak, just the emotional collapse. It's devastating. I can't imagine how you would move on from there."

I can't imagine it either. But Tatsuichi moved on. Despite his personal tragedies, he didn't give up. As a Japanese immigrant, he had very few rights. Although he had been living and working in the United States now for a quarter of a century, he was still classified as an alien ineligible for citizenship. He could have returned to Japan, but he did not. He chose to remain in America and rebuild his life. We found the complaint from a court case called "T. Yamaguchi vs. J. G. Shaw Company." The case was filed on April 14, 1925. In it, Tatsuichi pursued a certain J. G. Shaw, a fruit buyer, for an unpaid bond of $1,616. Despite Tatsuichi's uncertain status in America, he had enough faith in this country's system of justice to take his case to court. And he won. He was vindicated. The court ruled in his favor and made the fruit buyers pay their debt. Then, two years later, in 1927, Tatsuichi got married again, this time to a beautiful widow with three young children: Kristi's grandmother and namesake, Tsuya Ito Tanabe. She had come to California from Kumamoto prefecture with her first husband.

Tatsuichi and Tsuya went on to have six more children together, including Kristi's father, Jim. By 1941, the family was farming on 175 acres, earning enough to support themselves. The war changed everything, of course. When Tatsuichi and Tsuya were sent to the camps, all that they brought with them was what they could carry on their backs. They lost the farm and all their other possessions. And on August 7, 1945, the day after America dropped the atomic bomb on Hiroshima, the authorities at Poston interviewed Tatsuichi about his plans for relocation after the war. We found the notes taken by his interviewer, and they are chilling. They read, in part, "Mr. Y is 67 years old and questions his own employability. There are eight children, all at home, of whom three are employable. He states they have absolutely no resources and will need resettlement assistance."

Soon after the interview, Tatsuichi was given employment and as-signed to what was called "family housing" at the Santa Maria Berry Farms. According to Jim, the housing amounted to tents set up in a parking lot. Worse yet, after decades of running his own farm, Tatsuichi had to return to back-breaking manual labor—picking strawberries for a large, white-owned farm. "I don't know how he survived," said Kristi, "how not to have your spirit crushed by that: knowing that you've worked so hard, had a life, had it taken away, and now you have to face starting over again at that age."

Kristi remembers that when she was growing up her father would sometimes talk about farming as a young boy with his father and siblings in Santa Maria. "I remember stories of how before and after school they'd be in the fields picking strawberries. My father never really complained too much about it. But I know that he decided, 'Hey, this isn't what I'm going to do for the rest of my life.' I think it inspired him to go to dental school."

Tatsuichi did not have the option to do anything else with his life—all he knew was farming. But he refused to be broken by his experience. He worked as hard after the war as he had before it, toiling endlessly in the fields to give his family a better life. And he endured, paving the way for his children's and his grandchildren's success. Remarkably, on December 17, 1954, at the age of seventy-five, he became a citizen of the United States. By that date, Tatsuichi Yamaguchi had been in America for fifty-five years. For fifty-three of those years, he had been classified as an alien ineligible for citizenship. But in December 1952, the U.S. Congress passed the McCarran-Walter Act, which allowed Japanese immigrants finally to become naturalized citizens. And despite everything Tatsuichi had lived through, as soon as the law was passed, he immediately applied for citizenship. He died four years later on May 10, 1958, a seventy-nine-year-old American. "He really laid the foundation for our family," said Kristi. "He went through it all. Either he was running from something in Japan, or he just saw a future here for his family. Doesn't matter—he did it."

Tatsuichi's wife, Tsuya Yamaguchi, never applied for citizenship. She outlived her husband by seven years, dying peacefully in 1965, but she never saw the need to become an American citizen. "I didn't know that," said Kristi. "But I think it's great that he wanted it and got it. I'm sure he felt he earned it, that he had put his time in and paid his debt, so he deserves to have that stamp of approval. I think I wouldn't be here probably if he hadn't done that."

After everything we had learned about Tatsuichi Yamaguchi, I really wanted to know where he came from and why he left. So our researchers

Naturalization papers signed by Kristi's paternal grandfather, Tatsuichi Yamaguchi, on December 17, 1954. At that time, Tatsuichi was seventy-five years old and had lived in America for fifty-five of those years. (Public domain)

went searching for the records of the Yamaguchi family in Japan. It was very challenging to find them. We had no luck at all until we encountered, by chance, a man named Kenji Yamaguchi. He turned out to be Kristi's father's cousin, although the two had never met and did not know of each other's existence.

Kenji was born in 1936 in the town of Ureshino in Saga prefecture, and he lived there until he died in 2009. His grandfather Sahachi Yamaguchi was Tatsuichi's older brother. He told us that although he never met Tatsuichi, he grew up hearing stories about this uncle who had gone to America. Kenji said that Tatsuichi was a legendary figure in the family—the rebel who went away. His relatives even kept a photo of him—a photo that he had mailed to his mother in 1911—displayed in their home for almost a century. "That's amazing," said Kristi, "that the family back in Japan has kept it all these years. Maybe it shows how close they were and how hard it was for him to leave and find a new life."

Kenji told us that everyone in his family thought that Tatsuichi had been a big success in America. At first, this seemed sadly ironic to me. Kenji's family, I thought, would have been shocked to learn how hard Tatsuichi struggled just to survive in this country. But then we learned about Kenji's experience in World War II. Kenji's father, Zenroku Yamaguchi, was in the Japanese navy. He died while serving off the coast of Japan in 1944. He was Kristi's great-uncle, and when he died, Kenji became his family's official head of household. Kenji was only eight years old, a boy living in a small town that was very close to Nagasaki and depended on Nagasaki as its port. The devastation of the war, especially the atomic bombing, made it extremely difficult, as we might imagine, for the Yamaguchis to survive. But in those difficult postwar years, Kenji and his family received aid from a most unexpected source: Tatsuichi, the rebel uncle. Although he was struggling to support his own family in Santa Maria, Tatsuichi sent boxes of food, clothing, and toys to his relatives back home in Japan. Kenji remembers receiving Hawaiian shirts and jeans from his mysterious relative. Nobody in Ureshino had ever seen anything like them before. Kristi was dumbfounded. "Again, there's the character of Tatsuichi, taking care of his family that he really didn't know back home. He's still thinking of them."

Kristi's relatives in Ureshino had no idea that her grandfather and his family had been sent to an internment camp. And though they say they never talked to people about their American relatives during the war, once the war was over, they felt proud of them. They still do today—all thanks to a farm laborer who left Japan in 1899. Kenji's wife remembers seeing Kristi skate for the Olympic gold medal, against a Japanese skater. "Had we known she was a relative," she said, "we would have rooted for her!" They rooted, of course, for the Japanese skater, Midori Ito.

"It's very complex," said Kristi. "So many lives going in different directions during a strange time in history. I don't know where to even go from there. Each man was probably doing what he believed in. Mind-boggling how it all ended up like this in my family tree."

We tried to learn more about Kristi's Yamaguchi ancestors, but the Japanese approach to genealogy made this almost impossible. As I explained to Kristi, the key family-history document in Japan is the koseki, a household register listing family members and facts about these family members. The koseki system started during the Meiji era, with the first national recording taking place in the year 1871. But koseki law requires the destruction of old documents eighty years after a person's death—so the records are not permanent. And since Tatsuichi's father, Kensuke Yamaguchi, died in 1894, his koseki, which might have listed his parents or other relatives, would have been destroyed in the year 1974.

"I am surprised by that," said Kristi. "I would think with the rich history they've had in Japan they would want to keep their records accessible, to let people know their roots and their heritage and more about the country itself. It's unfortunate that they have that law of destroying the records, but I know that Japanese are very private people and very concerned about family honor, so it's maybe to protect their family name."

Since we'd reached a dead end with civil records, we turned to the records of the local Buddhist temple. The temple Kristi's family belonged to was established in the year 1369, and it moved to its current location 650 years ago. We asked the head monk there what he knew about the family. And he found the record of Kristi's great-grandfather Kensuke's death from 1894, but he also reminded us why we might not ever be able to figure out the names of Kensuke's parents: most Japanese people didn't use surnames until the government required them to do so at the time of the Meiji Restoration. In earlier times, people were known, for example, as Tatsuichi from the mountain or Kensuke who has the shop, just as Jewish people and Turks, as we have seen in the family stories of Mike Nichols and Mehmet Oz, were known by only one name or simply as the "son of" their fathers.

I told Kristi that since her great-grandfather Kensuke Yamaguchi was born around the year 1835, he may be the person who chose to take the surname Yamaguchi, which the family has used ever since. We can't know for sure, though. The only other thing we could glean about Kensuke from the temple record was the Buddhist name he received after his death. These posthumous names are recorded in household altars as well as in the temple, replacing the name that the person has used during his or her lifetime. They often reflect what the priest, who knew the person well, thought really described that person's individual character. After Kristi's great-grandfather Kensuke died, he was given the name Kenonjijo—which means "warm," "voluntary," and "giving to others." "Sounds like he embraced everyone around him," said Kristi.

Unfortunately, I told her, that's where her family's paper trail ends. "I'm amazed that you found as much as you have," she said. "This was very cool. I think it was an honor to be given that name that he was given posthumously."

Turning to Kristi's DNA, I told her that our admixture test revealed that she is 100 percent Asian—with no African or European ancestry. This, of course, reflects what her genealogy told us. Her mitochondrial DNA revealed no exact matches in the Family Tree DNA database. I told her that there are several possible explanations for this. Perhaps not enough Japanese people have taken these genetic tests yet and are thus not well reflected in the existing databases. Or perhaps there aren't many people with her unique genetic signature. This could occur if an event such as a famine or plague wiped out many of her ancient ancestors.

The closest matches that came up on the databases were what are called two-step mutations with two people living today in China and one living in Japan. These are very distant matches. The most recent common ancestor Kristi shares with these people would have lived thousands of years ago. This, again, speaks to the rarity of her maternal genetic signature.

Her mitochondrial haplogroup, M8a, also reflects her uniqueness. Haplogroup M is one of two branches of the mitochondrial DNA tree that arose about sixty thousand years ago, soon after human beings first left Africa. Scientists believe it spread rapidly along the coast of the Indian Ocean, probably reaching the coasts of southeastern Asia within a few thousand years. (Some scientists have speculated that haplogroup M traveled eastward at least in part by sea, because the route it took would have required a number of substantial ocean passages.) The harsh Ice Age sixty thousand years ago would have made life away from the coast extremely difficult for these new migrants. But with climatic improvements over the millennia, people gradually carried haplogroup M inland. Kristi's subset of haplogroup M, 8a, is now found mostly in southern Siberia, Korea, and the northern Chinese provinces of Liaoning, Xinjiang, and Qinghai. It is thought to have arisen in the Altay Mountains of southern Siberia about eighteen thousand years ago. At that time the Ice Age would have made the area comparable to Arctic regions today. That's where Kristi's people come from—a land covered under snow and ice with vast stretches of tundra and subfreezing temperatures for much of the year. "Maybe that's why I ice skate?" Kristi joked. "I love the ice—it pulled me in." This geographic location may also be why her genetic signature is so rare. It would have been very difficult to survive those harsh conditions. Her ancient ancestors were the strong ones who made it.

Since Kristi's group is so rare, I was surprised when one of our researchers discovered that someone else had been discovered with this haplogroup signature. It isn't anybody from this project, but it is an interesting story. The first emperor of China was a man named Qin Shihuangdi. He is famous for constructing a huge city-sized mausoleum including statues of over seven thousand terracotta soldiers to stand guard over it (known today as the Terracotta Army). Construction on the mausoleum began in the year 246 BC and required an estimated seven hundred thousand workers. One legend says that the statues, each of which is unique, were based on real soldiers who were buried with the emperor to protect him in the next life. Another legend says that the workers who built the necropolis were killed when they completed the work, in order to maintain the project's secrecy because Qin Shihuangdi did not want his tomb plundered. There is no way to assess the validity of either of these legends, but in recent years, archaeologists have found ancient human skeletons near the site. These are probably the remains of workers who died during the construction. Scientists were able to extract some DNA from nineteen of these skeletons, and our researchers determined that one of these workers is in fact a cousin of Kristi's by virtue of belonging to her rare haplogroup: M8a. This person was alive in 246 BC—and Kristi shares a maternal ancestor with him.

"That's just unbelievable," said Kristi, "to think that by looking inside your cells today we can travel back thousands of years through time and find your ancestors at this ancient site. Something you can't even see can tell so much."

Since Kristi's father, Jim, is alive, we were able to test his Y-DNA and learn about her direct paternal ancestry. His haplogroup, and that of the entire Yamaguchi clan, is called O3a. It is a branch of haplogroup O, the dominant haplogroup in eastern Asia. O3 appears to have originated about thirty thousand years ago in southeastern Asia and spread northward toward China and throughout China shortly afterward. It's the most common haplogroup among the Han Chinese; it is found in more than 50 percent of all Han Chinese men. It's found at similarly high frequencies among many other ethnic groups within China. And although O3 becomes less frequent as one moves further north or further south from central China, it's still quite common in other eastern Asian populations, reaching about 40 percent among Manchurian, Korean, and Vietnamese men, 35 percent among Filipinos and Malaysians, and about 20 percent among the Japanese. So, as I explained to Kristi, about 20 percent of the people in Japan are her very distant cousins.

"It makes you think further down through your life," said Kristi, "and through history. You think of the people you know, your grandparents and maybe your great-grandparents, but not much beyond that. It makes you realize that you are connected to all these people, more than you realize."

As we said goodbye, I think Kristi and I were both still stunned by the stories of her grandparents. They had all lived through such terrible hardship, and yet their will to survive—indeed, to thrive—was so deeply ennobling and inspiring. They evinced such contradictory emotions in me: awe and outrage. I couldn't find the words to describe my feelings. Kristi could.

"It reinforces the pride I have in being Japanese American," she said, "in both: Japanese and American. Because I think I will always respect and love and honor my Japanese heritage, but in the same breath, I'm very proud to be American. I've lived the American dream, and I know my family has gone through so much to establish a life here. And I've been the result of that hard work and those hardships. I'm hoping my children will continue on and appreciate this."

12

Eva Longoria

1975

EVA LONGORIA BECAME a household name when she was cast on the hit television show *Desperate Housewives* in 2004. Since then, she's built a remarkable career in Hollywood, all the while donating her time, money, and image to a host of worthy Latino causes. I asked her to participate in this series in no small part because I admire her for this. When she moved to Hollywood in the late 1990s, she was a very young woman, in her early twenties. She was trying to get work, and she could have done what countless other actors have done: pass as European—as Spanish or Italian. She declined to do that. Instead, she embraced her Mexican American roots at a point when there were virtually no well-known Latino actors or stars.

I was thrilled when she agreed to participate, but I had no idea what our researchers would find in her family tree. As it turned out, she has one of the most fascinating and most deeply documented family histories in the whole project. Her ancestors actually arrived in North America even before the Pilgrims did! They settled in Texas before there was a Texas—or a Mexico, for that matter. Their story is deeply illustrative of the complex history of America's settlement, as well as of the way in which we all construct ourselves as fragments of that history.

Eva Jacqueline Longoria was born on March 15, 1975, in Corpus Christi, Texas, one of four children born to Enrique Longoria, Jr., and Ella Eva Mireles. Her parents were both Mexican Americans, and Eva told me she had never been the least troubled by questions of identity or race. She has always, she said, felt comfortable with who she was and where she lived. "My family really has a strong sense of where it came from," she said. "Where we grew up, it's predominantly Hispanic, and so I felt right at home. I always felt really connected to my culture, whether it was through language, through religion, through tradition. It was just the way we grew up. If people ask me what I am, I say I'm a 'Texican.' Many of us do. The

Eva with her father, Enrique Longoria, Jr., on the family's ranch in Encino, Texas. (Used by permission of the Longoria family)

Texicans are the indigenous native people that were here before anybody else except the Indians. We were here for a long time."

Eva's sense of stability and culture is tied to her family's ranch in Encino, Texas, which is located in the very southernmost part of the state, less than a hundred miles from the Rio Grande. The ranch sits on a rural road that for years was actually called Longoria Road, because it was entirely occupied by her relatives. Eva grew up spending a tremendous amount of time on this ranch, and the experience helped shape her identity. "It was such fun," she said, "especially as a kid. We had pigs and chickens and cows; we had a little deer that we raised. When I think about the ranch I just think of freedom. I actually get claustrophobic now when I'm in a city, because I grew up having land and having such an appreciation for land. My father is such a man of the land. He would take us hunting and camping and teach us how to find water and how to find north and how to find our way back—survival skills. That was just who we were."

As with many of the families that I researched over the course of this project, I found that the acquisition of land was crucial to the Longorias' ultimate prosperity. I had a professor in college named John Morton Blum who wrote a brilliant book, *The Promise of America*. I first read it over thirty years ago, and I still remember the experience. It changed the way I thought about history. I remember looking at the title and thinking that I knew what it was about. The promise of America, I thought, was freedom, equality. I was wrong. Blum said the promise of America was land and the right and the capacity to own it. And he was right—and this project has confirmed his thesis a thousand times over. In Europe, unless you were part of a tiny privileged class, you couldn't possibly own land. But if you came to America, and you worked diligently, there was lots of land around, though much of it, of course, was occupied by Native Americans. The settlement and cultivation of this land, and the removal of Native Americans from it, shaped our country's early history quite profoundly. And in Eva's family, as in many other families, the acquisition of land was a leitmotif, a precursor to success, a prerequisite for survival.

Eva is well aware of this fact. "My ancestors have been in the same land and the same area of Texas for many, many generations," she said proudly. "People say, 'What generation are you: first generation, second generation?' And I say we've never moved. We settled a long, long time ago on this land. There's a really huge misconception that if you're a Latino in America, you're an immigrant. That's not true."

Surprisingly, however, Eva had no idea how her family's land came to be owned by Longorias. "All I've known is it's been in my family forever," she said. "But I've never known when it entered the family and how." The answer lies deep in the past. To find it, we had to go back to Eva's great-great-great-great-grandfather Pedro Longoria, who was born in 1733, near Monterrey, in what is today Mexico and was then part of Spain's colonial empire. Pedro was from a farming family, one of many in the region, working communal land. In 1749, he and his parents joined a mission led by the explorer and soldier Jose de Escandon and headed north in search of land for themselves. Commissioned by the Spanish king, Ferdinand VI, this mission was a part of a longstanding Spanish effort to settle the area along the Gulf Coast in what later became northern Mexico and Texas, colonizing the Indian tribes that occupied these lands and keeping British and French colonists out of them.

Jose de Escandon offered anyone who would join him the promise of land grants from Ferdinand VI and exemption from taxes for ten years. It was, the settlers knew, a once-in-a-lifetime opportunity to improve their social status. When the mission left from the town of Sierralvo, Escandon had forty pioneer families with him, the Longorias among them, as well

Patent record in the files of the Texas Land Office memorializing the fact that in 1767 the Spanish Crown granted Eva's fourth-great-grandfather Pedro Longoria title to forty-five hundred acres in what is today Starr County, Texas. (Public domain)

as cattle, sheep, goats, and a stock of provisions. After a long, hazardous journey, the mission finally settled the area around the town of Camargo in the Tamaulipas territory, along the Rio Grande on what is now the border between Mexico and Texas. Pedro Longoria, together with his father and his brothers, then worked their cattle on communal lands surrounding Camargo for almost two decades. But as their herds grew, they needed more fields for grazing, and they wanted to own the property themselves, as per the original offer made to them when they joined the Escandon mission. They ended up taking extraordinary measures to get it.

We found documents showing that Pedro petitioned the king of Spain for the land that had been promised to his family by Escandon. And in 1767, the Crown granted his request, awarding Pedro title to forty-five hundred acres just north of the Rio Grande in what is today Starr County, Texas. We found the patent for this grant as well as a summary of it in the records of the Texas Land Office. The summary reads, in part, "Following the same course and the margin of the said river, they stretched the cord twenty one times which make one thousand and fifty Mexican varas

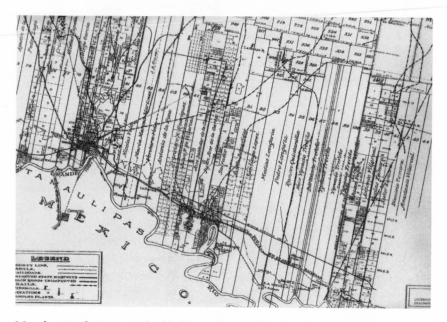

Map showing the Longoria land holdings along the Rio Grande that were granted to the family by Spain. (Public domain)

with so many more on the opposite headline and twenty five thousand in depth adjust a Porcion it was marked out and Pedro Longoria, an old settler petitioned for it as the son of a Primitive Colonist and it was adjudicated to him."

Eva had no idea that her family had been granted land by the Spanish Crown. "I thought we came and settled," she said. "I just thought it was yours if you were there first."

There is no indication that Pedro ever lived on his land. It seems that it was used primarily for cattle grazing, probably because it was in a very dangerous area. Native American tribes such as the Lipan Apache had hunted there for centuries and were fighting to keep it. The Spanish settlers were not yet numerous enough to subdue them. So Pedro Longoria and his descendants continued to live in Camargo, south of the Rio Grande, for another seventy years.

These seventy years were a time of tremendous political upheaval in the Spanish empire. Mexico became independent from Spain after the revolution of 1821, and then, in 1836, Texas won its own independence from Mexico. At some point in the turmoil, as Jim Bowie and Davy Crockett were getting ready to die in the Alamo, Pedro's grandson, Eva's third-great-grandfather Juan Santiago Longoria, moved across the Rio Grande and into the chaos of the new nation to set up residence on the land his grandfather had been granted by Spain. Juan was born in Camargo in 1808. He was twenty-eight years old when he crossed the river, and it is unlikely that he moved of his own accord. He was probably concerned that the family might actually lose the land to Anglo Texans and most likely wanted to establish settling rights.

Although Eva's family had been in what is now Mexico since 1603, Juan is her first American immigrant ancestor. He founded the town of La Grulla within his land grant and made sure that his family was not going to be dislodged anytime soon. He designed the town more like a fortress than a settlement, clearly worried about the violence that surrounded him. He and his siblings and cousins constructed houses and farm buildings hidden in the trees and shrubbery, and thick log fences were built around the yards. Armed men guarded the place day and night. Through a small peep hole in the fence, they could see anyone approaching.

These fears were well grounded. The area was still very dangerous. One of Juan's sons, Eugenio, was killed in 1870. According to oral history, he went riding on his horse to visit relatives and friends in Las Cuevitas and was not seen again. His family searched for him for weeks but never found him. Months later, his remains and those of his horse were discovered in the thick brush just off the trail near Penitas, Texas. The hand bones still had a gold ring with the initials E.L., identifying the remains as those of Eugenio. The skull of the horse had three bullet holes in it. The exact circumstances of Eugenio's death were never determined. We found his grave in the town cemetery in La Grulla.

We also discovered that there are actual buildings constructed by Eva's ancestors that still stand today in La Grulla. In fact, we were able to identify a house built in the early 1840s as the original Longoria homestead in the settlement. And the town's cemetery is filled with Longoria ancestors. There are even streets named after her relatives.

Juan Santiago lived through a remarkable period in history. Though he moved only once in his lifetime—from Camargo to La Grulla—because of the events that transformed his land, he lived under the rule of five different flags: Spain, Mexico, Texas, the Confederacy, and finally the flag of the United States. He preserved his family's property through revolution, the Civil War, Indian attacks, and a host of other dangers.

"It's very frustrating," Eva said. "I remember studying Texas history, studying the Alamo, and not seeing the Hispanic stories. I'd rather it not be in a history book unless you're going to put it in right. You can only know history through these stories and through these families."

She's right, of course. People like Juan Longoria are not recorded alongside Davy Crockett in the history of Texas. But they were there— and they built towns and shaped the land. They suffered, triumphed, and endured.

Juan's son, Ponciano Longoria, was born in July 1852 in La Grulla, Texas. He is Eva's great-great-grandfather and the first member of her family to be born in America. He married a woman named Maria Rita Villa-rreal, and by combining his assets with an inheritance from her family, he became a land baron of sorts and a Longoria family legend. We found census records and land documents related to Ponciano's many business dealings. They show that he bought and sold numerous parcels of land, including many owned by his in-laws, starting in 1884, growing the Longoria holdings out from the forty-five hundred acres around La Grulla to over thirteen thousand acres, primarily of grazing land but also including the ranch sites around Encino, Texas, where Eva spent so much of her childhood. The ranch that Eva's father grew up on, Santa Rita Ranch, was named in honor of Ponciano's wife, Maria. She was Eva's great-great-grandmother.

Ponciano and Maria raised six children in La Grulla. But he and his sons spent a great deal of time riding on horseback back and forth to remote ranches to tend to their cattle. This was still a very dangerous area in the late nineteenth century. The Apaches remained, and following the absorption of Texas into the United States in 1845 and accelerating at the end of the Civil War, a steady stream of white settlers began pouring in, hoping to lay claim to some of this vast land. By the late nineteenth century, conflicts between these new settlers and families like the Longorias were becoming increasingly frequent.

It was a classic confrontation between two very different cultures. The early Texas landholders like the Longorias were of Spanish and Mexican descent; they had dark skin, they were Catholic—all of which marked them as inferiors in the eyes of Anglo-Americans. They also had a developed technique of free-range cattle farming that required enormous tracts of open land. They never fenced in their cattle but rather allowed them to roam freely. The Anglo ranchers, by contrast, enclosed their livestock and had very little respect for the land claims of the Spanish and Mexican people they found in their way. And they brought with them three things that made life very difficult for Eva's ancestors: barbed wire, lawyers, and

Painting of Eva's great-great-grandparents Ponciano Longoria and
Maria Rita Villarreal. (Used by permission of the Longoria family)

a vigilante group known as the Texas Rangers. The Rangers today are celebrated as frontier lawmen who bravely provided stability and justice in a
wild, lawless corner of America. The reality is quite different. The Rangers evolved into lawmen over the course of their long history. When they
started out in the 1830s, and for much of the nineteenth century, they
were essentially hired guns, enforcers, working for the Anglo settlers who
were trying to take the land of people like the Longoria family. The Anglos
used barbed wire to build fences around the land, claiming whatever parcels they wanted for themselves. If they encountered resistance, they had
their lawyers figure out a way to take the land through the Texas courts.

Failing that, they had the Texas Rangers there to settle the argument on their behalf.

We found the graves of several of Eva's distant relatives testifying to the intensity of this conflict, including the grave of a man named Antonio Longoria, who was killed by a band of Texas Rangers. His body was buried along the road, where it still lies today.

"I've never heard that story," said Eva, saddened, "at least not that specific story. But there's always been animosity between the ranchers and all the Mexicans, not just Longorias but any Mexicans in south Texas. If you had a fence sign, the ranchers moved it. I remember my grandmother telling me stories that Ponciano would put guards at corners of the fencing so that they wouldn't come and move it."

Eva's great-great-grandfather Ponciano successfully navigated this conflict for more than forty years, maintaining the better part of his land, expanding it wherever possible, building ranches, and amassing a small amount of wealth. He was not rich by any means, but his family endured in the face of the massive influx of Anglo settlers. In the end, however, he paid the ultimate price for his stand. Sometime in 1913, Ponciano had an altercation with one of the ranch hands at the King Ranch, an Anglo-owned ranch on the border of his property near Encino. Ponciano was stabbed in the fight. He died of his wounds the following year. He was sixty-five years old.

Ponciano's wife, Maria, survived him by sixteen years, dying peacefully in 1929. In 1925, she divided up their land among their children—giving them roughly two hundred acres each. The three male children, including Mateo Longoria, Eva's great-grandfather, built homes on this land, and it has remained in the family ever since.

We interviewed Eva's Aunt Irma, who still lives on the family ranch in Encino. She described her ancestors' experience, based on the many stories she had heard about their struggle, saying, "All they did was just survive on this land, because there was nothing much here, and they had to make a living. I'm very thankful for all they left us. I cherish all they left us. I never met Papa Ponciano, and my dad never met him, but to me he's alive. When I think of him, I think of him as Papa Ponciano, and I remember all the stories about him. I think *survival* is the word that we all need to tell ourselves. They survived."

We had now followed Eva's family from Mexico to America. But there was far more to their story. First, we were able to trace Eva's family back to her eleventh-great-grandfather, a man named Pedro de Longoria, who was

Eva's great-grandparents Mateo and Maria Sabina Longoria (*standing at left*) at the family's ranch in Encino, Texas. (Used by permission of the Longoria family)

born in 1525 in Asturias, Spain. And we were actually able to identify the first member of the Longoria family to set foot on the continent of North America. His name was Lorenzo Suarez De Longoria, and he is Eva's ninth-great-grandfather, born in Oviedo, Spain, around the year 1592. He immigrated to the New World when he was just eleven years old, traveling as the servant of his uncle, Pedro Longoria (not the same Pedro as Eva's eleventh-great-grandfather), who had been appointed the magistrate of Mexico by the Spanish Crown. The Longorias arrived in Vera Cruz in the summer of 1603, thus landing in North America seventeen years before the *Mayflower*! Today, our society tends to stereotype Mexicans as recent immigrants; Eva's family predates even the Pilgrims on this continent, forcing us to reconceive the way we think about the place of Mexico and Mexicans in the history of the New World.

We could not determine exactly why Lorenzo left Spain at such a young age. But we found an incredible story about his family in the Oviedo archives—a story that prefigures the Longoria experience in the New World and that may shed some light on Lorenzo's decision to emigrate. Sometime in 1593, when Lorenzo was just a year old, the family became embroiled in a legal battle with their neighbors in northern Spain. We don't often uncover lawsuits from the sixteenth century, so this was a very unusual find for us. It seems that Lorenzo's father and his brothers had confronted the family of Diego Suarez in order to keep them from harvesting on their land. There are different versions of what happened, but all the accounts indicate that there was violence. The two families essentially fought a battle using farm implements as weapons. According to the lawsuit documents, Suarez said that the Longorias came armed with heavy wooden staffs, reinforced with iron, and pitchforks and that Pedro Longoria, then a cleric in holy orders, led the attack, "telling my sons that by God, he would see them sent to row in prison ships." The lawsuit also alleges that Pedro called the Suarez daughters "wicked shameless whores" and that he struck them several times with a pole. "Well, we know where I got my Latin temper now," said Eva, laughing. "Nice, guys."

On November 16, 1593, the magistrate ordered all the Longoria men to be arrested and imprisoned. Before this order could be fulfilled, however, the Longorias were able to produce a deed from 1568 proving that the land was legally theirs. And so Eva's family was exonerated, and they were set free—despite the violence. And ten years later, Pedro the pole-swinging cleric was appointed a magistrate in New Spain. Eva laughed again. "This is a movie! These people are crazy."

The lawsuit tells us that land was very scarce, of course, in Spain and quite precious to Eva's family even then. It also helps us understand why her ancestor might have come to Mexico when he was just eleven years old: his family may have thought he would benefit from a fresh start.

At this point, Eva and I began to discuss the fact that although she identifies herself as Mexican—or Texican—her genealogy shows that her ancestors for the bulk of their history were considered Spanish. This, as I told her, resonates in the family even today. When our researchers interviewed her Aunt Irma, she talked about being Spanish and, quite frankly, was not at all interested in being identified as Mexican.

"That's funny," said Eva, "because I through and through feel Mexican, but obviously we wouldn't speak Spanish if it wasn't for the Spaniards. We wouldn't be Catholic if it wasn't for the Spaniards. We wouldn't have this mentality of land ownership if it wasn't for the mother country, and I get that. But honestly, when I go to Mexico, I feel at home. When I go to Spain, I feel a connection, but I feel more at home in Mexico—maybe just because it's closer and it's what I know. In my family, I am the one who claims Mexico ancestry the strongest. Every time they ask, 'Where are you from?' my dad says, 'Spain.' 'Dad, we're from Corpus Christi.' We're not from Spain; we're from Texas. He would always talk about our ancestors, and I never really understood that when I was younger. But now I feel very proud that my family is from Spain. I feel very proud that the Longoria name has been so strong and unchanged."

I then told Eva that the admixture test of her DNA supported our genealogical research and her father's view. She is 70 percent European, 27 percent Native American, and 3 percent African.

"That makes sense," she said. "I'm European. And that's how I define Mexican, as a European that conquered the natives. It's a little surprising, because I thought the percentages would be flipped. I mean, the Spanish conquistadors were the minority when they conquered and eventually overtook the society of Aztecs and Mayans. I guess I thought I would be a little more native, because, like I said, I feel closer to Mexico. But this makes sense."

Watching her response to these findings, I was struck by something that had occurred to me many times over the course of this project: almost all the subjects hoped to see more "ethnic" in their ethnic identities —more evidence of racial mixing in their personal pie chart, even the ones who were most mixed. European ancestry, in our world today, is not the source of pleasure and pride that it was even a few decades ago. The reasons for this are understandable and perhaps obvious, but it has been fascinating for me to see it unfold on such a personal level.

I asked Eva how she felt about seeing 3 percent African ancestry in her admixture. "I love it," she said. And she knew what it meant, too. Many people don't realize that Mexico had a large slave population early on in its colonial history, and that African presence is still quite alive in the area around Vera Cruz.

I then asked her how she felt about her large amount of European ancestry. "Well," she said, "it's complicated. If I had had to guess, I would have written 70 percent Native American indigenous to Mexico and 30 percent European. To know that I have Spanish blood in me—everyone knows that in Mexico—but a majority of Spanish blood . . . You know, I've been so proud of being Mexican, of coming from the indigenous native people."

Eva's mitochondrial DNA belongs to the haplogroup A2. I told her I thought this would make her happy. Haplogroup A2 reflects the human migration from Africa to Asia and then to the Americas. Scientists believe that fifteen to twenty thousand years ago, a small band of humans, including Eva's ancestors, crossed from Asia to North America on land bridges that are today buried under the ocean. Within a few thousand years, possibly even faster, people within this haplogroup migrated all the way down to the tip of South America. It is a common haplogroup among Native American peoples, and the fact that Eva belongs to it suggests that her earliest ancestors along her maternal line were Native Americans who at some point interbred with Europeans. "This is wonderful," said Eva. "Obviously for me that's the definition of Mexican."

I wanted to find out more about Eva's Native American ancestors, so I spoke with Dr. Mark Shriver at Penn State University. He is a leading anthropological geneticist, and he compared Eva's DNA to that of other indigenous populations. The results show that she is more closely related to the Mayans than to any other indigenous group. "Really?" she said, delighted. "I love the Mayans. Smartest civilization of their time. They created the number zero, created our modern-day calendar."

Eva then told me she had a question for me, something that had been haunting her for as long as she could remember. "I want to know," she said, "my ancestors who came from Spain, did we enslave any Indians? We obviously bred with them. But did we mistreat anybody along the way? I'm really concerned about the native population and what my family had to do with that, as a Longoria, because I have sympathy for the oppression of the indigenous people of Mexico. I've studied their journey and their enslavement; I do so much advocacy for the Mexican American community today because there's still so much injustice done towards them. To this day I feel it's my responsibility to help."

I told her, without knowing any details, that the answer to her question was undoubtedly yes. The Spaniards destroyed the native populations they found just as the English and French did. But, of course, as I told her, this kind of oppression is not limited to Europeans. The Aztecs and Mayans themselves were slave societies, and the history of Africa is filled with black people who sold other black people into slavery. It's one of the ugliest but most common elements of human nature—part of the shared history of virtually every person alive today. And there's nothing we can do about it.

"It's just hard, though," said Eva, "because I have been so closely identified with the Mexican community—by choice. I've been so proud of being Mexican, coming from the indigenous native people, because I find it the most beautiful culture in the world. And to know that that's not really who I am or not only who I am—it's a little shaking through my foundation."

I tried to reassure Eva by telling her the truth: there is no doubt on her mother's line that she is descended from a Native American female—a native woman from Mexico long before it was Mexico. But there is also no doubt that she is heavily European, and there is simply no way to alter our genetic makeup or the history it reflects. Identity is a matter, to a great extent, of choice. Our genetic heritage is not, though how we interpret our genetic makeup, of course, is.

Since Eva's father is alive, we were able to test his DNA as well and get a fuller picture of her double heritage. Eva's father's admixture reveals that he is 80 percent European, 19 percent Native American, and 1 percent African. This means that Eva got much of her Native American ancestry from her mother. Her father's Y-DNA also shows that her paternal line is, without a doubt, descended from Europe. We found two exact matches for him with people living today in Spain. We also found an exact match for his Y-DNA in England. This is because his Y-DNA haplogroup is R1b1b2, which is a subgroup of the most common haplogroup in western Europe.

Turning to the Broad Institute's autosomal DNA testing, I told Eva that her results revealed that she shares an ancestor in common with Yo-Yo Ma as recently as the past 250 years. "How?" asked Eva, joking. "He's Mexican?"

I liked that joke, but I assured her it was no joke. She and the world's greatest cellist share DNA on chromosome 3, matching from base pair 49 to base pair 57, which translates into nine million base pairs, which is a significant number. I explained that they must share a person of Native American extraction, because he's 100 percent Asian, and as I mentioned, scientists believe that the earliest humans in North America came here by crossing land bridges from Asia about sixteen thousand years ago. "Amazing," she said. "I love it. I want to meet him."

Eva was also thrilled to learn that she has a common ancestor with Meryl Streep. The two share DNA on chromosome 2, matching from base pair 46 to 51, which is six million base pairs, less of a match, by a third, than her match with Yo-Yo Ma but a significant match nonetheless. This, I told Eva, was undoubtedly due to her European ancestry—as her father's haplotype is spread across the continent, and Streep's family is of German descent.

In closing, I asked Eva how this experience had changed her. Did she still identify herself as a Texican? Or would she say Spanish, like her father? Or would she prefer to focus on her Mayan ancestry?

"I'd go with Texican," she said, "still—Texican or Mexican American. I feel like it's a true dichotomy of who I am. Because I am through and through Mexican—we just made tamales yesterday, you know? We love mariachis, the music, the language are ingrained in me. It's where I'm from and my source of inspiration, my source of intelligence, my source of my acting. But yet I am so American. I made an apple pie yesterday, too. I went to college here. I speak perfect English. And I think there's a lot of us Texicans that are really just split down the middle, wanting to hold on to the heritage and the Mexican traditions and yet wanting to be seen as Americans. And that's me. And that's what I'll always be."

DNA Appendix

Dr. Nathan Pearson

Chromosomes: Distinctive Words in the "Book" of the Genome

The genome is often likened to a great book of information about the person who carries it. This metaphor proves fruitful on many levels, including clarifying the nature of the genome's twenty-three pairs of *chromosomes*. Each of those chromosomes is, extending the book metaphor, essentially a long chemical "word" made up of many millions of DNA "letters" strung together in a distinctive order.

Importantly, copies of a given chromosome, like printings of a given word, can come in differing "spellings," which are easily recognized, of alternative versions of the same underlying thing. Typically, the spelling differences between human chromosomes are slight: if, for example, we randomly pick two copies of a given chromosome (say, chromosome 7) from the human population and align them for comparison, we will find that their spellings tend to match at more than 999 out of every 1,000 letters.

This striking conformity of human chromosome spellings reflects two important facts of human biology. First, the cellular machinery that copies DNA from parent to child, via eggs and sperm, does so very faithfully; only rarely does the machinery miscopy a DNA letter (and so generate a new chromosomal spelling variant). Second, the human population has historically been notably small—much smaller, in fact, than today's rapidly expanding human population and much smaller than the relatively stable populations of other organisms, such as fruit flies, which harbor more genetic diversity, per head, than we do. Our low ancestral population size means that the many billion modern copies of a given human chromosome actually have relatively few distinct ancestors to potentially trace back to at earlier, but still evolutionarily recent, times. Ultimately, this means that two randomly picked copies of any human chromosome will tend to share relatively recent common ancestry; as such, the two copies will typically have descended along distinct chains of "copyings" for too few generations to have accumulated many spelling differences from each other, given the fidelity of our cells' DNA-copying machinery.

Yet the sprinkling of spelling differences that distinguish one copy of a human chromosome from another can nonetheless be quite informative clues about each copy's ancestry, helping us accurately guess where in the world it came from. Just as is true for written words, certain chromosomal spellings may be common in one part of the world, whereas others predominate elsewhere. To an experienced reader of English, for example, my usage of *recognized* two paragraphs up may signal that the passage was written by an American. Had it instead been written by a Briton, Indian, or Australian, the same word might well have been spelled *recognised*.

Haplotypes

Geneticists use handy jargon to talk about chromosomal spelling differences. In general, a distinctive DNA spelling variant can be called an *allele*, whether the variant in question is defined by a single letter (like the z in *recognized*) or by a combination of letters. For the latter case, in which multiple distinctive spelling variants jointly define a complex chromosomal spelling, geneticists reserve the special term *haplotype*. This term can refer to a combination of two closely spaced distinctive spelling variants—or, in the extreme, the complete spelling of a whole chromosome, including hundreds of thousands of distinctive letters scattered within it.

The combinations of variants that make up haplotypes can potentially be very distinctive; a chromosome carrying just thirty-three sites of simple "two-alternative" spelling variation, for example, could come in more distinct haplotypes than there are people on earth. Importantly, though, the spelling variants that make up haplotypes generally come in just a few, fairly robust combinations; one can picture an extreme version of this pattern, in which the thirty-three sites of spelling variation in the hypothetical example yielded just *two* overall spellings, because each variant at each site invariably appeared together with just one of the two possible variants at each other site.

Real human chromosomes show patterns of haplotype variation in between these two extremes. As we will see, in some parts of the genome—such as the approximately fifty-million-letter male-specific segment of the Y chromosome, for example—the spelling variants that define haplotypes stay linked together quite robustly; in other parts of the genome, a process called *recombination* plays a key role in breaking up haplotypes and quilting them together into new combinations.

Y Chromosomes and Mitochondrial DNA

The first finely resolved genetic portraits of human ancestral history—both for populations and for individuals—have come from studies of two special pieces of the genome, mitochondrial DNA (mtDNA) and the Y chromosome. Importantly, each of these modestly sized segments of DNA is passed down only from one parent: mtDNA from mother to child, and Y chromosome from father to son.

Such unusual inheritance means that neither mtDNA nor the Y[1] has a partner chromosome with which to undergo the process of *recombination* (discussed in the following section) that can scramble haplotypes and make them harder to interpret. As such, when a copy of the Y chromosome or mtDNA undergoes a new mutation (thanks to an error in cellular copying of DNA), that chromosome's existing haplotype acquires a new spelling variant that will remain firmly attached to that "background" haplotype. Over time, as more and more such new mutations happen, human Y and mtDNA lineages thus diversify into simply branching but richly detailed "trees" of haplotypes.

Moreover, mtDNA and Y haplotypes are particularly easy to read using current DNA-sequencing methods, because, with only one copy of the mtDNA or Y on hand (not a second copy from the other parent), there's no ambiguity about which spelling variant at one site of variation is attached to which variant at another site of variation. This easy, precise haplotype reading contrasts with the situation for the rest of the genome, for which the presence of two copies of each segment—one from Mom, one from Dad—can make it hard to figure out which variants are linked together on the same copy, as opposed to on different copies.

The simplicity and accessibility of mtDNA and Y haplotypes would be of little use for ancestral inference if each such haplotype were uniformly common all over the world. Luckily, the haplotype "branches" of the human mtDNA and Y trees tend to show strikingly clumped geographic distributions; that is, each such branch tends to be much more common in people from some parts of the world than from others. One can think of the branches of these trees as representing "flavors" of mtDNA or Y chromosomes; the worldwide distribution of those flavors reflects where particular mothers (mtDNA carriers) or fathers (Y carriers) were traveling in the past. Any big branch of the mtDNA or Y tree gathers together many smaller branches, whose mild similarity in flavor reflects ancient common ancestry through the movements of very early foremothers (mtDNA) or forefathers (Y). Smaller branches, at the tips of the trees, carry stronger and more distinctive flavors that may rarely be encountered in sampling human populations but whose presence strongly indicates recent common ancestry through the movement of recent forebears.

Because the geographic distributions of human mtDNA and Y haplotypes have now been very well surveyed, these unusual pieces of the genome can provide quick, clear, and detailed geographic insight into a person's matrilineal (mother's mother's mother's . . . mother's line) and (if male) patrilineal (father's father's father's . . . father's line) ancestry. In this sense, the mtDNA and Y are unique, telling us as much about the *identity* of particular early ancestors as we can ever know from genomic data. Other chromosomes, by contrast, tell us about ancestors who could have been of either sex and whose DNA has been handed down through lines of both mothers and fathers.

Yet, despite the appealingly precise inferences offered by mtDNA and Y data, it bears stressing that these two informative pieces of DNA make up less than 2 percent of the whole genome and tell us only about two lines among our myriad ancestors. Moreover, each generation of people hands down just one copy of mtDNA or the Y for every four or so copies of, say, chromosome 1. Just as the historically small human population is generationally shallower and less genetically diverse than the bigger population of, say, fruit flies, the small size of the mtDNA and Y "populations" means that the mtDNA and Y "family trees" are rooted quite shallowly in time. All people, for example, share a common matrilineal (mtDNA) ancestor who likely lived less than ten thousand generations ago in East Africa; by contrast, the last common ancestor of all copies of some parts of human chromosome 6 may well have lived more than four hundred thousand generations ago! To know more about our individual ancestry, and to dig deeper into the human past, we thus need to look beyond mtDNA and the Y, to the rest of the genome.

Recombination, Sex Chromosomes, and Autosomes

Geneticists speak of two main kinds of human chromosome: *sex chromosomes* (such as the Y and its larger, more-gene-rich partner, the X) and *autosomes* (chromosomes 1–22).[2] These classes are distinguished by how they behave when the cells carrying them divide to form new cells—especially the eggs and sperm that carry DNA to coming generations.

In particular, when eggs or sperm are made, the maternal and paternal copies of each autosome in the genome line up with each other, like partners at a dance, and randomly swap long segments, yielding newly stitched chromosomes that are each made up of part maternal, part paternal DNA. These new "patchwork" chromosomes then part, going their separate ways into newly formed eggs or sperm; a few such new cells will go on to found the next generation of a given family.

The process by which autosomes swap segments, *recombination,* is crucial to understanding what the genome can tell us about ancestry. Recombination breaks apart old haplotypes and joins their fragments together in new combinations, generating brand-new haplotypes. For geneticists trying to study ancestry, this process can be both frustrating (scrambling haplotypes that geneticists were trying to track as they spread from one part of the world to another) and informative (generating distinctive new haplotypes that can then be tracked, at least until they too are broken apart).

Admixture Tests

Ultimately, recombination means that neighboring segments of the same chromosome can have different ancestral histories, tracing to distinct people who may have lived far apart on the globe. Every genome is thus a mosaic of ancestry, in which not only whole chromosomes can trace back to different geographic regions but even segments of the *same* chromosome can do so. This "mosaicness" is important to bear in mind when thinking about ancestry. Ultimately, personal genetic tests don't tell us definitively that we "belong" to a particular ethnic group but rather offer richer, more complex insights into the ethnic mix—and it is always a mix, at some level (depending on how ethnicities are arbitrarily defined)—among our ancestors. It's healthy, and often surprising and enlightening, to bear this in mind when interpreting our own genome data.

Today, the basic approach to genetically assessing our ancestry—often called an "admixture test"—looks at the whole genome at once and seeks to answer a bottom-line sort of question: How much of this genome recently came from region A, how much from region B, and so on? At the expense of more precision about *which* parts of the genome came from which region, this simple approach boils down the "answer" to a small, easily understood set of numbers that sum to 100 percent. And, unlike some methods, this approach can be used effectively for anyone's genome, whether or not they have saliently "mixed" recent ancestry.

The actual computer methods used for admixture tests vary: some methods take into account not just the frequencies of individual spelling variants in different populations but the frequencies of relatively long haplotypes in those populations, as well as other important variables. Other, simpler methods may look only at smaller "windows"—even single sites of spelling variation—to compile an overall picture of similarity by tallying best guesses about the origin(s) of a person's copies of each such site/segment. Though simplistic, the latter approach is not complicated by assumptions about haplotypes—that is, about which spelling variants are linked together on the same copy of a chromosome and which are on separate copies—whereas more sophisticated admixture estimation methods require some assumptions on that front, because current DNA-sequencing methods do not allow unambiguous inference of haplotypes.

Genetic methods for guessing/summarizing a person's ancestral ethnic mix ultimately rely on publicly available data about the frequencies of particular genomic spelling variants in samples of DNA taken from people representing large regions, such as West Africa, East Asia, and northern Europe. Note that these data are not ideal: they come from modern people, who inevitably differ genetically from ancient people who lived in the same regions; they are finite samples, inevitably missing potentially informative facets of local genetic variation; they often suffer from sampling biases that distort the demographic prevalence of certain variants; and, currently, they are confined to sites in the genome that happen to have been included on "SNP chips," which are panels of sites scattered throughout the genome where spellings are already known to vary. Such panels are inevitably biased toward including only sites for which at least two spelling variants are both quite common; as such, they tend to include sites where both variants have spread relatively far and wide in the world and may miss sites that may have rarer, but potentially more geographically confined (and so potentially precisely informative) spelling variants.

In the future, the reference data used to infer details of personal ancestry will be based on *whole-genome* sequencing, raising the ceiling for how finely we can resolve the ancestral origins of particular segments of the genome.

Finding Autosomal Close Cousins

Though recombination is a random process, over time it reliably breaks up haplotypes in roughly the same way that cooking a stew breaks up its ingredients into smaller and smaller fragments. In a set of genomes descended from the same set of ancient ancestors, many or most of the ancestral "stew ingredients" may still be present; but, thanks to recombination, they will no longer be robustly attached to each other on the same copies of the chromosomes that carry them. Mulling this insight, one can see that, though both near and distant relatives may share genomic spelling variants, only close relatives should share long pieces of intact haplotypes. This is because their copies of the chromosomes in question will have been diverging, along separate ancestral lines, for too short a time for recombination to have broken up all the haplotypes passed down to them from one or more recent common ancestors.

It turns out that knowing how many haplotype fragments, of a given length, are shared by two people lets one estimate how closely related they are. In particular, pairings of parent and child, grandparent and child, aunt/uncle and niece/nephew, first cousins, second cousins, and so on, show accurately predictable patterns of haplotype segment sharing. Once the relationship becomes more distant than, say, third cousins, however, estimating the degree of cousinship becomes tougher, because the shared haplotype segments become, on average, too small to contain many distinctive spelling variants.

Even for people without a third-cousin or closer relationship, however, it's still possible to reliably infer that two people share a fairly recent ancestor, based on the fact that they share at least one sufficiently long haplotype segment. Such a segment is the shared remnant of a chromosome passed down by a real, living, individual ancestor fairly recently. How recently can be hard to say. Computer models allow estimation, based on what's known about recombination rates and other important parameters—but it's important to remember that such estimates are known to be imprecise (that is, subject to large "error"/uncertainty components), thanks in large part to the randomness of recombination itself.

Currently, however, the best available public SNP-chip reference data, and the best available sequencing methods, allow inferences that people who apparently share distinctive haplotype segments on autosomes probably share a common ancestor who lived in the past two to five centuries or so. In some populations, such estimates may take on different values, reflecting factors such as "founder" effects that greatly reduced genetic diversity among early ancestors, leading to more prevalent sharing of long haplotype segments than would otherwise be expected.

Eventually, the reference data used for inferring close cousinship will improve to include data from whole-genome sequencing (not just SNP chips), as well as more precise data on recombination rate variation in the genome. At the same time, sequencing methods will advance so that the linkage of spelling variants on the same chromosome can be unambiguously inferred. As such, in the future we will be able to make ever more precise inferences about the age of the last common ancestor shared by two people, based on their sharing of haplotype segments.

NOTES

1. The Y, however, does at its very tips recombine with the X chromosome; but these short regions are typically excluded from definitions of Y haplotypes.

2. Mitochondrial DNA (mtDNA) is usually classified separately, rather than as a chromosome, because (a) it is a short *ring* of DNA, unlike the long two-ended strings that we call chromosomes 1–22/X/Y, and (b) it is stored outside the chromosome-packed *nucleus* of the cell, inside little membrane-bound packets called *mitochondria*, which represent a line of symbiotic bacteria that established themselves inside other cells, helping to found the vast and ancient lineage of life, called *eukaryotes*, that we are part of.

Index

About the Author

HENRY LOUIS GATES, JR., is the Alphonse Fletcher University Professor and the Director of the W. E. B. Du Bois Institute for African and African American Research at Harvard University. An influential scholar in the field of African American studies, he is the author of twelve books and has hosted and produced ten documentaries, including the acclaimed PBS series *African American Lives*. Gates is coeditor, with Evelyn Brooks Higginbotham, of the *African American National Biography* (an eight-volume biographical dictionary), and his recent work has been instrumental in popularizing African American genealogical research and DNA testing. He is the recipient of fifty honorary degrees and many awards, including a MacArthur Foundation Fellowship and the National Humanities Medal, and was named to *Time* magazine's "25 Most Influential Americans" list in 1997 and to *Ebony* magazine's "100 Most Influential Black Americans" list in 2005 and its "Power 150" list in 2009.